Pope Pius IX, Herbert Vaughan

The Year of Preparation for the Vatican Council

including the original and English of the encyclical and syllabus, and of the papal documents connected with its convocation

Pope Pius IX, Herbert Vaughan

The Year of Preparation for the Vatican Council
including the original and English of the encyclical and syllabus, and of the papal documents connected with its convocation

ISBN/EAN: 9783337227852

Printed in Europe, USA, Canada, Australia, Japan

Cover: Foto ©Lupo / pixelio.de

More available books at **www.hansebooks.com**

THE

YEAR OF PREPARATION

FOR THE

VATICAN COUNCIL.

Including the Original and English of

the Encyclical and Syllabus,

and of the Papal Documents Connected with its

Convocation.

LONDON:
BURNS, OATES, AND CO., 17 AND 18, PORTMAN STREET, W.

1869.

CONTENTS.

	PAGE.
PREFACE	i

INTRODUCTION.—The effect produced upon the World and upon the Faithful by the summoning of the General Council—General Councils, from their nature called together but seldom.—They are signs of an unusual state of things.—The Indiction of a Council a very solemn act on the part of the Vicar of Jesus Christ 1

CHAPTER I.—What persons are commanded to attend the Council.—The schismatic Bishops of the East invited to be present.—Protestants invited to return to the Fold of Christ . . . 8

CHAPTER II.—The Pope alone has authority to summon a General Council.—He alone has authority to preside over it . . . 11

CHAPTER III.—The Pontifical Power necessary for the existence of a Council.—The order of precedence among the members.—Proxies.—Secular Princes.—Councils summoned by the Pope by virtue of his supreme Jurisdiction 14

CHAPTER IV.—False theories concerning the relation of a General Council to the Pope.—A Council without the Pope does not bind the Church.—Its jurisdiction derived from him . . . 20

CHAPTER V.—General Councils unlike all other assemblies.—The Pope not merely the president.—He is supreme.—Bishops not the delegates of the people, but the Pope's councillors . . 26

CHAPTER VI.—The desire for a Council long entertained by the Pontiff.—The expectations therefrom formed by the late Cardinal Wiseman.—The expressed desire of the Universal Episcopate—Consecration of the Council to the Immaculate Mother of God.—The Bull of Indiction 31

CHAPTER VII.—Visit of the Abate Carlo Testa to the Greek and Armenian Patriarchs.—Freedom of action of the Greek Bishops at the Council of Florence.—Dying testimony of John, Patriarch of Constantinople at that time.—Subservience of the Greek Bishops to their Patriarch.—Their futile objections to the Council,—These objections refuted.—Two Bishops honourably distinguished from the rest.—Despotism of the Patriarch.—Humiliation inflicted upon him by the Ottoman Government.—Proposed separation of Greek and Bulgarian Churches.—The Patriarch proposes to call a Council.—Objections to this on the part of both Turks and Greeks. 58

CHAPTER VIII.—Sentiments of the Catholicos of Echmiadzin.—Origin of his See and of its Title.—Its lapse into Schism, pretensions to dominion, and jealousy of the Armenian Patriarchate.—Apprehensions of the Catholicos with reference to the General Council.—His attempt to establish a Nuncio at Constantinople, and refusal of the Ottoman Government.—Proceedings of the Unionist and anti-Unionist party in the Armenian Church.—Intimidation of the Patriarch and his resignation.—Separation of the Bulgarians from the Greek Church and their contest with the Patriarch.—Consequent disturbances.—Reception of the Papal Letter by the Coptic Patriarch of Alexandria . . 70

CONTENTS.

CHAPTER IX.—Benefits which may be anticipated from the Council in respect to the Schismatic bodies.—Blindness of Catholic rulers to their true interests.—Behaviour of the French Government.—Its reservations in regard to the approaching Council.—Dispositions of the French Episcopate.—Desuetude of Canon Law in France.—Its causes and inconveniences.—The sentiments of liberal Catholics and of Catholics pure and simple. —Feeling and attitude of the non-Catholic body.—Aspirations and expectations of Catholics respecting dogmatic decisions . 84

CHAPTER X.—The Pope's conduct towards the Bishops of the Eastern Schism.—Their condition.—Necessity of their submission to the Holy See 97

CHAPTER XI.—Election of Gregory X. to the Pontificate.—He invites the Emperor to the Council of Lyons.—The Emperor professes the Roman faith.—The opening of the Council.— Sermon of S. Bonaventure.—Arrival and submission of the Eastern Deputies.—The Emperor (by proxy) and the Deputies abjure the Schism.—Death of S. Thomas and of S. Bonaventure.—Insincerity of the Easterns. — Excommunication of Michael Palæologus 101

CHAPTER XII.—Present aspect of affairs.—The great vice of the Oriental mind.—Usurpation on the part of the Bishop of Constantinople.—Eugenius IV. and the Council of Basle.—Reception of the Patriarch of Constantinople by the Pope.—Meeting of the Council at Ferrara.—Its adjournment to Florence.— Meeting in separate Synods of the Latins and Greeks . . 108

CHAPTER XIII.—The Pope's Address to Protestants—Differences between the Greeks and Protestants.—Heretics never summoned to a Council.—Conduct of the Protestant Princes when invited by Paul III.—Impossibility of discussion between Catholics and Heretics 115

CHAPTER XIV.—Difference between the Motives of the Greeks at Florence—and that of the Protestants at Trent.—Instructions of Julius III. touching the latter.—Defined Doctrines cannot again be discussed.— Therefore the Protestants abstained from the Council of Trent.—End of that Council . . . 120

CHAPTER XV.—The Sovereign Pontiff the only possible Convener of a Council.—His sanction necessary to its decrees.— The Council not superior to the Pope.—Supposed case of a Pope dying during the Session; the case of Antipopes.— Council of Pisa.—Conduct of the Cardinals.—Mutual relations between the Pope and a Council.—The Pope cannot be accused of Heresy.—Prejudices of certain Canonists . . . . 125.

CHAPTER XVI.—The work of Gratian.—The Canons "Anastasius" and "Si Papa."—Worthlessness of the former and non-authority of the latter.—Attempt of the Cardinals to call a Council.—Its failure.—The effect of opposition has been to make the Papal supremacy and infallibility more clear and certain 136

APPENDIX 141

PREFACE.

THE Assembly of the General Council of the Vatican is the greatest and most pregnant event of the last three hundred years. It is naturally, therefore, filling men's minds whether they will it or no.

The Church of God is a perfect kingdom, not *of* the world, but *in* it. It is a kingdom of souls, and has a divine mission to gather into itself the whole human race. It has a divine right to whatever is necessary for its perfect organization, and for the fulfilment of its divine mission. As there is no limit in point of time or place to its mission, so there is no exemption to the obedience due to its authority when once recognized.

The General Council is the reunion in one place of the Apostolate dispersed throughout the world, under the authority and direction of its divinely appointed head, whose office is "to confirm his brethren," and whose "faith shall not fail." Human society cannot but be affected by the decisions of the Council. Gainsay it as scoffers and unbelievers may, mankind will be influenced by its decision. Individuals may have eyes and see not, and ears and hear not: but God Himself will solemnly speak to the world through the infallible decisions of the Council of His Church, and the Spirit of the Lord will fill the face of the earth as the waters cover the sea.

There is much misconception as to the nature of a General Council. Subjects directly connected with it are ordinarily studied only by Theologians and Canonists. In the midst too of a Babel of tongues and newspapers in which we live circumstances attendant upon the Convocation of the Vatican Council have been continually reported inaccurately. The following pages, therefore, may be useful to all who desire correct and trustworthy information. They are reprinted chiefly from the Supplements on the Council which have appeared in THE TABLET newspaper during the past year. The theological and legal part of the work is due almost entirely to the pen of Mr. DAVID LEWIS, whose learning and accuracy are too well known to need commendation; while the narrative of current events has been prepared by other trustworthy and competent hands.

In order to make this volume on the Preparation for the General Council as useful and complete as possible, the originals and translations of the Encyclical and Syllabus (which may be considered as the remote preparation for the Council), as well as of the Apostolical Letters directed respectively by the Sovereign Pontiff to the Bishops of the Church, to the Schismatics of the East, and to the Protestants, have been here brought together into one place. The Letter of the Holy See to the Archbishop of Westminster has also been appended, as clearly connected with the same matter, and as completing the official documents published by Rome in preparation for the General Council.

And now I will end by repeating, and adopting in

my own name and in the name of those who are in any way responsible with me for the contents of this volume, the words of Thomas Bradwardine, an Archbishop of Canterbury, who died in 1349: "I know what I will do; I will commit myself to that ship which can never perish, the ship of Peter. For in it our only Head and Master Christ in safety sat and taught; to teach us mystically that in the boat of Peter, the Church of Rome, the authority and teaching of all Christian doctrine should abide. To the judgment, therefore, of so authentic and so great a teacher I submit, and subject fully and altogether myself and my writings, now and hereafter."*

     HERBERT VAUGHAN.
St. Joseph's Foreign Missionary College,
  Mill Hill, London.

The following is Cardinal Antonelli's Circular to the Cardinals and Bishops in forwarding to them the Encyclical and Syllabus:—

Our Holy Father, Pius IX., Sovereign Pontiff, being profoundly anxious for the salvation of souls and for sound doctrine, has never ceased from the commencement of his Pontificate to proscribe and condemn the chief errors and false doctrines of our most unhappy age, by his published Encyclicals, and Consistorial Allocutions, and other Apostolic Letters. But as it may happen that all the Pontifical acts do not reach each one of the ordinaries, the same Soverign Pontiff has willed that a Syllabus of the same errors should be compiled, to be sent to all the bishops of the Catholic world, in order that these bishops may have before their eyes all the errors and pernicious doctrines which he has reprobated and condemned.

He has consequently charged me to take care that

---

* Bradwardini de Causâ Dei. *Præf.*

this Syllabus, having been printed, should be sent to your [Eminence] on this occasion and at this time, when the same Sovereign Pontiff, from his great solicitude for the salvation and general good of the Catholic Church and of the whole flock divinely entrusted to him, has thought well to write another Encyclical Letter to all the Catholic bishops. Accordingly, performing, as is my duty, with all suitable zeal and submission the commands of the said Pontiff, I send your [Eminence] the said Syllabus, together with this letter.

I seize with much pleasure this occasion of expressing my sentiments of respect and devotion to your [Eminence], and of once more subscribing myself, while I humbly kiss your hands,

Your [Eminence's] most humble
and devoted servant,
G. Card. Antonelli.

Rome, Dec. 8, 1864.

[Translation.]
*VIII. December, MDCCCLXIV.
THE ENCYCLICAL LETTER
of Our most Holy Father the Pope, Pius IX.

To our Venerable Brethren, all Patriarchs, Primates, Archbishops, and Bishops having favour and communion of the Holy See.

PIUS PP. IX.

Venerable Brethren,

Health and Apostolic Benediction.

With how great care and pastoral vigilance the Roman Pontiffs, our predecessors, fulfilling the duty and office committed to them by the Lord Christ

---

*Die VIII. Decembris, MDCCCLXIV.
SS. Domini Nostri Pii IX.
EPISTOLA ENCYCLICA.*
Venerabilibus Fratribus Patriarchis, Primatibus, Archiepiscopis et Episcopis Universis Gratiam et Communionem Apostolicæ Sedis habentibus.

PIUS PAPA IX.

Venerabiles Fratres,

Salutem et Apostolicam Benedictionem.

Quanta cura ac pastorali vigilantia Romani Pontifices Prædecessores Nostri, exsequentes demandatum sibi ab ipso Christo Domino in persona

Himself in the person of most Blessed Peter, Prince of the Apostles, of feeding the lambs and the sheep, have never ceased sedulously to nourish the Lord's whole flock with words of faith and with salutary doctrine, and to guard it from poisoned pastures,—is thoroughly known to all, and especially to You, Venerable Brethren. And truly the same, Our Predecessors, asserters as they were and vindicators of the august Catholic religion, of truth, and of justice, being specially anxious for the salvation of souls, had nothing ever more at heart than by their most wise Letters and Constitutions to unveil and condemn all those heresies and errors which, being adverse to our Divine Faith, to the doctrine of the Catholic Church, to purity of morals, and to the eternal salvation of men, have frequently excited violent tempests, and have miserably afflicted both Church and State. For which cause the same our Predecessors, have, with Apostolic fortitude, constantly resisted the nefarious enterprises of wicked men, who, like raging waves of the sea foaming out their own confusion, and promising liberty whereas they are the slaves of corruption, have striven by their deceptive opinions and most pernicious writings to raze the foundations of the Catholic religion and of civil society, to remove from among men all virtue and justice, to deprave the mind and judgment of all, to turn away from true moral training unwary persons, and especially inexperienced youth, miserably

---

Beatissimi Petri Apostolorum Principis officium, munusque pascendi agnos et oves nunquam intermiscrint-universum Dominicum gregem sedulo enutrire verbis fidei, ac salutari doctrina imbuere, eumque ab venenatis pascuis arcere, omnibus quidem ac Vobis præsertim compertum, exploratumque est, Venerabiles Fratres. Et sane iidem Decessores Nostri, augustæ catholicæ religionis, veritatis ac justitiæ assertores et vindices, de animarum salute maxime solliciti nihil potius unquam habuere, quam sapientissimis suis Litteris, et Constitutionibus retegere et damnare omnes hæreses et errores, qui Divinæ Fidei nostræ, catholicæ Ecclesiæ doctrinæ, morum honestati, ac sempiternæ hominum saluti adversi, graves frequenter exeitarunt tempestates, et christianam civilemque rempublicam miserandum in modum funestarunt. Quocirca iidem Decessores Nostri Apostolica fortitudine continenter obstiterunt nefariis iniquorum hominum molitionibus, qui descumantes tamquam fluctus feri maris confusiones suas, ac libertatem promittentes, cum servi sint corruptionis, fallacibus suis opinionibus, et perniciosissimis scriptis catholicæ religionis civilisque societatis fundamenta convellere, omnemque virtutem ac justitiam de medio tollere, omniumque animos mentesque depravare, et incautos imperitamque præsertim juventutem a

to corrupt such youth, to lead it into the snares of error, and at length tear it from the bosom of the Catholic Church.

But now, as is well known to You, Venerable Brethren, already, scarcely had we been elevated to this Chair of Peter (by the hidden counsel of Divine Providence, certainly by no merits of Our own), when, seeing with the greatest grief of Our soul a truly awful storm excited by so many evil opinions, and [seeing also] the most grievous calamities never sufficiently to be deplored which overspread the Christian people from so many errors, according to the duty of Our Apostolic Ministry, and following the illustrious example of Our Predecessors, We raised Our voice, and in many published Encyclical Letters and Allocutions delivered in Consistory, and other Apostolic letters, we condemned the chief errors of this our most unhappy age, and we excited your admirable Episcopal vigilance, and we again and again admonished and exhorted all sons of the Catholic Church, to Us most dear, that they should altogether abhor and flee from the contagion of so dire a pestilence. And especially in Our first Encyclical Letter written to you on Nov. 9, 1846, and in two Allocutions delivered by us in Consistory, the one on Dec. 9, 1854, and the other on June 9, 1862, we condemned the monstrous portents of opinion which prevail especially in this age, bringing

---

recta morum disciplina avertere, eamque miserabiliter corrumpere, in erroris laqueos inducere, ac tandem ab Ecclesiæ catholicæ sinu avellere conati sunt.

Jam vero, uti Vobis, Venerabiles Fratres, apprime notum est, Nos vix dum arcano divinæ Providentiæ consilio nullis certe Nostris meritis ad hanc Petri Cathedram evecti fuimus, cum videremus summo animi Nostri dolore horribilem sane procellam tot pravis opinionibus excitatam, et gravissima, ac nunquam satis lugenda damna, quæ in christianum populum ex tot erroribus redundant, pro Apostolici Nostri Ministerii officio illustria Prædecessorum Nostrorum vestigia sectantes Nostram extulimus vocem, ac pluribus in vulgus editis Encyclicis Epistolis et Allocutionibus in Consistorio habitis, aliisque Apostolicis Litteris præcipuos tristissimæ nostræ ætatis errores damnavimus, eximiamque vestram episcopalem vigilantiam excitavimus, et universos catholicæ Ecclesiæ Nobis carissimos filios etiam atque etiam monuimus et exhortati sumus, ut tam diræ contagia pestis omnino horrerent et devitarent. Ac præsertim Nostra prima Encyclica Epistola die 9 Novembris anno 1846 Vobis scripta, binisque Allocutionibus, quarum altera die 9 Decembris anno 1854, altera vero 9 Junii anno 1862 in Consistorio a Nobis habita fuit, monstrosa opinionum portenta damnavimus, quæ hac potissimum

with them the greatest loss of souls and detriment of civil society itself; which are grievously opposed also, not only to the Catholic Church and her salutary doctrine and venerable rights, but also to the eternal natural law engraven by God in all men's hearts, and to right reason; and from which almost all other errors have their origin.

But, although we have not omitted often to proscribe and reprobate the chief errors of this kind, yet the cause of the Catholic Church, and the salvation of souls entrusted to us by God, and the welfare of human society itself, altogether demand that we again stir up your pastoral solicitude to exterminate other evil opinions, which spring forth from the said errors as from a fountain. Which false and perverse opinions are on that ground the more to be detested, because they chiefly tend to this, that that salutary influence be impeded and [even] removed which the Catholic Church, according to the institution and command of her divine Author, should freely exercise even to the end of the world—not only over private individuals, but over nations, peoples, and their sovereign princes; and [tend also] to take away that mutual fellowship and concord of counsels between Church and State which has ever proved itself propitious and salutary, both for religious and civil interests. For you well know, Venerable Brethren, that at this time men are found not a few who, applying to civil society the impious

---

ætate cum maximo animarum damno, et civilis ipsius societatis detrimento dominantur, quæque non solum catholicæ Ecclesiæ, ejusque salutari doctrinæ ac venerandis juribus, verum etiam sempiternæ naturali legi a Deo in omnium cordibus insculptæ, rectæque rationi maxime adversantur, et ex quibus alii prope omnes originem habent errores.

Etsi autem haud omiserimus potissimos hujusmodi errores sæpe proscribere et reprobare, tamen catholicæ Ecclesiæ causa, animarumque salus Nobis divinitus commissa, atque ipsius humanæ societatis bonum omnino postulant, ut iterum pastoralem vestram sollicitudinem excitemus ad alias pravas profligandas opiniones, quæ ex eisdem erroribus, veluti ex fontibus erumpunt. Quæ falsæ ac perversæ opiniones eo magis detestandæ sunt, quod eo potissimum spectant, ut impediatur et amoveatur salutaris illa vis, quam catholica Ecclesia ex divini sui Auctoris institutione et mandato, libere exercere debet usque ad consummationem sæculi non minus erga singulos homines, quam erga nationes, populos summosque eorum Principes, utque de medio tollatur mutua illa inter Sacerdotium et Imperium consiliorum societas et concordia, quæ rei cum sacræ tum civili fausta semper extitit ac salutaris. [Gregor. XVI. Epist. Encycl. "*Mirari.*" 15 Aug. 1832.] Etenim probe noscitis, Venerabiles Fratres, hoc tempore non paucos reperiri,

and absurd principle of *naturalism*, as they call it, dare to teach that "the best constitution of public society and [also] civil progress altogether require that human society be conducted and governed without regard being had to religion any more than if it did not exist; or, at least, without any distinction being made between the true religion and false ones." And, against the doctrine of Scripture, of the Church, and of the holy Fathers, they do not hesitate to assert that "that is the best condition of society, in which no duty is recognized, as attached to the civil power, of restraining, by enacted penalties, offenders against the Catholic religion, except so far as public peace may require." From which totally false idea of social government they do not fear to foster that erroneous opinion, most fatal in its effects on the Catholic Church and the salvation of souls, called by Our Predecessor, Gregory XVI., an *insanity*, viz., that "liberty of conscience and worships is each man's personal right, which ought to be legally proclaimed and asserted in every rightly-constituted society; and that a right resides in the citizens to an absolute liberty, which should be restrained by no authority, whether ecclesiastical or civil, whereby they may be able openly and publicly to manifest and declare any of their ideas whatever, either by word of mouth, by the press, or in any other way." But, while they rashly affirm this, they do not think and consider that they are preaching the *liberty of*

---

qui civili consortio impium absurdumque *naturalismi*, uti vocant, principium applicantes audent docere, "optimam societatis publicæ rationem, civilemque progressum omnino requirere, ut humana societas constituatur et gubernetur, nullo habito ad religionem respectu, ac si ea non existeret, vel saltem nullo facto veram inter falsasque religiones discrimine." Atque contra sacrarum Litterarum, Ecclesiæ, sanctorumque Patrum doctrinam, asserere non dubitant, "optimam esse conditionem societatis, in qua Imperio non agnoscitur officium coercendi sancitis pœnis violatores catholicæ religionis, nisi quatenus pax publica postulet." Ex qua omnino falsa socialis regiminis idea haud timent erroneam illam fovere opinionem catholicæ Ecclesiæ, animarumque saluti maxime exitialem a rec. mem. Gregorio XVI. Prædecessore Nostro *deliramentum* appellatam [Eadem Encycl. "*Mirari*"], nimirum "libertatem conscientiæ et cultuum esse proprium cujuscumque hominis jus, quod lege proclamari et asseri debet in omni recte constituta societate, et jus civibus inesse ad omnimodam libertatem nulla vel ecclesiastica, vel civili auctoritate coarctandam, quo suos conceptus quoscumque sive voce, sive typis, sive alia ratione palam publiceque manifestare ac declarare valeant." Dum vero id temere affirmant, haud cogitant et

perdition; and that "if human arguments are always allowed free room for discussion, there will never be wanting men who will dare to resist truth, and to trust in the flowing speech of human wisdom; whereas we know, from the very teaching of our Lord Jesus Christ, how carefully Christian faith and wisdom should avoid this most injurious babbling."

And, since where religion has been removed from civil society, and the doctrine and authority of divine revelation repudiated, the genuine notion itself of justice and human right is darkened and lost, and the place of true justice and legitimate right is supplied by material force, thence it appears why it is that some, utterly neglecting and disregarding the surest principles of sound reason, dare to proclaim that "the people's will, manifested by what is called public opinion or in some other way, constitutes a supreme law, free from all divine and human control; and that in the political order accomplished facts, from the very circumstance that they are accomplished, have the force of right." But who does not see and clearly perceive that human society, when set loose from the bonds of religion and true justice, can have, in truth, no other end than the purpose of obtaining and amassing wealth, and that [society under such circumstances] follows no other law in its actions, except the unchastened desire of ministering to its own pleasures

---

considerant, quod *libertatem perditionis* [S Aug. Epist. 105, al. 166] prædicant, et quod "si humanis persuasionibus semper disceptare sit liberum, nunquam deesse poterunt, qui veritati audeant resultare, et de humanæ sapientiæ loquacitate confidere, cum hanc nocentissimam vanitatem quantum debeat fides et sapientia christiana vitare, ex ipsa Domini nostri Jesu Christi institutione cognoscat. [S. Leonis Epist. 164, al. 133, § edit. Ball.]

Et quoniam ubi a civili societate fuit amota religio, ac repudiata divinæ revelationis doctrina et auctoritas, vel ipsa germana justitiæ humanique juris notio tenebris obscuratur et amittitur, atque in veræ justitiæ legitimique juris locum materialis substituitur vis, inde liquet cur nonnulli certissimis sanæ rationis principiis penitus neglectis posthabitisque audeant conclamare, "voluntatem populi, publica, quam dicunt, opinione vel alia ratione manifestatam constituere supremam legem ab omni divino humanoque jure solutam, et in ordine politico facta consummata, eo ipso quod consummata sunt vim juris habere." Verum ecquis non videt, planeque sentit, hominum societatem religionis ac veræ justitiæ vinculis solutam nullum aliud profecto propositum habere posse, nisi scopum comparandi, cumulandique opes, nullamque aliam in suis actionibus legem sequi, nisi indomitam animi cupiditatem

and interests? For this reason men of the kind pursue with bitter hatred the Religious Orders, although these have deserved extremely well of Christendom, civilization and literature, and cry out that the same have no legitimate reason for being permitted to exist; and thus [these evil men] applaud the calumnies of heretics. For, as Pius VI., Our Predecessor, taught most wisely, "the abolition of regulars is injurious to that state in which the Evangelical Counsels are openly professed; it is injurious to a method of life praised in the Church as agreeable to Apostolic doctrine; it is injurious to the illustrious founders themselves, whom we venerate on our altars, who did not establish these societies but by God's inspiration." And [these wretches] also impiously declare that permission should be refused to citizens and to the Church, "whereby they may openly give alms for the sake of Christian charity;" and that the law should be abrogated "whereby on certain fixed days servile works are prohibited because of God's worship;" on the most deceptive pretext that the said permission and law are opposed to the principles of the best public economy. Moreover, not content with removing religion from public society, they wish to banish it also from private families. For teaching and professing the most fatal error of *Communism* and *Socialism*, they assert that "domestic society or the family derives the whole principle of its existence from the civil law alone; and

---

inserviendi propriis voluptatibus et commodis? Eapropter hujusmodi homines acerbo sane odio insectantur Religiosas Familias quamvis de re christiana, civili, ac litteraria summopere meritas, et blaterant easdem nullam habere legitimam existendi rationem, atque ita hæreticorum commentis plaudunt. Nam ut sapientissime rec. mem. Pius VI. Decessor Noster docebat, "regularium abolitio lædit statum publicæ professionis consiliorum evangelicorum, lædit vivendi rationem in Ecclesia commendatam tamquam Apostolicæ doctrinæ consentaneam, lædit ipsos insignes fundatores; quos super altaribus veneramur, qui non nisi a Deo inspirati eas constituerunt societates." [Epist. ad Card. de la Rochefoucault, 10 Martii, 1791.] Atque etiam impie pronunciant, auferendam esse civibus et Ecclesiæ facultatem "qua eleemosynas christianæ caritatis causa palam erogare valeant," ac de medio tollendam legem "qua certis aliquibus diebus opera servilia propter Dei cultum prohibentur," fallacissime prætexentes, commemoratam facultatem et legem optimæ publicæ œconomiæ principiis obsistere. Neque contenti amovere religionem a publica societate, volunt religionem ipsam a privatis etiam arcere familiis. Etenim funestissimum *Communismi* et *Socialismi* docentes ac profitentes errorem asserunt "societatem domes-

consequently that from the civil law alone issue, and on it depend, all rights of parents over their children, and especially that of providing for education." By which impious opinions and machinations these most deceitful men chiefly aim at this result, viz., that the salutary teaching and influence of the Catholic Church may be entirely banished from the instruction and education of youth, and that the tender and flexible minds of young men may be infected and depraved by every most pernicious error and vice. For all who have endeavoured to throw into confusion things both sacred and secular, and to subvert the right order of society, and to abolish all rights divine and human, have always (as we above hinted) devoted all their nefarious schemes, devices, and efforts, to deceiving and depraving incautious youth and have placed all their hope in its corruption. For which reason they never cease by every wicked method to assail the clergy, both secular and regular, from whom (as the surest monuments of history conspicuously attest), so many great advantages have abundantly flowed to Christianity, civilization, and literature, and to proclaim that "the clergy, as being hostile to the true and beneficial advance of science and civilization, should be removed from the whole charge and duty of instructing and educating youth."

Others meanwhile, reviving the wicked and so often

ticam seu familiam totam suæ existentiæ rationem a jure dumtaxat civili mutuari; proindeque ex lege tantum civili dimanare ac pendere jura omnia parentum in filios, cum primis vero jus institutionis educationisque curandæ." Quibus impiis opinionibus, machinationibusque in id præcipue intendunt fallacissimi isti homines, ut salutifera catholicæ Ecclesiæ doctrina ac vis a juventutis institutione et educatione prorsus eliminetur, ac teneri flexibilesque juvenum animi perniciosis quibusque erroribus, vitiisquo misere inficiantur ac depraventur. Siquidem omnes, qui rem tum sacram, tum publicam perturbare, ac rectum societatis ordinem evertere, et jura omnia divina et humana delere sunt conati, omnia nefaria sua consilia, studia et operam in improvidam præsertim juventutem decipiendam ac depravandam, ut supra innuimus, semper contulerunt, omnemque spem in ipsius juventutis corruptela collocarunt. Quocirca nunquam cessant utrumque clerum, ex quo, veluti certissima historiæ monumenta splendide testantur, tot magna in christianam, civilem, et litterariam rempublicam commoda redundarunt, quibuscumque infandis modis divexare, et edicere, ipsum Clerum "utpote vero, utilique scientiæ et civilitatis progressui inimicum, ab omni juventutis instituendæ educandæque cura et officio esse amovendum."

At vero alii instaurantes prava ac toties damnata novatorum com-

condemned inventions of innovators, dare with signal impudence to subject to the will of the civil authority the supreme authority of the Church and of this Apostolic See given to her by Christ Himself, and to deny all those rights of the same Church and See which concern matters of the external order. For they are not ashamed of affirming "that the Church's laws do not bind in conscience unless when they are promulgated by the civil power; that acts and decrees of the Roman Pontiffs, referring to religion and the Church, need the civil power's sanction and approbation, or at least its consent; that the Apostolic Constitutions, whereby secret societies are condemned (whether an oath of secrecy be or be not required in such societies), and whereby their frequenters and favourites are smitten with anathema—have no force in those regions of the world wherein associations of the kind are tolerated by the civil government; that the excommunication pronounced by the Council of Trent and by Roman Pontiffs against those who assail and usurp the Church's rights and possessions, rests on a confusion between the spiritual and temporal orders, and [is directed] to the pursuit of a purely secular good; that the Church can decree nothing which binds the consciences of the faithful in regard to their use of temporal things; that the Church has no right of restraining by temporal punishments those who violate her laws; that it is conformable to the

---

menta, insigni impudentia audent, Ecclesiæ et hujus Apostolicæ Sedis supremam auctoritatem a Christo Domino ei tributam civilis auctoritatis arbitrio subjicere, et omnia ejusdem Ecclesiæ et Sedis jura denegare circa ea quæ ad exteriorem ordinem pertinent. Namque ipsos minime pudet affirmare " Ecclesiæ leges non obligare in conscientia, nisi cum promulgantur a civili potestate ; acta et decreta Romanorum Pontificum ad religionem et Ecclesiam spectantia indigere sanctione et approbatione, vel minimum assensu potestatis civilis ; constitutiones Apostolicas [Clement XII. "*In eminenti.*" Benedict XIV. "*Providas Romanorum.*" Pii. VII. "*Ecclesiam.*" Leonis XII. "*Quo graviora*"], quibus damnantur clandestinæ societates, sive in eis exigatur, sive non exigatur juramentum de secreto servando, earumque asseclæ et fautores anathemate mulctantur, nullam habere vim in illis orbis regionibus ubi ejusmodi aggregationes tolerantur a civili gubernio ; excommunicationem a Concilio Tridentino et Romanis Pontificibus latam in eos, qui jura possessionesque Ecclesiæ invadunt et usurpant, niti confusione ordinis spiritualis ordinisque civilis ac politici, ad mundanum dumtaxat bonum prosequendum ; Ecclesiam nihil debere decernere, quod obstringere possit fidelium conscientias in ordine ad usum rerum temporalium ;

principles of sacred theology and public law to assert and claim for the civil government a right of property in those goods which are possessed by the Church, by the Religious Orders, and by other pious establishments." Nor do they blush openly and publicly to profess the maxim and principle of heretics from which arise so many perverse opinions and errors. For they repeat that "the ecclesiastical power is not by divine right distinct from, and independent of, the civil power, and that such distinction and independence cannot be preserved without the civil power's essential rights being assailed and usurped by the Church." Nor can we pass over in silence the audacity of those who, not enduring sound doctrine, contend that "without sin and without any sacrifice of the Catholic profession assent and obedience may be refused to those judgments and decrees of the Apostolic See, whose object is declared to concern the Church's general good, and her rights and discipline, so only it do not touch the dogmata of faith and morals." But no one can be found not clearly and distinctly to see and understand how grievously this is opposed to the Catholic dogma of the full power given from God by Christ our Lord Himself to the Roman Pontiff of feeding, ruling, and guiding the universal Church.

Amidst, therefore, such great perversity of depraved opinions, We, well remembering Our Apostolic Office,

---

Ecclesiæ jus non competere violatores legum suarum pœnis temporalibus coercendi; conforme esse sacræ theologiæ, jurisque publici principiis, bonorum proprietatem, quæ ab Ecclesia, a Familiis religiosis, aliisque locis piis possidentur, civili gubernio asserere et vindicare." Neque erubescunt palam publiceque profiteri hæreticorum effatum et principium, ex quo tot perversæ oriuntur sententiæ, atque errores. Dictitant enim "Ecclesiasticam potestatem non esse jure divino distinctam et independentem a potestate civili, neque ejusmodi distinctionem et independentiam servari posse, quin ab Ecclesia invadantur et usurpentur essentialia jura potestatis civilis." Atque silentio præterire non possumus eorum audaciam, qui sanam non sustinentes doctrinam contendunt "illis Apostolicæ Sedis judiciis, et decretis quorum objectum ad bonum generale Ecclesiæ, ejusdemque jura, ac disciplinam spectare declaratur, dummodo fidei morumque dogmata non attingat, posse assensum et obedientiam detrectari absque peccato, et absque ulla catholicæ professionis jactura:" quod quidem quantopere adversetur catholico dogmati plenæ potestatis Romano Pontifici ab ipso Christo Domino divinitus collatæ universalem pascendi, regendi, et gubernandi Ecclesiam, nemo est qui non clare aperteque videat et intelligat.

In tanta igitur depravatarum opinionum perversitate, Nos Apostolici

and very greatly solicitous for our most holy Religion, for sound doctrine and the salvation of souls which is intrusted to Us by God, and [solicitous also] for the welfare of human society itself, have thought it right again to raise up Our Apostolic voice. Therefore, by Our Apostolic Authority we reprobate, proscribe, and condemn all and singular the evil opinions and doctrines severally mentioned in this letter, and will and command that they be thoroughly held by all children of the Catholic Church as reprobated, proscribed, and condemned.

And besides these things, You know very well, Venerable Brethren, that in these times the haters of all truth and justice and most bitter enemies of our religion, deceiving the people and maliciously lying, disseminate sundry other impious doctrines by means of pestilential books, pamphlets, and newspapers dispersed over the whole world. Nor are You ignorant, also, that in this our age some men are found who, moved and excited by the spirit of Satan, have reached to that degree of impiety as not to shrink from denying Our Ruler and Lord Jesus Christ, and from impugning his divinity with wicked pertinacity. Here, however, we cannot but extol You, Venerable Brethren, with great and deserved praise, for not having failed to raise, with all zeal, your episcopal voice against impiety so great.

Therefore, in this Our Letter, we again most lovingly

Nostri officii probe memores, ac de sanctissima nostra Religione, de sana doctrina, et animarum salute Nobis divinitus commissa, ac de ipsius humanæ societatis bono maxime solliciti, Apostolicam Nostram vocem iterum extollere existimavimus. Itaque omnes et singulas pravas opiniones ac doctrinas singillatim hisce Litteris commemoratas Auctoritate Nostra Apostolica reprobamus, proscribimus atque damnamus, easque ab omnibus catholicæ Ecclesiæ filiis, veluti reprobatas, proscriptas atque damnatas omnino haberi volumus et mandamus.

Ac præter ea, optime scitis, Venerabiles Fratres, hisce temporibus omnis veritatis justitiæque osores, et acerrimos nostræ religionis hostes, per pestiferos libros, libellos, et ephemerides toto terrarum orbe dispersas populis illudentes, ac malitiose mentientes alias impias quasque disseminare doctrinas. Neque ignoratis, hac etiam nostra ætate, nonnullos reperiri, qui Satanæ spiritu permoti et incitati eo impietatis devenerunt, ut Dominatorem Dominum Nostrum Jesum Christum negare, ejusque Divinitatem scelerata procacitate oppugnare non paveant. Hic vero haud possumus, quin maximis meritisque laudibus Vos efferamus, Venerabiles Fratres, qui episcopalem vestram vocem contra tantam impietatem omni zelo attollere minime omisistis.

Itaque hisce Nostris Litteris Vos iterum amantissime alloquimur,

address you, who, having been called unto a part of Our solicitude, are to us, among our grievous distresses, the greatest solace, joy, and consolation, because of the admirable religion and piety wherein you excel, and because of that marvellous love, fidelity, and dutifulness, whereby, bound as you are to Us, and to this Apostolic See in most harmonious affection, you strive strenuously and sedulously to fulfil your most weighty episcopal ministry. For from your signal Pastoral zeal we expect that, taking up the sword of the spirit which is the word of God, and strengthened in the grace of our Lord Jesus Christ, you will, with redoubled care, each day more anxiously provide that the faithful intrusted to your charge "abstain from noxious herbage, which Jesus Christ does not cultivate because it is not His Father's plantation." Never cease also to inculcate on the said faithful that all true felicity flows abundantly upon man from our august religion and its doctrine and practice; and that happy is the people whose God is their Lord. Teach that "kingdoms rest on the foundation of the Catholic Faith, and that nothing is so deadly, so hastening to a fall, so exposed to all danger [as that which exists] if, believing this alone to be sufficient for us that we received free will at our birth, we seek nothing further from the Lord; that is, if forgetting our Creator we abjure his power that we may display our freedom." And again do not fail to teach "that the royal power

---

qui in sollicitudinis Nostræ partem vocati summo nobis inter maximas Nostras acerbitates solatio, lætitiæ, et consolationi estis propter egregiam, qua præstatis religionem, pietatem, ac propter mirum illum amorem, fidem, et observantiam, qua Nobis et huic Apostolicæ Sedi concordissimis animis obstricti gravissimum episcopale vestrum ministerium strenue ac sedulo implere contenditis. Etenim ab eximio vestro pastorali zelo expectamus, ut assumentes gladium spiritus, quod est verbum Dei, et confortati in gratia Domini nostri Jesu Christi, velitis ingeminatis studiis quotidie magis prospicere, ut fideles curæ vestræ concrediti "abstineant ab herbis noxiis, quas Jesus Christus non colit, quia non sunt plantatio Patris." [S. Ignatius M. ad Philadelph. 3.] Atque eisdem fidelibus inculcare nunquam desinite, omnem veram felicitatem in homines ex augusta nostra religione, ejusque doctrina et exercitio redundare, ac beatum esse populum, cujus Dominus Deus ejus. [Psal. 143.] Docete "catholicæ Fidei fundamento regna subsistere [Cœlest. Epist. 22, ad Synod. Ephes. apud Coust., p. 1200], et nihil tam mortiferum, tam præceps ad casum, tam expositum ad omnia pericula, si hoc solum nobis putantes posse sufficere, quod liberum arbitrium, cum nasceremur, accepimus, ultra jam a Domino nihil quæramus, id

was given not only for the governance of the world, but most of all for the protection of the Church;" and that there is nothing which can be of greater advantage and glory to Princes and Kings than if, as another most wise and courageous Predecessor of Ours, St. Felix, instructed the Emperor Zeno, they "permit the Catholic Church to practise her laws, and allow no one to oppose her liberty. For it is certain that this mode of conduct is beneficial to their interests, viz., that where there is question concerning the causes of God, they study, according to His appointment, to subject the royal will to Christ's Priests, not to raise it above theirs."

But if always, Venerable Brethren, now most of all amidst such great calamities both of the Church and of civil society, amidst so great a conspiracy against Catholic interests and this Apostolic See, and so great a mass of errors, it is altogether necessary to approach with confidence the throne of grace, that We may obtain mercy and find grace in timely aid. Wherefore, We have thought it well to excite the piety of all the faithful in order that, together with Us and You, they may unceasingly pray and beseech the most merciful Father of light and pity with most fervent and humble prayers, and in the fulness of faith flee always to Our Lord Jesus Christ, who redeemed

---

est, auctoris nostri obliti, ejus potentiam, ut nos ostendamus liberos, abjuremus." [S. Innocent. I. Epist. 29 ad Episc. Conc. Carthag. apud Coust., p. 891.] Atque etiam ne omittatis docere "regiam potestatem non ad solum mundi regimen, sed maxime ad Ecclesiæ præsidium esse collatam" [S. Leonis Epist. 156, al. 125], et nihil esse quod civitatum Principibus, et Regibus majori fructui, gloriæque esse possit, quam si, ut sapientissimus fortissimusque alter Prædecessor Noster S. Felix Zenoni Imperatori præscribebat, "Ecclesiam catholicam . . . sinant uti legibus suis, nec libertati ejus quemquam permittant obsistere. . . . Certum est enim, hoc rebus suis esse salutare, ut, cum de causis Dei agatur, justa ipsius constitutam regiam voluntatem Sacerdotibus Christi studeant subdere, non præferre." [Pii VII. Epist. Encycl. "*Diu satis*," 15 Maii 1800.]

Sed si semper, Venerabiles Fratres, nunc potissimum in tantis Ecclesiæ, civilisque societatis calamitatibus, in tanta adversariorum contra rem catholicam, et hanc Apostolicam Sedem conspiratione tantaque errorum congerie, necesse omnino est, ut adeamus cum fiducia ad thronum gratiæ, ut misericordiam consequamur, et gratiam inveniamus in auxilio opportuno. Quocirca omnium fidelium pietatem excitare existimavimus, ut una Nobiscum Vobisque clementissimum luminum et misericordiarum Patrem ferventissimis humillimisque precibus sine intermissione orent, et obsecrent, et in plenitudine fidei

us to God in His blood, and earnestly and constantly supplicate His most sweet Heart, the victim of most burning love towards us, that He would draw all things to Himself by the bonds of His love, and that all men inflamed by His most holy love may walk worthily according to His Heart, pleasing God in all things, bearing fruit in every good work. But since without doubt men's prayers are more pleasing to God if they reach Him from minds free of all stain, therefore we have determined to open to Christ's faithful, with Apostolic liberality, the Church's heavenly treasures committed to our charge, in order that the said faithful, being more earnestly enkindled to true piety, and cleansed through the Sacrament of Penance from the defilement of their sins, may with greater confidence pour forth their prayers to God, and obtain His mercy and grace.

By these Letters therefore, in virtue of Our Apostolic authority, We concede to all and singular the faithful of the Catholic world, a Plenary Indulgence in form of Jubilee, during the space of one month only for the whole coming year 1865, and not beyond; to be fixed by You, Venerable Brethren, and other legitimate Ordinaries of places, in the very same manner and form in which We granted it at the beginning of Our supreme Pontificate by Our Apostolic Letters in the form of a Brief, dated November 20, 1846, and all

semper confugiant ad Dominum Nostrum Jesum Christum, qui redemit nos Deo in sanguine suo, Ejusque dulcissimum Cor flagrantissimæ erga nos caritatis victimam enixe jugiterque exorent, ut amoris sui vinculis omnia ad seipsum trahat, utque omnes homines sanctissimo suo amore inflammati secundum Cor Ejus ambulent digne Deo per omnia placentes, in omni bono opere fructificantes. Cum autem sine dubio gratiores sint Deo hominum preces, si animis ab omni labe puris ad ipsum accedant, idcirco cælestes Ecclesiæ thesauros dispensationi Nostræ commissos Christifidelibus Apostolica liberalitate reserare censuimus, ut iidem fideles ad veram pietatem vehementius incensi, ac per Pœnitentiæ Sacramentum a peccatorum maculis expiati, fidentius suas preces ad Deum effundant, ejusque misericordiam et gratiam consequantur.

Hisce igitur Litteris auctoritate Nostra Apostolica omnibus et singulis utriusque sexus catholici orbis fidelibus Plenariam Indulgentiam ad instar Jubilæi concedimus intra unins tantum mensis spatium usque ad totum futurum annum 1865 et non ultra, a Vobis, Venerabiles Fratres, aliisque legitimis locorum Ordinariis statuendum, eodem prorsus modo et forma qua ab initio supremi Nostri Pontificatus concessimus per

dressed to all your Episcopal Order, beginning, "Arcano Divinæ Providentiæ consilio," and with all the same faculties which were given by Us in those Letters. We will, however, that all things be observed which were prescribed in the aforesaid Letters, and those things be excepted which We there so declared. And We grant this, notwithstanding anything whatever to the contrary, even things which are worthy of individual mention and derogation. In order however that all doubt and difficulty be removed, We have commanded a copy of the said Letters to be sent you.

"Let us implore," Venerable Brethren, "God's mercy from our inmost heart and with our whole mind: because He has Himself added, 'I will not remove my mercy from them.' Let us ask and we shall receive; and if there be delay and slowness in our receiving because we have gravely offended, let us knock, because to him that knocketh it shall be opened, if only the door be knocked by our prayers, groans, and tears, in which we must persist and persevere, and if the prayer be unanimous: . . . . let each man pray to God, not for himself alone, but for all his brethren, as the Lord hath taught us to pray." But in order that God may the more readily assent to the prayers and desires of Ourselves, of You, and of all the faithful, let us with all confidence employ as

---

Apostolicas Nostras Litteras in forma Brevis die 20 mensis Novembris anno 1846 datas, et ad universum episcopalem vestrum Ordinem missas, quarum initium "Arcano Divinæ Providentiæ consilio," et cum omnibus eisdem facultatibus, quæ per ipsas Litteras a Nobis datæ fuerunt. Volumus tamen, ut ea omnia serventur, quæ in commemoratis Litteris præscripta sunt, et ea excipiantur, quæ excepta esse declaravimus. Atque id concedimus, non obstantibus in contrarium facientibus quibuscumque, etiam speciali et individua mentione ac derogatione dignis. Ut autem omnis dubitatio et difficultas amoveatur, earumdem Litterarum exemplar ad Vos perferri jussimus.

"Rogemus, Venerabiles Fratres, de intimo corde et de tota mente misericordiam Dei, quia et ipse addidit dicens: Misericordiam autem meam non dispergam ab eis. Petamus et accipiemus, et si accipiendi mora et tarditas fuerit quoniam graviter offendimus, pulsemus, quia et pulsanti aperietur, si modo pulsent ostium preces, gemitus, et lacrymæ nostræ, quibus insistere et immorari oportet, et si sit unanimis oratio, . . . unusquisque oret Deum non pro se tantum, sed pro omnibus fratribus, sicut Dominus orare nos docuit. [S. Cyprian.

our advocate with Him the Immaculate and most holy Virgin Mary, Mother of God, who has slain all heresies throughout the world, and who, the most loving Mother of us all, "is all sweet . . . . and full of mercy . . . . shows herself to all as easily entreated: shows herself to all as most merciful; pities the necessities of all with a most large affection;" and standing as a Queen at the right hand cf her only begotten Son, our Lord Jesus Christ, in gilded clothing, surrounded with variety, can obtain from Him whatever she will. Let us also seek the suffrages of the Most Blessed Peter, Prince of the Apostles, and of Paul his Fellow-apostle, and of all the Saints in Heaven, who having now become God's friends, have arrived at the heavenly kingdom, and being crowned bear their palms, and being secure of their own immortality are anxious for our salvation.

Lastly, imploring from Our heart for You from God the abundance of all heavenly gifts, We most lovingly impart the Apostolic Benediction from Our inmost heart, a pledge of our signal love towards You, to Yourselves, Venerable Brethren, and to all the clerics and lay faithful committed to your care.

Given at Rome, from S. Peter's, the 8th day of December, in the year 1864, the tenth from the Dog-

---

Epist. II.] Quo vero facilius Deus Nostris, Vestrisque, et omnium fidelium precibus, votisque annuat, cum omni fiducia deprecatricem apud Eum adhibeamus Immaculatam sanctissimamque Deiparam Virginem Mariam, quæ cunctas hæreses interemit in universo mundo, quæque omnium nostrum amantissima Mater "tota suavis est . . . ac plena misericordiæ . . . omnibus sese exorabilem, omnibus clementissimam præbet, omnium necessitates amplissimo quodam miseratur affectu" [S. Bernard. Serm. de duodecim prærogativis B.M.V. ex verbis Apocalyp.], atque utpote Regina adstans a dextris Unigeniti Filii Sui Domini Nostri Jesu Christi in vestitu deaurato circumamicta varietate nihil est, quod ab Eo impetrare non valeat. Suffragia quoque petamus Beatissimi Petri Apostolorum Principis, et Coapostoli ejus Pauli, omniumque Sanctorum Cælitum, qui facti jam amici Dei pervenerunt ad cælestia regna, et coronati possident palmam, ac de sua immortalitate securi, de nostra sunt salute solliciti.

Denique cælestium omnium donorum copiam Vobis a Deo ex animo adprecantes, singularis Nostræ in Vos caritatis pignus Apostolicam Benedictionem ex intimo corde profectam Vobis ipsis, Venerabiles Fratres, cunctisque Clericis, Laicisque fidelibus curæ vestræ commissis peramanter impertimus.

Datum Romæ apud S. Petrum die VIII. Decembris anno 1864,

matic Definition of the Immaculate Conception of the Virgin Mary, Mother of God.

In the nineteenth year of Our Pontificate.

---

*SYLLABUS,

EMBRACING THE PRINCIPAL ERRORS OF OUR TIME WHICH ARE CENSURED IN CONSISTORIAL ALLOCUTIONS, ENCYCLICALS, AND OTHER APOSTOLIC LETTERS OF OUR MOST HOLY FATHER, POPE PIUS IX.

[It must be remembered, in regard to these propositions, that they were addressed by the Pontiff immediately not to laymen but to the Bishops; and that it is the office of those Bishops, or of theologians writing under their sanction, to set forth the true interpretation of them. For want of remembering this persons unacquainted with theological language have before now fallen into serious misapprehension.

One particular instance of this may be mentioned. When some given proposition is condemned, it by no means follows that what logicians call the "contrary" proposition is thereby asserted, but only the "contradictory." If some misbelievers, *e. g.*, were censured for saying that "all men will be finally saved," the Church would not thereby teach that *no* man will be finally saved, but only that not *all* men will be so blessed. By a blunder parallel to what we have now exposed a recent writer has actually understood the Syllabus as teaching that it is a wicked error to admit Protestants to equal political rights with Catholics, or to allow Protestant immigrants the free use of their worship.

---

decimo a Dogmatica Definitione Immaculatæ Conceptionis Deiparæ Virginis Mariæ.
Pontificatus Nostri anno decimonono.

Pius PP. IX.

---

*SYLLABUS

COMPLECTENS PRÆCIPUOS NOSTRÆ ÆTATIS ERRORES QUI NOTANTUR IN ALLOCUTIONIBUS CONSISTORIALIBUS, IN ENCYCLICIS ALIISQUE APOSTOLICIS LITTERIS SANCTISSIMI DOMINI NOSTRI PII PAPÆ IX.

" But the condemnation of Prop. 77 only teaches that in *some* places even at this time it is expected that the Catholic religion should be treated as the only religion of the State, all other worships being excluded." And the condemnation of Prop. 78 only implies that in *some* places (and particularly in New Grenada, to which the original Allocution referred) it is not laudable to tolerate Protestant immigrants in the public exercise of their worship. Various very important lessons undoubtedly follow from these condemnations; but it is simply monstrous to interpret them as has been done by the writer above cited.—EDITOR.]

§ I.

Pantheism, Naturalism, and absolute Rationalism.

I. There exists no supreme all-wise and most provident divine Being distinct from this universe, and God is the same as the nature of things, and therefore liable to change; and God is really made both in man and in the world, and all things are God and have the self-same substance of God; and God is one and the same thing with the world, and therefore spirit is the same thing with matter, necessity with liberty, truth with falsehood, good with evil, and just with unjust.

II. All action of God on mankind and on the world is to be denied.

III. Human reason, without any regard whatever being had to God, is the one judge of truth and falsehood, of good and evil; it is a law to itself, and

---

§ I.

Pantheismus, Naturalismus, et Rationalismus absolutus.

I. Nullum supremum, sapientissimum, providentissimumquæ Numen divinum exsistit ab hac rerum universitate distinctum, et Deus idem est ac rerum natura, et iccirco immutationibus obnoxius; Deusque reapse fit in homine et mundo, atque omnia Deus sunt et ipsissimam Dei habent substantiam; ac una eademque res est Deus cum mundo, et proinde spiritus cum materia, necessitas cum libertate, verum cum falso, bonum cum malo, et justum cum injusto.

Alloc. *Maxima quidem* 9 iunii 1862.

II. Neganda est omnis Dei actio in homines et mundum.

Alloc. *Maxima quidem* 9 iunii 1862.

III. Humana ratio, nullo prorsus Dei respectu habito, unicus est

suffices by its natural strength for providing the good of men and peoples.

IV. All the truths of religion flow from the natural force of human reason ; hence reason is the chief rule whereby man can and should obtain the knowledge of all truths of every kind.

V. Divine revelation is imperfect, and therefore subject to a continuous and indefinite progress corresponding to the advance of human reason.

VI. The faith of Christ is opposed to human reason; and divine revelation not only nothing profits, but is even injurious to man's perfection.

VII. The prophecies and miracles recorded and narrated in Scripture are poetical fictions, and the mysteries of christian faith a result of philosophical investigations ; and in the books of both Testaments are contained mythical inventions; and Jesus Christ himself is a mythical fiction.

§ II.
Moderate Rationalism.

VIII. Since human reason is on a level with religion

---

veri et falsi, boni et mali arbiter, sibi ipsi est lex, et naturalibus suis viribus ad hominum ac populorum bonum curandum sufficit.

Alloc. *Maxima quidem* 9 iunii 1862.

IV. Omnes religionis veritatis ex nativa humanæ rationis vi derivant ; hinc ratio est princeps norma qua homo cognitionem omnium cujuscumque generis veritatum assequi possit ac debeat.

Epist. encycl. *Qui pluribus* 9 novembris 1846.
Epist. encycl. *Singulari quidem* 17 martii 1856.
Alloc. *Maxima quidem* 9 iunii 1862.

V. Divina revelatio est imperfecta et iccirco subjecta continuo et indefinito progressui qui humanæ rationis progressioni respondeat.

Epist. encycl. *Qui pluribus* 9 novembris 1846.
Alloc. *Maxima quidem* 9 iunii 1862.

VI. Christi fides humanæ refragatur rationi ; divinaque revelatio non solum nihil prodest, verum etiam nocet hominis perfectioni.

Epist. encycl. *Qui pluribus* 9 novembris 1846.
Alloc. *Maxima quidem* 9 iunii 1862.

VII. Prophetiæ et miracula in sacris Litteris exposita et narrata sunt poetarum commenta, et christianæ fidei mysteria philosophicarum investigationum summa ; et utriusque Testamenti libris mythica continentur inventa ; ipseque Jesus Christus est mythica fictio.

Epist. encycl. *Qui pluribus* 9 novembris 1846.
Alloc. *Maxima quidem* 9 iunii 1862.

§ II.
Rationalismus moderatus.

VIII. Quum ratio humana ipsi religioni æquiparetur, iccirco theologicæ disciplinæ perinde ac philosophicæ tractandæ sunt.

itself, therefore theological studies are to be handled in the same manneras philosophical.

IX. All the dogmas of the Christian religion are without distinction the object of natural science or philosophy ; and human reason, with no other than an historical cultivation, is able from its own natural strength and principles to arrive at true knowledge of even the more abstruse dogmas, so only these dogmas hvae been proposed to the reason itself as its object.

X. Since the philosopher is one thing, philosophy another, the former has the right and duty of submitting himself to that authority which he may have approved as true ; but philosophy neither can nor should submit itself to any authority.

XI. The Church not only ought never to animadvert on philosophy, but ought to tolerate the errors of philosophy, and leave it in her hands to correct herself.

XII. The decrees of the Apostolic See and of Roman Congregations interfere with the free progress of science.

XIII. The method and principles whereby the ancient scholastic doctors cultivated theology are not suited to the necessities of our time and to the progress of the sciences.

Alloc. *Singulari quadam perfusi* 9 decembris 1854.
IX. Omnia indiscriminatim dogmata religionis Christianæ sunt objectum naturalis scientiæ seu philosophiæ ; et humana ratio historice tantum exculta potest ex suis naturalibus viribus et principiis ad veram de omnibus etiam reconditoribus dogmatibus scientiam pervenire, modo hæc dogmata ipsi rationi tamquam objectum proposita fuerint.
Epist. ad Archiep. Frising. *Gravissimas* 11 decembris 1862.
Epist. ad eumdem *Tuas libentur* 21 decembris 1863.
X. Quum aliud sit philosophus, aliud philosophia, ille jus officium habet se submittendi auctoritati, quam veram ipse probaverit ; at philosophia neque potest, neque debet ulli sese submittere auctoritati.
Epist ad Archiep. Frising. *Gravissimas* 11 decembris 1862.
Epist. ad eumdem *Tuas libenter* 21 decembris 1863.
XI. Ecclesia non solum non debet in philosophiam unquam animadvertere, verum etiam debet ipsius philosophiæ tolerare errores, eique relinquere ut ipsa se corrigat.
Epist. ad Archiep. Frising. *Gravissimas* 11 decembris 1862.
XII. Apostolicæ Sedis Romanarumque Congregationum decreta liberum scientiæ progressum impediunt.
Epist. ad Archiep. Frising. *Tuas libenter* 21 decembris 1863.
XIII. Methodus et principia, quibus antiqui doctores scholastici Theologiam excoluerunt, temporum nostrorum necessitatibus scientiarumque progressui minime congruunt.
Epist. ad Archiep. Frising. *Tuas libenter* 21 decembris 1863.

XIV. Philosophy should be treated without regard had to supernatural revelation.

N.B.—To the system of Rationalism belong mostly the errors of Antony Günther, which are condemned in the epistle to the Cardinal-Archbishop of Cologne: "Eximiam tuam," June 15, 1857, and in that to the Bishop of Breslau, "Dolore haud mediocri," April 30, 1860.

§ III.
Indifferentism, Latitudinarianism.

XV. Every man is free to embrace and profess that religion which, led by the light of reason, he may have thought true.

XVI. Men may in the practice of any religion whatever find the path of eternal salvation, and attain eternal salvation.

XVII. At least good hopes should be entertained concerning the salvation of all those who in no respect live in the true Church of Christ.

XVIII. Protestantism is nothing else than a different form of the same Christian religion, in which it is permitted to please God equally as in the true Catholic Church.

XIV. Philosophia tractanda est nulla supernaturalis revelationis habita ratione.
  Epist. ad Archiep. Frising. *Tuas libenter* 21 decembris 1863.
  N.B. Cum rationalismi systemate cohærent maximam partem errores Antonii Günther, qui damnatur in Epist. ad Card. Archiep. Coloniensem *Eximiam tuam*, 15 iunii 1847, et in Epist. ad Episc. Wratislaviensem *Dolore haud mediocri,* 30 aprilis 1860.

§ III.
Indifferentismus, Latitudinarismus.

XV. Liberum cuique homini est eam amplecti ac profiteri religionem, quam rationis lumine quis ductus veram putaverit.
  Litt. Apost. *Multiplices inter* 10 iunii 1851.
  Alloc. *Maxima quidem* 9 iunii 1862.

XVI. Homines in cujusvis religionis cultu viam æternæ salutis reperire æternamque salutem assequi possunt.
  Epist. encycl. *Qui pluribus* 9 novembris 1846.
  Alloc. *Ubi primum* 17 decembris 1847.
  Epist. encycl. *Singulari quidem* 17 martii 1856.

XVII. Saltem bene sperandum est de æterna illorum omnium salute, qui in vera Christi Ecclesia nequaquam versantur.
  Alloc. *Singulari quadam* 9 decembris 1854.
  Epist. encycl. *Quanto conficiamur* 17 augusti 1863.

XVIII. Protestantismus non aliud est quam diversa ejusdem Christianæ religionis forma, in qua æque ac in Ecclesia Catholica Deo placere datum est.
  Epist. encycl. *Nostis et Nobiscum* 8 decembris 1849.

§ IV.

Socialism, Communism, Secret Societies, Bible Societies, Clerical Liberal Societies.

Pests of this kind are often reprobated, and in the most severe terms in the Encyclical "Qui pluribus," November 9, 1846; the Allocution "Quibus Quantisque," April 20, 1849; the Encyclical "Noscitis et Nobiscum," December 8, 1849; the Allocution "Singulari quâdam," December 9, 1854; the Encyclical "Quanto conficiamur," August 10, 1863.

§ V.

Errors concerning the Church and her rights.

XIX. The Church is not a true and perfect society fully free, nor does she enjoy her own proper and permanent rights given to her by her divine Founder, but it is the civil power's business to define what are the Church's rights, and the limits within which she may be enabled to exercise them.

XX. The ecclesiastical power should not exercise its authority without permission and assent of the civil government.

XXI. The Church has not the power of dogmatically defining that the religion of the Catholic Church is the only true religion.

---

§ IV.

Socialismus, Communismus, Societates clandestinæ, Societates biblicæ, Societates clerico-liberales.

Ejusmodi pestes sæpe gravissimisque verborum formulis reprobantur in Epist. encycl. *Qui pluribus*, 9 novemb. 1846; in Alloc. *Quibus quantisque*, 20 april. 1849; in Epist. encycl. *Noscitis et Nobiscum*, 8 dec. 1849; in Alloc. *Singulari quadam*, 9 decemb. 1854; in Epist. encycl. *Quanto conficiamur mœrore*, 10 augusti 1863.

§ V.

Errores de Ecclesia ejusque juribus.

XIX. Ecclesia non est vera perfectaque societas plane libera, nec pollet suis propriis et constantibus juribus sibi a divino suo Fundatore collatis, sed civilis potestatis est definire quæ sint Ecclesiæ jura ac limites, intra quos eadem jura exercere queat.

    Alloc. *Singulari quadam* 9 decembris 1854.
    Alloc. *Multis gravibusque* 17 decembris 1860.
    Alloc. *Maxima quidem* 9 iunii 1862.

XX. Ecclesiastica potestas suam auctoritatem exercere non debet absque civilis gubernii venia et assensu.

    Alloc. *Meminit unusquisque* 30 septembris 1861.

XXI. Ecclesia non habet potestatem dogmatice definiendi, religionem Catholicæ Ecclesiæ esse unice veram religionem.

    Litt. Apost. *Multiplices inter* 10 iunii 1851.

XXII. The obligation by which Catholic teachers and writers are absolutely bound, is confined to those things alone which are propounded by the Church's infallible judgment, as dogmas of faith to be believed by all.

XXIII. Roman Pontiffs and Œcumenical Councils have exceeded the limits of their power, usurped the rights of Princes, and erred even in defining matters of faith and morals.

XXIV. The Church has no power of employing force, nor has she any temporal power direct or indirect.

XXV. Besides the inherent power of the episcopate, another temporal power has been granted expressly or tacitly by the civil government, which may therefore be abrogated by the civil government at its pleasure.

XXVI. The Church has no native and legitimate right of acquiring and possessing.

XXVII. The Church's sacred ministers and the Roman Pontiff should be entirely excluded from all charge and dominion of temporal things.

XXVIII. Bishops ought not, without the permis-

XXII. Obligatio, qua catholici magistri et scriptores omnino adstringuntur, coarctatur in iis tantum, quæ ab infallibili Ecclesiæ judicio veluti fidei dogmata ab omnibus credenda proponuntur.
Epist. ad Archiep. Frising. *Tuas libenter* 21 decembris 1863.

XXIII. Romani Pontifices et Concilia œcumenica a limitibus suæ potestatis recesserunt, jura Principum usurparunt, atque etiam in rebus fidei et morum definiendis errarunt.
Litt. Apost. *Multiplices inter* 10 iunii 1851.

XXIV. Ecclesia vis inferendæ potestatem non habet, neque potestatem ullam temporalem directam vel indirectam.
Litt. Apost. *Ad apostolicae* 22 augusti 1851.

XXV. Præter potestatem episcopatui inhærentem, alia est attributa temporalis potestas a civili imperio vel expresse vel tacite concessa, revocanda propterea, cum libuerit, a civili imperio.
Litt. Apost. *Ad apostolicae* 22 augusti 1851.

XXVI. Ecclesia non habet nativum ac legitimum jus acquirendi ac possidendi.
Alloc. *Nunquam fore* 15 decembris 1856.
Epist encycl. *Incredibili* 17 septembris 1863.

XXVII. Sacri Ecclesiæ ministri Romanusque Pontifex ab omni rerum temporalium cura ac dominio sunt omnino excludendi.
Alloc. *Maxima quidem* 9 iunii 1862.

sion of the Government, to publish even letters apostolic.

XXIX. Graces granted by the Roman Pontiff should be accounted as void, unless they have been sought through the Government.

XXX. The immunity of the Church and of ecclesiastical persons had its origin from the civil law.

XXXI. The ecclesiastical forum for the temporal causes of clerics, whether civil causes or criminal, should be altogether abolished, even without consulting, and against the protest of, the Apostolic See.

XXXII. Without any violation of natural right and equity, that personal immunity may be abrogated, whereby clerics are exempted from the burden of undertaking and performing military services; and such abrogation is required by civil progress, especially in a society constituted on the model of a free rule.

XXXIII. It does not appertain exclusively to ecclesiastical jurisdiction by its own proper and native right to direct the teaching of theology.

XXXIV. The doctrine of those who compare the

XXVIII. Episcopis sine Gubernii venia, fas non est vel ipsas apostolicas litteras promulgare.
    Alloc. *Nunquam fore* 15 decembris 1856.

XXIX. Gratiæ a Romano Pontifice concessæ existimari debent tamquam irritæ, nisi per Gubernium fuerint imploratæ.
    Alloc. *Nunquam fore* 15 decembris 1856.

XXX. Ecclesiæ et personarum ecclesiasticarum immunitas a jure civili ortum habuit.
    Litt. Apost. *Multiplices inter* 10 iunii 1851.

XXXI. Ecclesiasticum forum pro temporalibus clericorum causis sive civilibus sive criminalibus omnino de medio tollendum est etiam inconsulta et reclamante Apostolica Sede.
    Alloc. *Acerbissimum* 27 septembris 1852.
    Alloc. *Nunquam fore* 15 decembris 1856.

XXXII. Absque ulla naturalis juris et æquitatis violatione potest abrogari personalis immunitas, qua clerici ab onere subeundæ exercendæque militiæ eximuntur; hanc vero abrogationem postulat civilis progressus, maxime in societate ad formam liberioris regiminis constituta.
    Epist. ad Episc. Montisregal. *Singularis nobisque* 29 septembris 1864.

XXXIII. Non pertinet unice ad ecclesiasticam jurisdictionis potestatem proprio ac nativo jure dirigere theologicarum rerum doctrinam.
    Epist. ad Archiep. Frising. *Tuas libenter* 21 decembris 1863.

XXXIV. Doctrina comparantium Romanum Pontificem Principi

Roman Pontiff to a Prince, free and acting in the Universal Church, is the doctrine which prevailed in the middle age.

XXXV. Nothing forbids that by the judgment of some general Council, or by the act of all peoples, the supreme Pontificate should be transferred from the Roman Bishop and City to another Bishop and another state.

XXXVI. The definition of a national Council admits no further dispute, and the civil administration may fix the matter on this footing.

XXXVII. National Churches separated and totally disjoined from the Roman Pontiff's authority may be instituted.

XXXVIII. The too arbitrary conduct of Roman Pontiffs contributed to the Church's division into East and West.

§ VI.

Errors concerning Civil Society, considered both in itself and in its relations to the Church.

XXXIX. The State, as being the origin and fountain of all rights, possesses a certain right of its own, circumscribed by no limits.

---

libero et agenti in universa Ecclesia, doctrina est quæ medio ævo prævaluit.
    Litt. Apost. *Ad apostolicae* 22 augusti 1851.
    XXXV. Nihil vetat, alicujus Concilii generalis sententia aut universorum populorum facto, summum Pontificatum ab Romano Episcopo atque Urbe ad alium Episcopum aliamque civitatem transferri.
    Litt. Apost. *Ad apostolicae* 22 augusti 1851.
    XXXVI. Nationalis Concilii definitio nullam aliam admittit disputationem, civilisque administratio rem ad hosce terminos exigere potest.
    Litt. Apost. *Ad apostolicae* 22 augusti 1851.
    XXXVII. Institui possunt nationales Ecclesiæ ab auctoritate Romani Pontificis subductæ planeque divisæ.
    Alloc. *Multis gravibusque* 17 decembris 1860.
    Alloc. *Iamdudum cernimus* 18 martii 1861.
    XXXVIII. Divisioni Ecclesiæ in orientalem atque occidentalem nimia Romanorum Pontificum arbitria contulerunt.
    Litt. Apost. *Ad apostolicae* 22 augusti 1851.

§ VI.

Errores de societate civili tum in se, tum in suis ad Ecclesiam relationibus spectata.

    XXXIX. Reipublicæ status, utpote omnium jurium origo et fons, jure quodam pollet nullis circumscripto limitibus.
    Alloc. *Maxima quidem* 9 iunii 1862.

XL. The doctrine of the Catholic Church is opposed to the good and benefit of human society.

XLI. The civil power, even when exercised by a non-Catholic ruler, has an indirect negative power over things sacred; it has consequently not only the right which they call *exequatur*, but that right also which they call *appel comme d'abus*.

XLII. In the case of a conflict between laws of the two powers, civil law prevails.

XLIII. The lay power has the authority of rescinding, of declaring null, and of voiding solemn conventions (commonly called Concordats), concerning the exercise of rights appertaining to ecclesiastical immunity, which have been entered into with the Apostolic See, without this See's consent, and even against its protest.

XLIV. The civil authority may mix itself up in matters which appertain to religion, morals and spiritual rule. Hence it can exercise judgment concerning those instructions which the Church's pastors issue according to their office for the guidance of consciences: nay, it may even decree concerning the administration of the holy sacraments, and concerning the dispositions necessary for their reception.

XL. Catholicæ Ecclesiæ doctrina humanæ societatis bono et commodo adversatur.
    Epist. encycl. *Qui pluribus* 9 novembris 1846.
    Alloc. *Quibus quantisque* 20 aprilis 1849.

XLI. Civili potestati vel ab infideli imperante exercitæ competit potestas indirecta negativa in sacra; eidem proinde competit nedum jus quod vocant *exequatur*, sed etiam jus *appellationis*, quam nuncupant *ab abusu*.
    Litt. Apost, *Ad apostolicae* 22 augusti 1851.

XLII. In conflictu legum utriusque potestatis, jus civile prævalet.
    Litt. Apost. *Ad apostolicae* 22 augusti 1851.

XLIII. Laica potestas auctoritatem habet rescindendi, declarandi ac faciendi irritas solemnes conventiones (vulgo *Concordata*) super usu jurium ad ecclesiasticam immunitatem pertinentium cum Sede Apostolica initas, sine hujus consensu, immo et ea reclamante.
    Alloc. *In Consistoriali* 1 novembris 1850.
    Alloc. *Multis gravibusque* 17 decembris 1860.

XLIV. Civilis auctoritas potest se immiscere rebus quæ ad religionem, mores et regimen spirituale pertinent. Hinc potest de instructionibus judicare, quas Ecclesiæ pastores ad conscientiarum normam pro suo munere edunt, quin etiam potest de divinorum sacramentorum administratione et dispositionibus ad ea suscipienda necessariis decernere.
    Alloc. *In Consistoriali* 1 novembris 1850.
    Alloc. *Maxima quidem* 9 iunii 1862.

XLV. The whole governance of public schools wherein the youth of any Christian State is educated, episcopal seminaries only being in some degree excepted, may and should be given to the civil power; and in such sense be given, that no right be recognized in any other authority of mixing itself up in the management of the schools, the direction of studies, the conferring of degrees, the choice or approbation of teachers.

XLVI. Nay, in the very ecclesiastical seminaries, the method of study to be adopted is subject to the civil authority.

XLVII. The best constitution of civil society requires that popular schools which are open to children of every class, and that public institutions generally which are devoted to teaching literature and science and providing for the education of youth, be exempted from all authority of the Church, from all her moderating influence and interference, and subjected to the absolute will of the civil and political authority [so as to be conducted] in accordance with the tenets of civil rulers, and the standard of the common opinions of the age.

XLVIII. That method of instructing youth can be approved by Catholic men, which is disjoined from

---

XLV. Totum scholarum publicarum regimen, in quibus juventus christianæ alicujus Reipublicæ instituitur, episcopalibus dumtaxat seminariis aliqua ratione exceptis, potest ac debet attribui auctoritati civili, et ita quidem attribui, ut nullum alii cuicumque auctoritati recognoscatur jus immiscendi se in disciplina scholarum, in regimine studiorum, in graduum collatione, in delectu aut approbatione magistrorum.

Alloc. *In Consistoriali* 1 novembris 1850.
Alloc. *Quibus luctuosissimis* 5 septembris 1851.

XLVI. Immo in ipsis clericorum seminariis methodus studiorum adhibenda civili auctoritati subjicitur.

Alloc. *Nunquam fore* 15 decembris 1856.

XLVII. Postulat optima civilis societatis ratio, ut populares scholæ, quæ patent omnibus cujusque e populo classis pueris, ac publica universim Instituta, quæ litteris severioribusque disciplinis tradendis et educationi juventutis curandæ sunt destinata, eximantur ab omni Ecclesiæ auctoritate, moderatrice vi et ingerentia, plenoque, civilis ac politicæ auctoritatis arbitrio subjiciantur, ad imperantium placita et ad communium ætatis opinionum amussim.

Epist. ad Archiep. Friburg. *Quum non sine* 14 iulii 1864.

XLVIII. Catholicis viris probari potest ea juventutis instituendæ ratio, quæ sit a catholica fide et ab Ecclesiæ potestate sejuncta, quæque

the Catholic faith and the Church's power, and which regards exclusively, or at least principally, knowledge of the natural order alone, and the ends of social life on earth.

XLIX. The civil authority may prevent the Bishops and faithful from free and mutual communication with the Roman Pontiff.

L. The lay authority has of itself the right of presenting Bishops, and may require of them that they enter on the management of their dioceses before they receive from the Holy See canonical institution and apostolical letters.

LI. Nay, the lay government has the right of deposing Bishops from exercise of their pastoral ministry; nor is it bound to obey the Roman Pontiff in those things which regard the establishment of Bishoprics and the appointment of Bishops.

LII. The government may, in its own right, change the age prescribed by the Church for the religious profession of men and women, and may require religious orders to admit no one to solemn vows without its permission.

LIII. Those laws should be abrogated which relate to protecting the condition of religious orders and their

---

rerum dumtaxat naturalium scientiam ac terrenæ socialis vitæ fines tantum modo vel saltem primarium spectet.
    Epist. ad Archiep. Friburg. *Quum non sine* 14 iulii 1864.
    XLIX. Civilis auctoritas potest impedire quominus sacrorum Antistites et fideles populi cum Romano Pontifice libere ac mutuo communicent.
    Alloc. *Maxima quidem* 9 iunii 1862.
    L. Laica auctoritas habet per se jus præsentandi Episcopos, et potest ab illis exigere ut ineant diœcesium procurationem, antequam ipsi canonicam a S. Sede institutionem et apostolicas litteras accipiant.
    Alloc. *Nunquam fore* 15 decembris 1856.
    LI. Immo laicum gubernium habet jus deponendi ab exercitio pastoralis ministerii Episcopos, neque tenetur obedire Romano Pontifici in iis quæ episcopatum et Episcoporum respiciunt institutionem.
    Litt. Apost. *Multiplices inter* 10 iunii 1851.
    Alloc. *Acerbissimum* 27 septembris 1852.
    LII. Gubernium potest suo jure immutare ætatem ab Ecclesiæ præscriptam pro religiosa tam mulierum quam virorum professione, omnibusque religiosis familiis indicere, ut neminem sine suo permissu ad solemnia vota nuncupanda admittant.
    Alloc. *Nunquam fore* 15 decembris 1856.
    LIII. Abrogandæ sunt leges quæ ad religiosarum familiarum statum tutandum, earumque jura et officia pertinent; immo potest civile guber-

rights and duties; nay, the civil government may give assistance to all those who may wish to quit the religious life which they have undertaken, and to break their solemn vows; and in like manner it may altogether abolish the said religious orders, and also collegiate churches and simple benefices, even those under the right of a patron, and subject and assign their goods and revenues to the administration and free disposal of the civil power.

LIV. Kings and Princes are not only exempted from the Church's jurisdiction, but also are superior to the Church in deciding questions of jurisdiction.

LV. The Church should be separated from the State, and the State from the Church.

§ VII.

Errors concerning natural and Christian Ethics.

LVI. The laws of morality need no divine sanction, and there is no necessity that human laws be conformed to the law of nature, or receive from God their obligatory force.

LVII. The science of philosophy and morals, and also the laws of a state, may and should withdraw themselves from the jurisdiction of Divine and ecclesiastical authority.

---

nium iis omnibus auxilium præstare, qui a suscepto religiosæ vitæ instituto deficere ac solemnia vota frangere velint; pariterque potest religiosas easdem familias perinde ac collegiatas Ecclesias et beneficia simplicia etiam juris patronatus penitus extinguere, illorumque bona et reditus civilis potestatis administrationi et arbitrio subjicere et vindicare.

Alloc. *Acerbissimum* 27 septembris 1852.
Alloc. *Probe memineritis* 22 ianuarii 1855.
Alloc. *Cum saepe* 26 iulii 1855.

LIV. Reges et Principes non solum ab Ecclesiæ jurisdictione eximuntur, verum etiam in quæstionibus jurisdictionis dirimendis superiores sunt Ecclesiæ.

Litt. Apost. *Multiplices inter* 10 iunii 1851.
LV. Ecclesia a Statu, Statusque ab Ecclesia sejungendus est.
Alloc. *Acerbissimum* 27 septembris 1852.

§ VII.

Errores de Ethica naturali et Christiana.

LVI. Morum leges divina haud egent sanctione, minimeque opus est ut humanæ leges ad naturæ jus conformentur aut obligandi vim a Deo accipiant.

Alloc. *Maxima quidem* 9 iunii 1862.

LVII. Philosophicarum rerum morumque scientia, itemque civiles leges possunt et debent a divina et ecclesiastica auctoritate declinare.

Alloc. *Maxima quidem* 9 iunii 1862.

LVIII. No other strength is to be recognized except material force; and all moral discipline and virtue should be accounted to consist in accumulating and increasing wealth by every method, and in satiating the desire of pleasure.

LIX. Right consists in the mere material fact; and all the duties of man are an empty name, and all human facts have the force of right.

LX. Authority is nothing else but numerical power and material force.

LXI. The successful injustice of a fact brings with it no detriment to the sanctity of right.

LXII. The principle of non-intervention (as it is called) should be proclaimed and observed.

LXIII. It is lawful to refuse obedience to legitimate princes, and even rebel against them.

LXIV. A violation of any most sacred oath, or any wicked and flagitious action whatever repugnant to the eternal law, is not only not to be reprobated, but is even altogether lawful, and to be extolled

---

LVIII. Aliæ vires non sunt agnoscendæ nisi illæ quæ in materia positæ sunt, et omnis morum disciplina honestasque collocari debet in cumulandis et augendis quovis modo divitiis ac in voluptatibus explendis.
  Alloc. *Maxima quidem* 9 iunii 1862.
  Epist encycl. *Quanto conficiamur* 10 augusti 1863.

LIX. Jus in materiali facto consistit, et omnia hominum officia sunt nomen inane, et omnia humana facta juris vim habent.
  Alloc. *Maxima quidem* 9 iunii 1862.

LX. Auctoritas nihil aliud est nisi numeri et materialium virium summa.
  Alloc. *Maxima quidem* 9 iunii 1862.

LXI. Fortunata facti injustitia nullum juris sanctitati detrimentum affert.
  Alloc. *Iamdudum cernimus* 18 martii 1861.

LXII. Proclamandum est et observandum principium quod vocant de *non interventu*.
  Alloc. *Novos et ante* 28 septembris 1860.

LXIII. Legitimis principibus obedientiam detrectare, immo et rebellare licet.
  Epist. encycl. *Qui pluribus* 9 novembris 1846.
  Alloc. *Quisque vestrum* 4 octobris 1847.
  Epist. encycl. *Nostis et Nobiscum* 8 decembris 1849.
  Litt. Apost. *Cum catholica* 26 martii 1860.

LXIV. Tum cujusque sanctissimi juramenti violatio, tum quælibet scelesta flagitiosaque aetio sempiternæ legi repugnans, non solum haud

with the highest praise when it is done for love of country.

§ VIII.
Errors concerning Christian Matrimony.

LXV. It can in no way be tolerated that Christ raised matrimony to the dignity of a sacrament.

LXVI. The sacrament of marriage is only an accessory to the contract, and separable from it; and the sacrament itself consists in the nuptial benediction alone.

LXVII. The bond of matrimony is not indissoluble by the law of nature; and in various cases divorce, properly so called, may be sanctioned by the civil authority.

LXVIII. The Church has no power of enacting diriment impediments to marriage ; but that power is vested in the civil authority, by which the existing impediments may be removed.

LXIX. In later ages the Church began to enact diriment impediments, not in her own right, but through that right which she had borrowed from the civil power.

---

est improbanda, verum etiam omnino licita, summisque laudibus efferenda, quando id pro patriæ amore agatur.
 Alloc. *Quibus quantisque* 20 aprilis 1849.

§ VIII.
Errores de Matrimonio Christiano.

LXV. Nulla ratione ferri potest, Christum evexisse matrimonium ad dignitatem sacramenti.
 Litt. Apost. *Ad apostolicae* 22 augusti 1851.

LXVI. Matrimonii sacramentum non est nisi contractui accessorium ab eoque separabile, ipsumque sacramentum in una tantum nuptiali benedictione situm est.
 Litt. Apost. *Ad apostolicae* 23 augusti 1851.

LXVII. Jure naturæ matrimonii vinculum non est indissolubile, et in variis casibus divortium proprie dictum auctoritate civili sanciri potest.
 Litt. Apost. *Ad apostolicae* 22 augusti 1851.
 Alloc. *Acerbissimum* 27 septembris 1852.

LXVIII. Ecclesia non habet potestatem impedimenta matrimonium dirimentia inducendi, sed ea potestas civili auctoritati competit, a qua existentia impedimenta tollenda sunt.
 Litt. Apost. *Multiplices inter* 10 iunii 1851.

LXIX. Ecclesia sequioribus sæculis dirimentia impedimenta inducere cœpit, non jure proprio, sed illo jure usa, quod a civili potestate mutuata erat.

LXX. The Canons of Trent, which inflict the censure of anathema on those who dare to deny the Church's power of enacting diriment impediments, are either not dogmatical, or are to be understood of this borrowed power.

LXXI. The form ordained by the Council of Trent does not bind on pain of nullity wherever the civil law may prescribe another form, and may will that, by this new form, matrimony shall be made valid.

LXXII. Boniface VIII. was the first who asserted that the vow of chastity made at ordination annuls marriage.

LXXIII. By virtue of a purely civil contract there may exist among Christians marriage, truly so called; and it is false that either the contract of marriage among Christians is always a sacrament, or that there is no contract if the sacrament be excluded.

LXXIV. Matrimonial causes and espousals belong by their own nature to the civil forum.

N.B. To this head may be referred two other errors: on abolishing clerical celibacy, and on preferring the

---

Litt. Apost. *Ad apostolicae* 22 augusti 1851.
LXX. Tridentini canones qui anathematis censuram illis inferunt qui facultatem impedimenta dirimentia inducendi Ecclesiæ negare audeant, vel non sunt dogmatici vel de hac mutuata potestate intelligendi sunt.
Litt. Apost. *Ad apostolicae* 22 augusti 1851.
LXXI. Tridentini forma sub infirmitatis pœna non obligat, ubi lex civilis aliam formam præstituat, et velit ac nova forma interveniente matrimonium valere.
Litt. Apost. *Ad apostolicae* 22 augusti 1851.
LXXII. Bonifacius VIII. votum castitatis in ordinatione emissum nuptias nullas reddere primus asseruit.
Litt. Apost. *Ad apostolicae* 22 augusti 1851.
LXXIII. Vi contractus mere civilis potest inter christianos constare veri nominis matrimonium; falsumque est, aut contractum matrimonii inter christianos semper esse sacramentum, aut nullum esse contractum, si sacramentum excludatur.
Litt. Apost. *Ad apostolicae* 22 augusti 1851.
Lettera di SS. Pio IX al Re di Sardegna, 9 settembre 1852.
Alloc. *Acerbissimum* 27 septembris 1852.
Alloc. *Multis gravibusque* 17 decembris 1860.
LXXIV. Caussæ matrimoniales et sponsalia suapte natura ad forum civile pertinent.
Litt. Apost. *Ad apostolicae* 22 augusti 1851.
Alloc. *Acerbissimum* 27 septembris 1852.
N.B. Huc facere possunt duo alii errores: de clericorum cœlibatu

state of marriage to that of virginity. They are condemned, the former in the Encyclical "Qui pluribus," Nov. 9, 1846; the latter in the Apostolic Letters, "Multiplices inter," June 10, 1851.

§ IX.

Errors concerning the Roman Pontiff's civil princedom.

LXXV. Children of the Christian and Catholic Church dispute with each other on the compatibility of the temporal rule with the spiritual.

LXXVI. The abrogation of that civil power, which the Apostolic See possesses, would conduce in the highest degree to the Church's liberty and felicity.

N.B. Besides these errors explicitly branded, many others are implicitly reprobated in the exposition and assertion of that doctrine which all Catholics ought most firmly to hold concerning the Roman Pontiff's civil princedom. This doctrine is clearly delivered in the Allocution "Quibus quantisque," April 20, 1849; in the Allocution, "Si semper antea," May 20, 1850; in the Apostolic Letters, "Cum Catholica Ecclesia," March 26, 1860; in the Allocution, "Novos," Sept. 28, 1861; in the Allocution "Jamdudum," March 18, 1861; in the Allocution, "Maxima quidem," June 9, 1862.

---

abolendo et de statu matrimonii statui virginitatis anteferendo. Confodiuntur, prior in Epist. Encycl. *Qui pluribus*, 9 Novembris 1846, posterior in Litteris Apost. *Multiplices inter*, 10 Junii 1851.

§ IX.

Errores de civili Romani Pontificis Principatu.

LXXV. De temporalis regni cum spirituali compatibilitate disputant inter se christianæ et catholicæ Ecclesiæ filii.

Litt. Apost. *Ad apostolicae* 22 augusti 1851.

LXXVI. Abrogatio civilis imperii, quo Apostolica Sedes potitur, ad Ecclesiæ libertatem felicitatemque vel maxime conduceret.

Alloc. *Quibus quantisque* 20 aprilis 1849.

N.B.—Præter hos errores explicite notatos, alii complures implicite reprobantur proposita et asserta doctrina, quam catholici omnes firmissime retinere debeant, de civili Romani Pontificis principatu. Ejusmodi doctrina luculenter traditur in Alloc. *Quibus quantisque*, 20 April. 1849; in Alloc, *Si semper antea* 20 Maii 1850; in Litt. Apost. *Cum catholica Ecclesia*, 26 Mart. 1860; in Alloc. *Novos*, 28 Sept. 1860; in Alloc. *Jamdudum*, 18 Mart. 1861; in Alloc. *Maxima quidem*, 9 Junii 1862.

§ X.

Errors which have reference to the Liberalism of the day.

LXXVII. In this our age it is no longer expedient that the Catholic religion should be treated as the only religion of the State, all other worships whatsoever being excluded.

LXXVIII. Hence it has been laudably provided by law in some Catholic countries, that men thither immigrating should be permitted the public exercise of their own several worships.

LXXIX. For truly it is false that the civil liberty of all worships, and the full power granted to all of openly and publicly declaring any opinions or thoughts whatever, conduces to more easily corrupting the morals and minds of peoples and propagating the plague of indifferentism.

LXXX. The Roman Pontiff can and ought to reconcile and harmonize himself with progress, with liberalism, and with modern civilization.

---

§ X.
Errores qui ad Liberalismum hodiernum referuntur.

LXXVII. Ætate hac nostra non amplius expedit religionem catholicam haberi tanquam unicam status religionem, ceteris quibuscumque cultibus exclusis.

Alloc. *Nemo vestrum* 26 iulii 1855.

LXXVIII. Hinc laudabiliter in quibusdam catholici nominis regionibus lege cautum est, ut hominibus illuc immigrantibus liceat publicum proprii cujusque cultus exercitium habere.

Alloc. *Acerbissimum* 27 septembris 1852.

LXXIX. Enimvero falsum est, civilem cujusque cultus libertatem, itemque plenam potestatem omnibus attributam quaslibet opiniones cogitationesque palam publiceque manifestandi, conducere ad populorum mores animosque facilius corrumpendos, ac indifferentismi pestem propagandam.

Alloc. *Nunquam fore* 15 decembris 1856.

LXXX. Romanus Pontifex potest ac debet cum progressu, cum liberalismo et cum recenti civilitate sese reconciliare et componere.

Alloc. *Iamdudum cernimus* 18 martii 1861.

THE FIRST COUNCIL OF THE VATICAN;

OR,

THE NINETEENTH GENERAL COUNCIL.

INTRODUCTION.

THE EFFECT PRODUCED UPON THE WORLD AND UPON THE FAITHFUL BY THE SUMMONING OF THE GENERAL COUNCIL.—GENERAL COUNCILS, FROM THEIR NATURE, CALLED TOGETHER BUT SELDOM.—THEY ARE SIGNS OF AN UNUSUAL STATE OF THINGS.—THE INDICTION OF A COUNCIL A VERY SOLEMN ACT ON THE PART OF THE VICAR OF JESUS CHRIST.

Conciliorum originem ab Apostolis petere debemus, a quibus primum Concilium Jerosolymis fuit celebratum, cum Antiochiæ exorta esset controversia de necessitate circumcisionis, legisque Mosaicæ servandæ: cujus Concilii acta referuntur a Sancto Luca in cap. xv. Actorum. Quamobrem Ecclesia ab Apostolis edocta, eorumque exemplum secuta, quoties aut in rebus fidei aut disciplinæ aliquid in controversiam venit, quod, etsi sola Romani Pontificis perscripta auctoritate definiri posset, pro temporum tamen vel causarum aut personarum ratione, multo facilius coactis in unum Episcopis, atque collatis consiliis expediri posse videretur, concilia habere consuevit.—*Bartholi, Inst. Juris Canonic.,* c. 21.

THE convocation of a General Council is a fact that has come upon this generation in a manner so unexpected that it has deprived it, in one sense, of the power of discussing its meaning. There is in the minds of some a certain feeling akin to that of fear, for they cannot imagine any reasons why the Sovereign Pontiff, amid all his troubles, should voluntarily add to them. It is true that these people have notions of General Councils not likely to be realized at present, for they imagine the Prelates, who will come together from the four corners of the earth, to be under the dominion of ideas and prejudices long ago extinct in the ecclesiastical mind. It is, perhaps, impossible to persuade these people of confused knowledge, that the Bishops of the Church understand their position, know their work, and are ready to do it. But there are also many persons, unhappily for themselves and to their grievous spiritual loss, who have heard without much sympathy of this great Pontifical act, and therefore remain indifferent to the issues. Every action of the Sovereign Pontiff concerns the Church over which he rules as the Vicar of God, and every member of that Church ought to feel, and those who realize their state do feel, some more, some less, a most constant and abiding sense of the supernatural power and influence which every Pontifical act involves. As in civil life, the acts of the sovereign power in making laws and decrees, by which the rights or possessions of the subject are touched, reach in a thousand ways through the whole body politic, so is it in the Church, but in a far greater degree and to far nobler ends; for the aims of the Pope are higher than temporal and material good, seeing that the whole action of the Church—and he is its supreme ruler—tends to the salvation of human souls.

When the world first heard a rumour from Rome that his Holiness the Pope was seriously thinking of calling a General Council, and of holding it in the Eternal City, daily menaced by the lawless men who have tried to banish civil government out of the world as well as the holy name of Christ, it received that rumour with incredulity, and then treated the story with the contemptuous indifference which it gives only to the things of God. Good people too wondered, and were not wholly without fear; but as time went on, and they had time to think, their minds underwent a change, and they found themselves not only willing to accept the Council, but even eager to welcome the Indiction of it. It was a change wrought by the hand of the Highest, and an earnest of coming good, for the soil was undergoing the fitting preparation for the Great Husbandman, who in due time will sow the corn of God, into whose storehouses his successors will have to gather the harvest when the time shall have come for its ripening.

Since the publication of the Bull of Indiction

on the Feast of SS. Peter and Paul, 1868, many prayers have ascended up to Heaven for the intention of his Holiness from pious and humble souls, who probably, if they were questioned, would be able to give but poor answers to any one that might be tempted to ask them what they know about a General Council. They know very likely nothing to be wondered at, but they know that the Pope is set over them by God, and that every act of his concerns them; they feel that they are interested in the Pope, that he is more to them than any other man on earth, and that they wish more keenly for his prosperity than they wish for their own. They feel and know that the Sovereign Pontiff is not acting from caprice, without reflection, or for other ends than those he acknowledges, and so they go simply to their prayers like dutiful children when father or mother asks them to pray.

On the other hand, the powers of this world, moved by the powers of hell, are more or less troubled, for the voice of the great Shepherd has been heard calling his sheep together, and they do not care to be of the number. They have indulged themselves in many speculations about the Pontiff's intentions, but they have not given him credit for any that are good. They suspect him, watch him, and are ready to entrap him if they can. Their scribes are busy, but with them we have nothing to do. There is nothing to make us afraid, and the world is now more afraid of the Church than it has been in the memory of living men, and stands before her not altogether unlike the old pagan world in the presence of the Faith during the time that intervened between one persecution and another.

From the beginning of the Church to this day there have been but eighteen General Councils, and in nine of these the Popes presided in person, in the other nine by their Legates. His Holiness now reigning has convoked the Nineteenth General Council, which will be known as the First Council of the Vatican. It is to begin its work in public on the Feast of the Immaculate Conception this year, and it will be one of the great acts of his reign. The Council of Trent is the last of the General Councils, and the last session of that assembly was held on the fourth day of December, 1563. It is now three hundred years since the last General Council was held, and we are living as far from that day as the Fathers of Nice who assembled for the first time in an Œcumenical Synod were from the foundation of the Church. Nine generations of men and thirty-one Popes have passed away since the close of the Council of Trent.

His Holiness calls the Council because of the calamities of the times, and also because the Bishops throughout the world desire to hear his judgment. *Nihil antiquius habent quam sua Nobiscum communicare et conferre consilia, ac salutaria tot calamitatibus adhibere remedia.* It is plain from this that there is no danger or risk to the Pope, as some have suggested, in the assembling of the Prelates, for they are going to Rome, not to teach the Pope, but to learn, to be "confirmed," and to receive new strength from their visit to the holy place, where the body of the first Pope is waiting for the resurrection of the just.

There have been times of calamity before our day, and the Popes have been in grievous straits, but no Pope since St. Peter has had such an Episcopate under him as God has given to Pius IX. There is no suspicion anywhere that there are Bishops going to Rome to be troublesome, Bishops more in the service of the State than in the service of the Church; all the Prelates summoned are men of good-will, men whom the Pope describes as *singulari in Catholicam ecclesiam amore incensi*—Prelates whose hearts are burning with a special love of Holy Church; men, too, *eximia erga Nos et Apostolicam hanc Sedem pietate et observantia spectati*—loyal Bishops of tried fidelity, and of tender reverence for the Holy See and the Pope. The unity of the Church is a feeling here as well as a fact, and amid the multitude of dolours which are surging up over the soul of the Pontiff, God has given him one consolation on earth, he (and in this, unlike many of his predecessors) cannot say *filios enutrivi et exaltavi, ipsi autem spreverunt me.* His children, whom he has raised to high dignities, have not despised him. The Bishops of Holy Church are faithful and true, and the Pope is glad to bear that testimony in their favour.

General Councils, then, are not of common occurrence, nor is there any rule or law about them. They are held when the Pontiff thinks it fitting, for it cannot be said that they are in any way necessary. They were at no time thought essential to the well-governing of the Church, though there was a time when some persons thought it wise to make their convocation imperative once in ten years. A General Council was called together for the condemnation of the Arian heresy, but it was not thought necessary to call one for the condemnation of Jansenism. The Church is not bound to have recourse to a General Council in every trouble. Viewed as remedies for great evils, they are even in that sense not had recourse to, for Europe has been in sore distress more than once during the last 300 years, but the Pope did not judge it right to assemble the Prelates in a General Council. It would be easy to say that at such or such a time a General Council might have been desirable, as, for instance, at the time of the Treaty of Westphalia, for the times were evil as they are now, yet the Holy See did not call a Council. The reasons for convocation must be sought elsewhere, and it may not be given to man even to discover why the Holy Ghost moves the Pope at particular times to call to his side his distant brethren, who have a share in his heavy anxieties, but are not possessed with the fullness of his power.

General Councils are signs, at least, of something unusual. The Church seems to break through her daily round of work; there is a change and a stir; the waters of the pool are disturbed, and to people who have faith there must come great graces, if only they look for them. There must be some reason for this inspiration of the Pope, and we had better take the matter to heart, lest we should miss something that we might otherwise have had. All the Bishops of the Church travelling to Rome from all parts of the earth are something more than ordinary travellers—more than common pilgrims. They are not going to visit the tomb of the Apostles merely out of devotion, for they are summoned; they are obedient to a heavenly voice, and the act of going is meritorious. They are the sheep of the great Shepherd; the brethren going to be confirmed, strengthened, and inspired anew for their daily labour and harassing work. They go to receive light, and they will find it; for strength, and will get it; their flocks, when they return, will profit by them, and the power of St. Peter's shadow will be seen once more miraculous.

The Pope calls the Council because the world is sick; he sends for the Prelates of the Church because he is anxious for the correction of men's morals, which are now corrupt: *ad corruptos populorum mores corrigendos*. Civil governments are powerless to stem an evil which they have never seriously tried to check; but the Pope will try; he will do his work; and leaving success in the hands of God, he does his duty. His business is to show men and help them on the road to Heaven; but in order to do this he has to fight against the world, and to proclaim anew, year by year, even the elementary principles of justice. He, whose work is primarily to guard and teach the supernatural doctrines of the Faith and the morals of the Gospel, finds that he has to teach also the precepts of the natural law, the common maxims of honesty, because men are so perverse, and so ready to sink to a lower level than the brutes, who never fail in obedience to their natural instincts. For doing this, men rise and sit in judgment on his acts, question his motives, and denounce his reasons. At first there were rumours that certain Governments would lay restraints upon the Bishops within their reach, and hinder them from obeying the summons of the Pope; but there were no rumours about disobedient Bishops, and the heart of the Pontiff must have been glad when he knew that his own servants were faithful.

The Indiction of a General Council is a very grave and solemn act, for the Pope is not thereby merely inviting the Prelates to attend him. It is true, he does that in a most fatherly and tender way, and almost descends to supplication, but the majesty of the Pontiff is not obscured by the gracious humility of the invitation. The Sovereign Pontiff, in all his acts, never forgets who he is—the Vicar of God, invested with the fullness of power and authority, and the holder of the keys of Heaven. So, in the Indiction of the Council, after determining the day whereon it is to meet, and proclaiming the reasons for that Indiction, the Pope says—*Volumus, jubemus, omnes ex omnibus locis tam Venerables Fratres Patriarchas, archiepiscopos, episcopos quam dilectos filios Abbates, omnesque alios, quibus jure, aut privilegio, Conciliis generalibus residendi, et sententias in eis dicendi facta est potestas, ad hoc Œcumenicum Concilium a Nobis indictum venire debere, requirentes hortantes admonentes ac nihilominus eis vi jurisjurandi, quod Nobis et huic sanctæ Sedi præstiterunt, ac sanctæ obedientiæ virtute, ut sub pœnis jure aut consuetudine in celebrationibus Conciliorum adversus non accedentes ferri et proponi solitis, mandantes arcteque præcipientes, ut ipsimet nisi forte justo detineantur impedimento, quod tamen per legitimos Procuratores Synodo probare debebunt, Sacro huic Concilio omnino adesse et interesse teneantur.* That is, the Supreme Pastor of the flock of God wills and commands the attendance of all the Prelates; he reminds them of their obedience due to him, and of the sanctions guarding that obedience; moreover, as the Sovereign Ruler, he sets before them the penalties due to disobedience, and the absolute necessity of proof that their absence, if so it shall be, is due not to negligence, but to the impossibility of their personal attendance.

A General Council, then, is not an assembly into which a Prelate may go or not go, at his own pleasure or convenience. It is a far more serious affair at all times, and to every one summoned it is the most serious affair for him. The ordinary work of his daily life, however important it may be, must be intermitted, so far as he is concerned, because his presence is required in the great congregation which comes together at the bidding of one whom all the powers of the world must obey.

Chapter I.

WHAT PERSONS ARE COMMANDED TO ATTEND THE COUNCIL.—THE SCHISMATIC BISHOPS OF THE EAST INVITED TO BE PRESENT.—PROTESTANTS INVITED TO RETURN TO THE FOLD OF CHRIST.

Concilium Generale est Congregatio Episcoporum et aliorum indicta, congregata continuata et approbata in suis actibus a Romano Pontifice in ea præsidente personaliter, vel per suos Legatos, ad tractandum canonice et capitulariter de rebus universam religionem Christianam tangentibus.—*Bordoni, Sacr. Tribunal.*, c. vi. 2, 15.

A GENERAL Council is an assembly of ecclesiastical, not of lay persons, not of all ecclesiastics, but only of Prelates; those who are in authority. Ecclesiastics under subjection to other ecclesiastics are not summoned, such as parish priests and religious, not even canons. Bishops are summoned, and Bishops are the chief persons who constitute a Council, under the Chief of all the Bishops. But they are summoned, not because of their rank, so far as that depends on their Orders, but because they are called to a share in the anxieties of the Pope: *in partem solicitudinis vocati;* in other words, because they have jurisdiction in the places where they habitually dwell, or whence they derive their titles. Thus, a Bishop who has resigned his See, and has retired to a monastery, is not summoned, for he has ceased to be a Prelate; but a Bishop whose See is occupied by the Infidels, or who is in exile, or in any way hindered from the active exercise of his jurisdiction, which he has not himself abandoned or forfeited, is summoned together with his brethren, for he is still a Prelate, possessed of his authority and rank in the Church. A Bishop, too, who resigns his see, from any cause, and is then translated, or nominated to a bishopric *in partibus infidelium*, retains his dignity, and is liable to be summoned with the others. Primarily, all persons who have received episcopal consecration are the constituent elements of a General Council.

But Bishops are not the only members of the Council: the Cardinals are members of it, so also are Abbots, and Generals of the Regulars, for all these are invested with a jurisdiction quasi-episcopal. They are summoned because of the dignities to which they have been raised, not because of any Orders they may have received, for they may be Priests only, and the Cardinals may not be even Priests, all of them. Though this be so, it is denied that there is any right in the matter beyond that of custom: but it is not necessary, nor would it be useful, to discuss the question here; it is enough for us to know that persons not in the Orders of a Bishop have a right to sit, and a right to give their suffrages, in a General Council,* whatever the nature of that right may be.

The Council is said to be General or Œcumenic, because all the Prelates are summoned who have jurisdiction in any part of the Church, but the non-attendance of any or of many of those who were summoned would not deprive the Council of its character of universality; whether a hundred or ten Bishops came together would make no difference; the Council is General because of the summons sent forth by the Pope. Thus, in the several Councils that have been held, the number of attending Prelates has varied, but the authority or dignity of the Council was never questioned because the attendance was scanty or intermittent.

The Pope has summoned the Prelates from the four corners of the earth, and it is possible that the attendance will be larger than it ever has been before. It is true that many countries are laid waste by heresy and schism, and that from them not many Bishops may be expected; but in spite of all his trials, perhaps in consequence of them, there are now so many new sees that, in the next Council, Bishops will be seen of whom none could prophesy in any of the Councils that have gone before. Bishops will come from the United States of America, where there was not a single Prelate when the Fathers of the Church were assembled in Trent. They will also

---

* Præter Episcopos solent insuper Cardinales non episcopi, Abbates et Præpositi Generales Ordinum Regularium suffragium ferre, quippe qui jurisdictione quasi Episcopali potiuntur. Sed ex mera Ecclesiæ concessione et privilegio factum est, ut quam facultatem vi characteris non habent, eandem vi dignitatis obtinerent.—*Card. Soglia, Institut. Jun. Publ.*, c. ii., sec. 35.

come from the distant colonies of England, into which the Faith has been carried, and where there was not one Christian when this country rose in rebellion against the Vicar of Christ, and cast the commandments of God behind its back.

His Holiness has also invited, not summoned, the rebel Bishops of the Oriental rites. Upon them he lays no command, nor does he threaten them with pains and penalties; not, however, because they are not his subjects, but because they are contumacious. They must repent and return with the prodigal son before the Father will indulge them so far as to command them. *Obsecramus, monemus et obtestamur*, he entreats, admonishes, and earnestly adjures them to present themselves at Rome on the Feast of the Immaculate Conception, as their forefathers did at Lyons and Florence, now more than four hundred years ago.

But the Greek Prelates, in heresy and schism, are not invited to take part in the discussions of the Council. They are not constituent elements of a Council while they remain in their errors. His Holiness calls them to penance, to be reconciled to the Church from which they have gone away, and confess the supremacy of St. Peter, and the lawful rule of his successor. If they come in any number, no doubt a fitting reception would be given them, as Pope Eugenius did before in Ferrara and Florence, but they would not sit in the Council among the Bishops who have kept the Faith. It may be that a place apart from the Council might be assigned them, as was done in Florence, where they could hear and see, and, if they had any difficulties, they might be allowed to address the assembled Prelates; but they would not be in the Vatican, any more than they were in Florence, members of the Synod before they made confession of the Catholic Faith, and submitted themselves and their Churches to the fatherly Supremacy of his Holiness Pius IX.

In the same way, and for the same end, the Sovereign Pontiff has sent his messengers to bid other guests to the feast: the unhappy sectaries who have filled Europe, and who, unlike their Eastern brethren, have rid themselves even in appearance of all ecclesiastical fashion. These are invited, not of course to become members of the Synod, but rather to consider their position, and examine themselves in the light which this great Pontifical act throws upon it. They are sheep without shepherds even in name. They hold principles subversive of obedience, and are careless of all things; but they are nevertheless lost sheep. They are the sheep of the Good Shepherd that have gone astray and lost themselves in the wilderness of sin, and the Vicar of Our Lord would willingly bring them back, if he could; so he addresses even them, and bids them welcome to the feast, for he has room enough and food enough for all, for he is the great steward of the House of God.

Chapter II.

The Pope alone has authority to summon a General Council.—He alone has authority to preside over it.

Relatum est ergo ad Apostolicam Sedem, Johannem Constantinopolitanum episcopum universalem se subscribere, vosque ex hac sua præsumptione ad Synodum convocare generalem, cum generalium synodorum convocandi auctoritas Apostolicæ Sedi beati Petri singulari privilegio sit tradita, et nulla unquam synodus rata legatur quæ Apostolica auctoritate non fuerit fulta. Qua propter quicquid in prædicto vestro conventiculo— quia synodus taliter præsumpta esse non potuit—statuistis, ex auctoritate Sancti Petri Apostolorum Principis et Domini Salvatoris voce, qua beato Petro potestatem ligandi atque solvendi ipse Salvator dedit, quæ etiam potestas in successoribus ejus indubitanter transivit, præcipio omnia quæ ibi statuistis, et vana et cassata esse, ita ut deinceps nunquam appareant, nec ventilentur.—*Pelagii* ii. Ep.

A GENERAL Council is not a tumultuous assembly of men coming together of their own will and of their own mere motion. The Bishops do not invite one another, neither does any one among them take upon himself the task of inviting his brethren to meet, for none of them have any right or power to do so. The Bishops are in one sense independent of each other, and for the most part not in subjection to each other. A Patriarch may call together the Bishops within his patriarchate, and a Metropolitan his suffragans, but that convocation cannot make a General, such assemblies would be no more than Provincial, Synods. The Bishops of the whole Church must therefore be convoked by one who has authority and jurisdiction over them all, for they are not bound to respect any other summons. There have been people who said that a General Council is to be convoked by the Emperor, but the Emperor, whoever he may be, has no power to summon Bishops not within his territories, so that on this supposition a General Council would never be held. The civil power is incompetent for such a work, for one State has no authority to summon Bishops living in another State; and without entering upon the question of right and jurisdiction, it is plain at once that the civil power and no State whatever is competent ever practically to send out a summons for a General Council.

As no Council can be General to which all the Prelates entitled to be summoned have not been summoned—it being clear that a summons can be sent forth only by one having the power and the right to do it—the General Councils must be the work of the Pope, for it is he only that has jurisdiction over all the Bishops of the Church. Thus a Council, then, cannot be a General Council if it has met without the Papal bidding, and if, under some circumstances, all the Bishops did meet, and formed themselves into a Council, their acts would be null, unless the Pope consented to them. Their assembling together in that way would be illegal, and their deliberations wasted; no act would have any authority whatever. On the other hand, if the Pope sanctioned the assembly, no matter how it came together, and confirmed their acts, the Synod would become lawful. It is not necessary that the Pope should be present in person; but it is absolutely-necessary that his authority should be respected.

It is absolutely necessary for the legal inception of a General Council that it be convoked by the Papal authority; none other can do it, not even the Cardinals; nor can the Cardinals do so during the vacancy of the Holy See. The right is in the Pontiff alone, and can be usurped by none. It is true that in troublous times, some Cardinals forgetting themselves did take upon themselves to do acts which belong to the

Pontiff, but the judgment of the Church has ever since been against them. Thus a General Council is reserved for the Pontiff alone; and from that fact by itself, without taking any other into account, we may judge of how grave a matter, and how fraught with consequences, is the convocation of a General Council. It is one of those Pontifical acts which are rarely done, for which there can be no reasons assigned till the time has come, and which can never be foretold, because they proceed immediately from the inspirations of the Holy Ghost.

As the Pope alone can call a General Council, so it is he alone that can preside over it; he does so either in person, or through his Legates, as he sees fit. When he dissolves it, it is ended; and if the Council should persist in sitting after the Papal order for its dissolution shall have gone forth, it then becomes an illegal and schismatical assembly, suspected of heresy—in the language of that great lawyer, though a saint, St. John Capistran, *basiliscorum spelunca dæmonumque caterva,** in allusion to the Council of Basle, the Prelates there assembled having rebelled against Eugenius IV. There are many assemblies of Prelates recorded in the history of the Church, and among these are some which have failed in their primary duties. They stood up against Moses, and became schismatical; some of them professed heresies; all of them were guilty of schism, because they refused to submit themselves to the authority of the Pope, without whose countenance they could never be anything—shadows of antipopes, who are always and everywhere regarded as the lieutenants of Satan, because they have placed themselves in opposition to the Vicar of Christ, and sat in the "chair of pestilence."

At this day there is no one who would seriously maintain that a General Council can be convoked by any other than the Sovereign Pontiff; but it has not been always so. The change of men's minds, and the conversion, if we may so speak, of men accounted learned, are in one sense a remarkable testimony to the doctrine ever held in Rome. The Popes have

---

* S. Joh. a Capistrano, *De Auctoritate Papæ*, par 3, 2dæ, n. 68.

yielded nothing, they have had nothing to recant, nothing to withdraw; they, at least, always believed Our Lord's words, and to the utmost of their power enforced His law. They have had to contend not only with the civil power, ever hostile, more or less, but with disloyal Prelates, faithless Cardinals, and, most grievous trial of all, the faint-heartedness of good men. They, always true to themselves as Vicars of God, and having always before their eyes, as only Saints could have it, the strict discussion of the final judgment, maintained, without hesitation or misgiving, the great prerogatives with which they are invested. They have had the learning of a whole generation arrayed against them. Universities and schools invented theories whereby their power might be diminished, but they never wavered. They kept their place, their dignity and power, for these things were not really theirs, but gifts of the Most High, graces not to be thrown away. Pius IX., perhaps, is the first of the Popes who sees his authority over the consciences of the faithful admitted without question throughout the whole world.

Chapter III.

The Pontifical Power necessary for the existence of a Council.—The order of precedence among the members. — Proxies. — Secular Princes. — Councils summoned by the Pope by virtue of his supreme Jurisdiction.

Cum igitur in concilio peculiare forum sit, non secretissimum, aut pœnitentiæ, sed publicum, propterea necesse est, ut patres in concilio teneant claves non ordinis sed potestatis, acceptas a Romano Pontifice : et quamvis Papa soleat has claves nominatim contribuere episcopis, quia cum existant suarum ecclesiarum pastores, tenentur omni studio procurare, ut salutare ovibus suis pabulum porrigatur, tamen integrum habet pro arbitrio suo has claves committere Abbatibus, et Præfectis Generalibus Ordinum Regularium, quippe quia sunt ipsi quoque Summi Pontificis auctoritate gregum suorum Pastores. Immo Papa in manu habet dare has claves iis omnibus, quos ad earum usum idoneos cognoverit cum salutari beneficio, atque utilitate universalis ecclesiæ, quamvis illi nequaquam essent initiati sacerdotio, quandoquidem hæ non sunt claves ordinis sed tantummodo potestatis.—*Anton. Delphin. de Concil Œcumen.*, c. 5.

WHEN the Bishops and others have come together in obedience to the Papal Summons, they do not proceed, as in secular assemblies, to elect their President, nor is it any part of their prerogative or duty to do so. The President of the Synod is the Pope, and if he cannot be present in person, or, for reasons that to him seem good, remains away from the assembly, then he appoints one or more persons who shall represent him, and preside over the Council in his name and by his authority, because the Council would cease to be a Council the instant it was forsaken by the Pope. The Pontifical power is necessary therefore throughout, for the convocation, for the continuation, and for the final dissolution of a General Council. One of the Canonists has expressed the whole doctrine in a few words, terse and clear—*Concilium est factura manuum Papalium*,* a Council is the work of the Papal hands, and of none other, for the calling all the Bishops of the world together can be done only by him who has authority over them.

From this fact flows necessarily the determination of the rights and powers of a Council, as well as of the character of those who shall be members of it, and of the precedence to be given to some in it over others. The chief seat therein belongs to the Sovereign Pontiff, and the next to the Cardinal Bishop of Ostia, Dean of the Sacred College. In former ages, the Patriarchs sat next to the Pope, but the custom of many centuries has now established the right of the Cardinals to sit above all others, immediately next to the Pope, being as they are, in the language of the law, "members of his body,"† and of the highest dignity in the Church. During the time in which Bishops looked upon the dignity of a Cardinal as less than their own, they declined it, especially about the end of the thirteenth, and the beginning of the fourteenth, centuries.‡ Nevertheless in General Councils, such as the first and the second of Lyons, the higher place had been assigned to the Cardinals, who sat above the Archbishops and Bishops. In the fifteenth century, during the time of

---

* Barbat. in Clem. de Electione, c. *Ne Romani.*

† Anton. de Butrio, de Privileg., c. *Antiqua.* Cum sint pars corporis Papæ.

‡ Johan. Andreæ, in 6to de Rescriptis, c. *Cum aliquibus.*

the Council of Florence, Henry Chicheley, Archbishop of Canterbury, made an attempt to deprive the Cardinals of their privilege, and, refusing to acknowledge the higher rank of the Archbishop of York as Cardinal of S. Balbina, carried his complaint to Eugenius IV. The Pope issued a Bull, *Non mediocri*, and set the question at rest. Chicheley's hands were not clean, even in this, for he had never attempted to set himself above Cardinal Beaufort, though as Bishop of Winchester that Cardinal was one of his Suffragans, and as such had always given way to the Archbishop till he was made Cardinal by Martin V. The Archbishop of York was, like the Bishop of Winchester, a Cardinal Priest, and the Pope was naturally surprised, if surprised he could be, at these proceedings of Chicheley, who during his episcopate was never on the side of the authority of the Church, when the State attempted to usurp her jurisdiction. Eugenius IV., in the Bull already mentioned, gave a clear decision of the question submitted to him, and from that day to this no serious attempt has ever been made, except once, to disturb the order established, and which was then in force, as the Pope showed* by the acts of the two Councils of Lyons under Innocent IV. and Gregory X., as well as by the order observed in the Council of Florence then sitting, over which he presided in person, as the Popes he referred to had presided over the two Councils of Lyons. From the time of Clement V. Bishops began to be made Cardinal Priests, and the dispute about the pre-eminence of the Cardinals became in consequence of more easy solution, for the Bishops themselves were in practice solving it, by their reversal of the policy they had till then observed in relation to the higher dignity of the Church.

After the Cardinals sit the Patriarchs who are not Cardinals, then the Archbishops, and the Bishops in

---

* Idem in antiquis generalibus conciliis, præsertim in duobus Lugdunensibus, in uno, præsidente Innocentio IV., in altero, Gregorio X., quorum adhuc extant acta, usitatum fuit. Sic et in his synodis nostris nostra ætate celebratis—de quibus etiam apud regnum Angliæ non pauci adhuc supersunt testes—observatum esse palam est, absentibus etiam summis Pontificibus. Idem et nunc nobis præsidentibus in hoc sacro œcumenico servatur Florentino Concilio.

their order of seniority of consecration, with the exception of those Bishops who are assistants of the Pontifical throne. These Prelates, if the Pope be present in person, will sit near him, on his left hand; and if he be absent, will take their places among the other bishops. After the Bishops come the mitred Abbots having episcopal or *quasi*-episcopal jurisdiction, with the Generals of the Religious Orders, who have all their places and their rights duly secured by the law.

A Bishop unable to attend in person may constitute a proxy, who will, however, have no place in the General Council; yet as the representative of the absent Prelate, he will have a voice in the discussions, but not a voice in the decisions. The Bishops are summoned to appear in person, and not by their attorneys, and it is a matter of grace to allow a Bishop, even lawfully hindered, to send a priest to represent him among his brethren. In a Provincial Council a Bishop may appear by his proctor, and if the Council think it expedient, that proctor may have also a decisive voice,* but it rests with the Council to decide as it may please. As to General Councils, the question is settled by the authority of the Holy See. It was raised during the Council of Trent, and those to whom the examination of it was then intrusted were nearly unanimous in refusing every right to the proctors but that of being present as spectators. Pius IV. then gave his decision, and allowed the representatives of the absent Prelates the faculty of expressing their opinion, but not the power of a decisive voice.†

Bishops also not consecrated may enter the Council

---

* In the first Synod of Oscott, A.D. 1852, the Bishop of Liverpool, unable to be present in person, sent one of his priests as his proxy, but the assembled Fathers allowed him to have no voice in the final decisions, for they admitted him only to a share in the preliminary consultation. *Admittimus cum voce deliberativa.*

† Bened. XIV., De Synod, Dioces., lib. iii. c. 12, §. 5. Sed cum, jubentibus Apostolicis Legatis, singulæ discussæ fuerint a selectis sacrorum canonum Peritis, hi fere unanimiter censuerunt, integrum quidem esse episcopis, legitime absentibus, suos procuratores ad concilium mittere, sed procuratoribus, neque decisivam, neque consultivam vocem, neque locum in sessionibus, de jure competere. Omnem demum controversiam composuit Pius IV. concedendo absentium episcoporum procuratoribus votum mere consultivum. Secus est de Conciliis Provincialibus.

if they have been confirmed by the Sovereign Pontiff, for they have power to do all acts of a Bishop excepting those for which Orders are necessary; but they will sit below the Prelates who have received the gift of consecration. In former times there were occasionally Bishops who delayed their consecration for years, as a Bishop of Lincoln did in the twelfth century, who governed that See for seven years, though he was not even a priest. Under the present discipline of the Church, no Bishop could remain long in a Council if not already in the orders of a Bishop, because, by the Council of Trent, Sess. 23, cap. 2, he would lose his See if unconsecrated for six months.

But in a Council many more are found than those who are strictly members of it; the Theologians of the Prelates are present, and contribute by their wisdom and learning to the final decisions of the grave questions which are submitted for discussion.

In former times, too, the secular powers of the earth were invited to be present either in person or by ambassadors; some of them were intrusted with the duty of protecting the Council from hostile attacks, and all were permitted to learn what was going on, because every Christian has a deep and abiding interest, whether he cares for it or not, in all matters appertaining to his eternal salvation. His Holiness now reigning is living in evil times, anticipations of the great apostasy coming on the earth, and has found himself unable to send forth the customary invitations to Catholic sovereigns, because he could not be sure of them. Anarchic doctrines have taken possession of men's minds so universally, that it is not possible now to discover a single state in Europe that is not governed upon theories hostile to the faith. Though the Pope has not respected the old tradition of inviting secular princes, he has not said nor felt that this is a state of things in any way desirable. It is not he who has given up the State; it is the State that has revolted from him; the old days of the Passion have returned; the nations will not have this man to rule over them, so they give themselves to Cæsar.

A General Council, then, is an assembly of men

having authority in the Church; for if its members had no authority its decisions would have no weight, other than that we attribute to the opinions of men we respect. The convocation of it is an act of authority; for the members are commanded, not merely invited, to assemble. The power of Order is the same in a Bishop and the Pope, for His Holiness can do no act of Order that cannot be done by a Bishop. All Bishops throughout the Church, including the Sovereign Pontiff himself, are equal in the matter of Orders, and so must always remain. The convocation of a General Council, therefore, is not made in virtue of any authority derived from the sacrament of Orders, because of its being equal in all who receive it. It is in virtue of his supreme jurisdiction, then, that the Pope calls Councils, and not because he is a bishop. His act in calling it together is an exercise of his supreme authority, which is shared by none, and might be made even if he were not in the Orders of a Bishop.* The power of Order is not necessary for the Pope, who summons, nor for the Prelates, who attend, deliberate, and decide; and thus we have in the convocation of a General Council another manifestation of the distinction that there is between the power of order and the power of jurisdiction. We have a shadow of this difference in the old law, *Moyses et Aaron in sacerdotibus ejus.* Aaron offered the sacrifices, and performed the duties of the priesthood, analogous to those of the power of order in the Church, but he was not invested with the power of his brother, nor was he the ruler and judge of Israel; the power analogous to that of jurisdiction was vested in Moses, not in Aaron, and it was the former, not the latter, who convoked the elders and governed the people of God, who appointed the judges, and made Josue his lieutenant to lead the armies of Israel into battle.† Jurisdiction is the power over the mystical

---

* Benedict XVI. de Synodo Diocesan., lib i. c. 4, § 2. Quod nostra interest, illud duntaxat est, nimirum statuere, jus Synodum convocandi, non ad Ordinis sed ad jurisdictionis episcopalis potestatem pertinere; quod profecto, semel percepto inter utramque discrimine, unusquisque facile deprehendet.

† Michael de Aninyon, de Unitate Ovilis et Pastoris, c. 27, n. 5. Sicut et Petrus fecit in conciliis—sicut et Moyses in Lege Veteri.

body of Christ; and the power of order has been subordinated to it, is directed by it, and dependent on it; if the exercise of the latter were not under the control of the former, that exercise would be sinful, and the acts thereof sacrilegious.

Chapter IV.

FALSE THEORIES CONCERNING THE RELATION OF A GENERAL COUNCIL TO THE POPE.—A COUNCIL WITHOUT THE POPE DOES NOT BIND THE CHURCH.—ITS JURISDICTION DERIVED FROM HIM.

Episcopi in concilio universali, aut sunt oves Christi, aut ovile Christi, aut Pastor universalis ecclesiæ: non Pastor, nam quomodo unus pastor tot pastores? Quomodo omnes oves Christi traditæ sunt Petro, si tot sunt ipsi antepositæ? Et quandonam data est illis in Evangelio talis potestas pascendi Petrum, ejusque sucessores? Si autem oves aut ovile Christi sunt debent ergo Pontificem totius ovilis Pastorem generalem agnoscere pro capite, atque ideo illi subjici, nisi dicant, se oves esse sine Pastore, et consequenter nec Christi.—Card. Petra, comm. in Pii II. Const. *In minoribus.*

IN past ages men's minds were busy about the relations of the Council to the Pope, and many evils, no doubt, sprung from the contentions and disputes: but we are living in a happier age, and in this generation it is not probable that any questions will be raised touching the nature of that jurisdiction which belongs to a General Council. All Catholics now agree that the Pope alone can convoke a universal synod, and that the confirmation of its decrees by the Pope is necessary to their validity. There have been grave scandals, for Bishops, Abbots, and simple priests, have met together before now, called themselves a General Council, and pretended to impose their will upon the Sovereign Pontiff and his faithful subjects. This has passed away, and we are now living in the full light of the Catholic doctrine on the sovereign authority of the Holy See.

Those doctors who formerly contended for the superiority of a General Council over the Pope, held also that the Council received its powers immediately from God, and was therefore supreme over all powers in the Church. The Pope was said to be bound by its decisions, and its canons, in consequence, were beyond his power to modify or dispense with. This doctrine may be resolved ultimately into the opinion which some of its professors held on the ecclesiastical jurisdiction: namely, that it was vested in the Church diffusive. Therefore when all the Prelates, or a majority of them, met together in General Council, their united jurisdiction, so to speak, was held to prevail over all, and their decisions were to be binding even on the Pope. But none of the professors of this theory ever explained how the Bishops could have had jurisdiction out of their own dioceses, and over persons never committed to their rule, for no Bishop, other than the Pope, ever pretended to have any jurisdiction whatever over the Roman Church.

It is probable that the maintainers of this opinion were misled by unconsciously arguing from the powers of a Provincial Council to those of a General Council. A Provincial Synod is convoked by the Archbishop or Primate, who is himself bound by the decision arrived at by the majority of the Bishops present in it. The Provincial Council cannot be dissolved by the Archbishop at his own pleasure without the assent of his suffragans, for the members of a Provincial Synod are more on an equality one with another, than are the Bishops of the whole Church assembled in a General Council by the Pope.* But be the grounds of the opinion whatever they may be, much evil arose out of it, and was fostered by it while it prevailed ; now it has disappeared from the schools, as it has from the minds of the faithful at large, if ever it had any home in men's hearts who were not by the necessity of their unhappy position driven to defend it, or to abstain from attacking it.

A General Council is an assembly that has no likeness on earth ; no senate or parliament resembles it ; judges in their courts, deliberating and deciding, are not an image, even faintly, of it ; learned doctors in the congregations of their universities, disputing and determining questions of theology, furnish us with no

---

* Fagnan. in Cap. *Sicut Olim.* de Accusationibus. Cum quæreretur, an Archiepiscopus solus justis de causis posset absque aliis Episcopis dissolvere concilium, S. Congregatio censuit non posse, nisi de consilio et assensu Co-Episcoporum.

shadows of the great congregation of the Church. That is wholly a supernatural assembly, using supernatural means for the attainment of supernatural ends.

Senates and parliaments and courts of law and faculties of theology come together at stated seasons, not so the Councils of the Church; these are summoned at the will of one man, who is not accountable to men for his acts, and who, so far as we can see, may convoke, or not convoke, them at his own absolute pleasure. All human assemblies together can never reach the rank and dignity of a Council, still less attain to its powers; and though it be now admitted that it has not, and never had, certain powers claimed for it in former ages, it is plain that it must have some authority, for otherwise there could be no visible reason for its convocation.

Many questions once hotly disputed may now be pretermitted altogether, such as the infallibility attributed to a Council as such; that opinion is, in our day, abandoned, for it is clear that a Council alone, without the Pope, has no authority to bind the Church, whereas an infallible authority would certainly bind her. Once too it was debated, and by some maintained in the affirmative, whether a General Council could depose the Sovereign Pontiff. In the strange evolutions of that notion it came to pass that many learned men, apparently out of human respect, held that a Council could depose the Pope for heresy; but as they disliked the opinion while they held it, they escaped from the consequences of it by saying that the case had never occurred.* Others maintained, and they have the common law on their side, that as the Pope is higher than all Bishops, none of them could have jurisdiction over him; and moreover, he could not submit to their jurisdiction voluntarily, because his power is a Divine gift. In this country the opinion

---

* Fagnan. in C. *Significasti* de Elect. Sed quidquid sit de veritate utrinoque opinionis, illud certum est, hunc casum in Ecclesia divinæ gratiæ præsidio nunquam hactenus contigisse, ut fatentur omnes. Suarez de Legg., iv. 8, § 10. Ad tertiam de Summo Pontifice possimus respondere, negando posse dari talem eventum juxta opinionem asserentem Pontificem Romanum ex divino privilegio non posse errare in fide, *etiam ut particularem personam quam opinionem probabiliter* defendunt aliqui, vindicando ab hac nota omnes Pontifices qui hactenus præcesserant.

of the infallibility of General Councils seems not to have been accepted, at least in the first centuries after the Conquest, for the Bishops maintained that they were not all bound to attend General Councils, and that it was enough for them if four of the English prelates attended.* It is not credible that in those days any were found, at least among the English Bishops, who held the infallibility of a General Council or its supremacy over the Pope; for if they did, they would not have been so eager to absent themselves.

But the Council has nevertheless a great and high authority, though not what has been claimed for it. To define the nature and extent of that authority may be difficult, and perhaps the best way, and therefore the safest, of ascertaining in some degree what the powers of a General Council are, is to ascertain, first of all, whence it derives its high jurisdiction. There have been two opinions on this point, both eagerly maintained, and which have made men forget two others, which never were long popular. Of these latter, one is, that the Councils derived their jurisdiction or powers from the State; the other from the whole body of the Church, which they represented, or rather were by the maintainers of that opinion said to represent. But the chief opinions were, one, that these General Councils derived their authority immediately from God; and the other, that their jurisdiction was derived from the Pope. These two opinions were long and keenly debated: the first belongs to the Gallicans, the other is held in Rome. Those who held that a General Council is above the Pope were compelled to hold, in their own defence, that the jurisdiction of a Council is divine; for if they did not, they could not possibly compass their ends of subjecting the Papal authority to an assembly which is not any portion of the divine constitution of the Church. The doctors of this school expressed themselves with a

---

* Hoveden. ad an. 1179, p. 582. Episcopi autem Angliæ constanter asseruerunt quod ad Concilium Generale Domini Papæ quatuor Episcopi de Anglia tantum Romam mittendi sunt. This was the Eleventh General Council and the third of the Lateran. The Bishops also had excused themselves from attending the previous Council of the Lateran under Innocent II. in 1139. V. Gesta Abbatum S. Albani, vol. i. p. 104.

clearness that could not be mistaken, and, apparently, were not disturbed by the certain dangers involved in the practice of their doctrine.* Of the same character, and held in the same school, were those opinions, namely, that appeals might be carried from the Sovereign Pontiff to a General Council, and that people might appeal to a future General Council, and that the Pope might be called upon to justify his acts before the Prelates, who had no authority in fact, other than that they receive from him. These opinions, though on the surface favourable to the authority of General Councils, are in reality utterly fatal to them; for no Pope would ever summon a General Council, because he would thereby raise a power above himself and beyond his control. The doctors who thus taught furnished, in reality, an answer to their own opinions, for while they held the superiority of a Council over the Pope, they admitted that the opinion was never heard of before the Council of Constance. They were also hampered by another objection; that the constitution of the Church upon their view of it was imperfect, for there is no provision in the Christian religion for the convocation of Councils, whereas it is otherwise with the Papacy, which is one of its most prominent doctrines; they unconsciously admitted this objection to be unanswerable, for they made a decree that two General Councils should be held within twelve years of the close of the Council of Constance, and then one every ten years for ever after.† The anarchy into which learned men had fallen in those days was not got rid of for many years afterwards, and the jealousy with which they regarded the Pontifical jurisdiction served as an excuse for kings and their ministers in their disastrous inroads upon the ecclesiastical jurisdiction throughout Europe.

A General Council held in Rome can scarcely be supposed by any one to possess any authority over the Pope, in whose diocese it assembles. If it met

---

* Almain de Authorit. Ecclesiæ et Concilii, c. 8. Sed postquam concilia generalia sunt authoritate Papæ *vel aliter* congregata, tum non habent suam authoritatem a Papa sed immediate a Christo, et illi potestati subjicitur summus Pontifex, sicut minister dominæ.

† Concil. Const., Sess. 39, cap. *Frequens*.

anywhere else, it could not be held that it superseded the local Bishop. A Bishop who enters the diocese of one of his brethren respects the jurisdiction of his brother; all Bishops always do so, and it is impossible to maintain that a hundred Bishops could do collectively what not one of them can do separately. The assembling together of a thousand Bishops in one cathedral city would not deprive the local Bishop of his right, merely because they were so many, or because they were met together in his city. But if the Bishops were assembled in that city by authority and commandment of the Pope, they would have authority, whatever that authority might be, and would be in a different condition from that in which they would be if they had come together of their own will, or at the invitation of the State, or of one of themselves.

The Bishops are in the Council judges; they have a great authority, as is confessed by all; but their authority as members of the Council must come to them from some other source than from the fact of their meeting, because none of them have any authority out of their own dioceses. The Pope is the supreme Bishop; he convokes the Council, and it must be from him that the members of it derive their jurisdiction.* The power of the Sovereign Pontiff is manifested, as it were, anew, and the Prelates of Holy Church are elevated to a higher position, and discharge grander functions, because they are now sitting together as the assessors and councillors of the supreme judge.†

---

* Card. Jacobat. de Conciliis, lib. ii. art 2, n. 72. Episcopi existentes in Concilio recipiunt jurisdictionem omnes in genere a Papa, et non ratione alicujus particularis ecclesiæ.

† Bened. XIV. de Synodo, lib. xiii., c. 2, § 3. Ex eo porro quod episcopi in Concilio generali sint veri judices, cave, ne inferas, teneri Romanum Pontificem in ferenda sententia majorem partem judicum sequi, eorumque doctrinam opprobare.

Chapter V.

GENERAL COUNCILS UNLIKE ALL OTHER ASSEMBLIES.—THE POPE NOT MERELY THE PRESIDENT.—HE IS SUPREME.—BISHOPS NOT THE DELEGATES OF THE PEOPLE, BUT THE POPE'S COUNCILLORS.

Cum etiam solum Romanum Pontificem pro tempore existentem, tanquam auctoritatem super omnia concilia habentem, tam conciliorum indicendorum, transferendorum ac dissolvendorum plenum jus et potestatem habere, nedum ex sacræ scripturæ testimonio, dictis sanctorem Patrum ac aliorum Romanorum Pontificum etiam prædecessorum nostrorum, sacrorumque canonum decretis, sed propria etiam eorundem conciliorum confessione manifeste constet.—*Pastor æternus*, Leo. x.

BISHOPS assembled in Council being subjects of the Pope, and even in that venerable congregation receiving from him the high jurisdiction which they wield, exercise all their powers as children of the Church their mother, though they are at the same time rulers of the chosen people of God. They are under the law of charity, for it is not their own interests, not even the interests of their own dioceses exclusively, that they are seeking. They are deliberating on the affairs of the whole Church, and their end is the greater glory of God. They differ herein from secular assemblies, and in degree from all ecclesiastical convocations whatever, because it is not the particular good of a province, or of an order, but the good of the whole Church throughout the world, that occupies their attention. They come together at the call of the Chief Shepherd, and remain together under his care and direction, helping him, even encouraging him, if need be, in the bearing of his great burden. At this day the old questions will not arise about conflicting opinions in the Council; for the former controversies are gone to their rest touching the value of the decisions arrived at by the Bishops, being unanimous, and by the Pope alone on the other side. These, with many others of the like nature, have disappeared, for even learned men have given up their prejudices with the traditions of their schools, for the simpler teaching which makes the Church our mother, and all the faithful little children listening to the voice of St. Peter.*

While men regarded Councils as mere human assemblies—for those really did so who insisted on their frequent convocations, in spite of their notion that the Council on its assembling together received its jurisdiction from God—it was very natural that they should attempt to make the Pope himself subject to its authority. They thought it unreasonable that the Bishops of the whole Church, sitting as judges in Council, should not have the plenary powers of a Council, if they were all of one mind, though the Pope was of another. But their objection to the doctrine which Cardinal Petra calls *communis et inconcussa*, rested really on a false theory of the Church; they may never have confessed even to themselves that they held that false theory, but it is plain that they held it, for without it they could not have held their positions. That theory seems to have been that the Pope was only the first in rank among his brethren, and not supreme over them. Having that notion in their minds, they regarded a General Council, even one presided over by the Pope in person, as an assembly of men of equal power, and one in which, as in all other assemblies, the majority ought to bear sway. But the Pope in a General Council is still the Pope, for he never ceases to be the Pope from the moment of his election till his resignation or death, and is therefore sovereign. He is not simply the President of the Council, but he is the Pope; and he is there as the Pope, and not as the ordinary President of ordinary assemblies. The whole authority resides really in himself, for though he communicates of his powers to the assembled Prelates, yet he does not divest himself of his own. Thus in the Council of Florence, after the long discussions, the final resolution of the ques-

---

* Azor. Inst. Mor. par. 2, lib. iv. c. 13, p. 456. At vera et certa sententia est eorum, qui oppositum tradiderunt, siquidem Romanus Pon.ifex est caput ecclesiæ, et ipsi unum datum est, ut pascat gregem, ovile custodiat Christi, fratres confirmet, et tanquam fundamentum Ecclesiam sustineat; ergo est majoris ponderis auctoritas Romani Pontificis, ut ei sit adhærendum potius quam generali concilio secus sentienti. Petro enim, ejus successoribus data est potestas, quæ ad fidem quæque ad mores pertinent, definiendi alligandi et solvendi.

tions discussed came from the Pope alone : " Ego Eugenius Catholicæ ecclesiæ Episcopus *ita definiens* subscripsi." The definition was the act of the Sovereign Pontiff ; all the Prelates—Cardinals, Patriarchs, and Bishops—of both rites, accepted the definition, but not one of them used any word equivalent to " define " ; they only " subscribed." their names. John Palæologus the Greek Emperor himself, though ruling his own Bishops till that day, did no more than the rest ; he simply " subscribed."

Thus the supreme jurisdiction of the Church never passes away from the Supreme Pontiff, and does not vest even in a General Council. The Government of the Church remains what Our Lord made it in the beginning, and cannot be changed, because it is divine. The Council's authority is great, and they will most magnify it, and most respect it, who think most of his authority who convokes it.* The reception of the Council of Trent was contested in those countries where the notion prevailed that a General Council was above the Pope, and least disputed there, or rather not disputed, where the supremacy of the Holy See was loyally maintained. In a word, the greatest enemies of General Councils are those who unduly magnify their authority, and derogate from the authority of the Pope.

When the Council shall have deliberated, and fashioned the decrees to which the Prelates assent by signing their names, its work is done. It has no power to publish the decrees, still less to make them laws of the Church. If the Pontiff be present in the Council, and signs them himself, they become laws before the Prelates testify their assent in writing ; and if he be absent in person, they must have his sanction and confirmation before they acquire any binding force on the consciences of the faithful. The reason assigned for this lies in the fact that the gift of infallibility is not communicated to the Council, but abides in the Pope,†

---

* F. Faber. Blessed Sacrament, book i. p. 35, 3rd Edit. " Every word of that queen of Councils, the blessed and glorious assembly of Trent, is more precious to us than a mine of gold."

† Fagnan. in cap. *Mejores*, de Baptismo. At infallibilitas in determinationibus non est hujusmodi [*i. e.* alteri delegabilis] quia fuit divinitus collata ipsi Petro, et ex Petri persona illius successoribus.

who is even then, while the Council is sitting, the Chief Shepherd of the sheep. Those who maintained that the gift of infallible teaching is given to the whole Church, were really unable, though they attempted, to maintain that the decrees of a Council, before the Pope has allowed them, are infallible truth, and of certain obligation,* because the whole Church has not given her voice in the Council, and because it cannot be proved, contrary to the visible fact, that the Bishops in Councils are delegates of the Church at large. The Bishops, being delegates of none, cannot have any authority from those below them; they are not deputies sent, but rather princes summoned by their sovereign Lord, to give their own counsel, and not to deliver instructions given them by their supposed constituents, of whom they are the supposed representatives.

Innocent III.† has determined the question, in the Decretal *Majores Ecclesiæ*, according to which all the greater questions, especially matters of faith, are to be referred to the supreme Pontiff;‡ and since the Council of Trent the question can never be raised again; for there the assembled Fathers resolved in their last session that the definitions and decrees of the Council should be sent to the Pope for confirmation; and no future Council is likely to transgress the bounds of the

---

* Azor. ibid, col. 457. Parisienses doctores negant generale Concilium ulla indigere Rom. Pontificis confirmatione. At enim concilia hactenus celebrata, Romani Pontificis confirmationem postularunt, et ab eo confirmata sunt, quotquot nunc in Ecclesia Concilia auctoritatem habent. The two Dominicans, Francis a Victoria and Dominic Soto, the first in his Relect. 2da. de Potestate Ecclesiæ; the second in his Commentaries on the 4th Book of the Sentences, Disp. 20, art. 4, qu. i., seem to say that the confirmation of a Council is not necessary, but the opinion is not held now.

† De Baptismo, cap. *Majores*. Majores ecclesia causas, præsertim articulos fidei contingentes, ad Petri sedem referendas intelligit, qui eum quærenti Domino, quem discipuli dicerent ipsum esse, respondisse notabat: Tu es Christus filius Dei vivi, et pro eo Dominum exorasse, ne deficiat fides ejus.

‡ Bull Pii IV. *Benedictus Deus*. Quum autem ipsa sancta synodus pro sua erga Sedem Apostolicam reverentia, antiquorum etiam conciliorum vestigiis inhærens, decretorum suorum omnium . . . . confirmationem a Nobis petierit, decreto de ea re in publica sessione facto, Nos . . . . hodie confirmavimus.

Fathers by neglecting to submit all their acts to the sovereign revision of the Holy See.

A General Council, then, is called together by the Pope, deliberates under his direction and in subordination to him, and finally submits to him, as the "Father and Teacher of all Christians," the decisions at which it may have arrived.* It is a manifestation of the visible unity of the Church, and a jubilee of brotherly love. The elders of Israel were not delegates of the people, nor did they derive their authority from those over whom they ruled, and whose difficult questions they determined in judgment. They had been appointed by Moses, and it was with "the spirit of Moses," *de spiritu qui erat in Moyse*, that God filled them to fit them for their work. They were admitted to a share in the responsibilities and anxieties of Moses, but not to the fulness of his powers. When the judges of Israel were unequal to the task assigned them, and questions arose which were too hard for them to solve, they brought them before the sovereign judge : *quicquid autem gravius erat, referebant ad eum, faciliora tantummodo judicantes*. What was thus begun by Moses was made a law in Israel, and the people went up to the place which God had chosen, and to the priests of the Levitical race, and to the judge then living. It is the same in the Church: the difficult questions of the people of God are carried up to the Eternal City, which God has chosen for the seat of His visible rule, and to the sovereign judge there sitting, the Vicar of Him who is a priest for ever after the order of Melchisedech, and who unites in his own person the jurisdiction of Moses and the order of Aaron, but in both is greater than Moses and Aaron, for to him have been intrusted the keys of the king-

---

* Gonzalez in ii. Sent. disp. 3, n. 370. Statuta facta a concilio legitime congregato sunt conditionata, "si Sanctissimo placuerit," et nullam vim obligendi habent antequam a Summo Pontifice accipiant confirmationem et robur. Tum etiam quia hoc ipsum probat constans traditio, qua constat, concilia generalia semper postulasse confirmationem a Summo Pontifice, et novissime Conc. Trid., Sess. 25, in fine censuit petendam confirmationem per legatos, quam et obtinuit. Concilia vero generalia, etsi authoritate Summi Pontificis congregata, si tamen conformationem non obtinuerunt a Papa, nec vim obligandi habent, nec inter legitima recensentur, et sunt exposita erroribus in perniciem ecclesiæ.

dom of Heaven,* and from whom no power on earth can take them.

Chapter VI.

The desire for a Council long entertained by the Pontiff.—The expectations therefrom formed by the late Cardinal Wiseman.—The expressed desire of the Universal Episcopate.—Consecration of the Council to the Immaculate Mother of God.—The Bull of Indiction.

THE Sovereign Pontiff has long entertained the desire to hold an Œcumenical Council as one of the most efficacious remedies that can be applied to the evils which afflict the Church throughout the world. H. E. the late Cardinal Wiseman, when in Rome in 1863, urged upon the Pope his own view of the great blessings which might flow from a General Council. The Pontiff then replied that the subject was occupying his mind, and that he was recommending it to God; but that he feared his own great age offered an obstacle to his beginning so anxious and laborious an undertaking. The Cardinal felt persuaded that, among other results which would flow from the Council, would be the reconciliation to the Church of many of the sincere and earnest non-Catholics in England who professed not to be able to submit themselves to the supremacy of the Pope, but to be willing to obey the injunctions of a General Council. The life and vigour of the Sovereign Pontiff have been wonderfully preserved: the meetings of the Bishops in 1854, 1863, and 1867, proved how easily the Bishops of the world might be brought together. On the 26th

---

* Innocent III., cap. *Per Venerabilem.* Sane cum Deuteronomium lex secunda interpretetur, ex vi vocabuli comprobatur, ut quod ibi decernitur, in Novo Testamento debeat observari, locus enim quem elegit Dominus, Apostolica Sedes esse cognoscitur. . . . Sunt autem Sacerdotes Levitici generis fratres nostri, qui nobis jure Levitico in executione sacerdotalis officii coadjutores existunt. Is vero super eos sacerdos, sive Judex existit, cui Dominus inquit in Petro, Quodcunque ligaveris. . . . Ejus vicarius qui est sacerdos in æternum secundum ordinem Melchisedech. Eugenius IV., Bull. *Non mediocri.* Id quod Deuter. 17, dicitur . . . de Summo Pontifice intelligendum esse et fratribus ejus, id est, Sanctæ Romanæ ecclesiæ Cardinalibus, qui ei jure Levitico in executione sacerdotalis officii coadjutores existunt.

of June, 1867, the Pope held a Secret Consistory in the Vatican, at which were present the Bishops who had hastened to Rome for the celebration of the Centenary of St. Peter's martyrdom. In this he pronounced an Allocution, publicly manifesting for the first time his desire to hold a Council as a further means of dissipating error, propagating Catholic truth, and bringing back the enemies of the Church into the way of salvation. The five hundred Bishops assembled from the four corners of the earth, and now surrounding the Pontiff as a crown of glory, answered this intimation by declaring with one heart and voice their persuasion that the Sovereign Pontiff spoke as with the voice of God, and that, under the blessing of God, and with the all-powerful intercession of His Immaculate Mother, the future Council would infallibly be a wonderful source of unity, peace, and holiness. To this declaration from the Bishops assembled at the Vatican was soon added the unanimous consent of all those Bishops who had been lawfully prevented from leaving their Dioceses; and thus the whole Episcopate expressed its desire for the convocation of a General Council. The address of the assembled Bishops, which was read to the Pontiff on the 1st of July, 1867, in the great Hall above the Portico of St. Peter's, was replied to in that same place, on the same day, by the Sovereign Pontiff. He said that their unanimity had filled him with consolation; and their suggestion that the Council should be placed in a special manner under the protection of Her whose foot from the beginning of the world had crushed the serpent's head and destroyed all heresies, had but anticipated his own desire. He therefore there and then decreed that the future Council should be placed under the august patronage of the Immaculate Virgin Mother of God, and that in whatever year it should open, it should be on the 8th of December, the Feast of Her Immaculate Conception.

On the 29th of June, 1868, the Bull of Indiction of the General Council, for the 8th of December, 1869, was duly published. Such a narrative as we propose to give of the preparation and action of the Council would be incomplete unless we printed the text and translation of all official documents relating to it. We therefore make no further apology, though they are not of recent date, for their publication in these pages.

*LETTERS APOSTOLIC OF HIS HOLINESS POPE PIUS IX.
BY WHICH THE ŒCUMENICAL COUNCIL IS PROCLAIMED, TO BE HELD AT ROME,
AND TO BEGIN ON THE DAY SACRED TO THE IMMACULATE CONCEPTION OF THE VIRGIN MOTHER OF GOD, IN THE YEAR MDCCCLXIX.

PIUS BISHOP,
SERVANT OF THE SERVANTS OF GOD.
In perpetual remembrance.

The Only-Begotten Son of the Eternal Father, because of the exceeding charity wherewith He hath loved us, and in order that in the fulness of time He might deliver the whole human race from the yoke of sin, from slavery to the devil, and from the darkness of error, by which through the fault of our first parent it had long been miserably oppressed, came down from His heavenly throne, and, without parting from His Father's glory, was clothed in human nature from the Immaculate and Most Holy Virgin Mary. He manifested a doctrine and a rule of life

---

* Sanctissimi Domini Nostri Pii Divina Providentia Papae IX. Litterae Apostolicae Quibus Indicitur Oecumenicum Concilium Romae Habendum et Die Immaculatae Conceptioni Deiparae Virginis Sacro An. MDCCCLXIX Incipiendum.

Pius Episcopus Servus Servorum Dei Ad Futuram rei Memoriam.

Aeterni Patris Unigenitus Filius propter nimiam, qua nos dilexit, caritatem, ut universum humanum genus a peccati jugo, ac daemonis captivitate, et errorum tenebris, quibus primi parentis culpa jamdiu misere premebatur, in plenitudine temporum vindicaret, de caelesti sede descendens, et a paterna gloria non recedens, mortalibus ex Immaculata Sanctissimaque Virgine Maria indutus exuviis, doctrinam, ac vivendi disciplinam e caelo delatam manifestavit, eamdemque tot admirandis operibus testatam fecit, ac semetipsum tradidit pro nobis, oblationem et hostiam Deo in odorem suavitatis. Antequam vero, devicta morte,

brought down by Him from heaven, giving witness to the same by many wonderful works, and delivering Himself up for us an Oblation and Victim unto God in the odour of sweetness. And, having conquered death, He ascended triumphant into heaven, to sit at the right hand of the Father, having first sent the Apostles into the whole world to preach the Gospel to every creature. He gave them the power of ruling the Church—*the pillar and ground of the truth*—which had been purchased and established by His blood, and which, enriched with heavenly treasures, shows to all nations the safe way of salvation and the light of true doctrine, and, like to a ship, *is so borne upon the waves of this present time as, while the world perishes, to preserve unhurt all whom she receives* (S. Max. Serm. 89). But in order that the government of that same Church should always proceed rightly and in order, and that the whole Christian people should ever stand firm in one faith, doctrine, charity, and communion, He both promised that He would Himself be present with her even to the consummation of the world, and also chose one out of all, Peter, whom He appointed Prince of the Apostles and His Vicar here on earth, and head, foundation, and centre of the Church; that both in the grade of rank and honour, and in the amplitude of chief and most full

---

triumphans in caelum consessurus ad dexteram Patris conscenderet, misit Apostolos in mundum universum, ut praedicarent evangelium omni creaturae, eisque potestatem dedit regendi Ecclesiam suo sanguine acquisitam, et constitutam, quae est *columna et firmamentum veritatis*, ac caelestibus ditata thesauris totum salutis iter, ac verae doctrinae lucem omnibus populis ostendit, et instar *navis in altum saeculi hujus ita natat, ut, pereunte mundo, omnes quos suscipit, servet illaesos* (S. Max. Semon. 89). Ut autem ejusdem Ecclesiae regimen recte semper, atque ex ordine procederet, et omnis christianus populus in una semper fide, doctrina, caritate, et communione persisteret, tum semetipsum perpetuo affuturum usque ad consummationem saeculi promisit, tum etiam ex omnibus unum selegit Petrum, quem Apostolorum Principem, suumque hic in terris Vicarium, Ecclesiaeque caput, fundamentum ac centrum constituit, ut cum ordinis et honoris gradu, tum praecipuae, plenissimaeque auctoritatis, potestatis, ac jurisdictionis amplitudine pasceret agnos, et oves, confirmaret fratres, universamque regeret Ecclesiam, et esset *caeli janitor, ac ligandorum, solvendorumque arbiter, mansura etiam*

authority, power, and jurisdiction, he should feed the lambs and the sheep, strengthen his brethren, and rule the whole Church, and should be *the keeper of the gate of heaven, and the arbiter of things to be bound and loosed, so that the determination of his judgments should abide hereafter even in heaven.* And because the unity and integrity of the Church, and the government thereof, as established by the same Christ, are for ever to remain unchanged, therefore in the Roman Pontiffs, successors of Peter, who are placed on this same Roman Chair of Peter, the very same supreme power, jurisdiction, and primacy, possessed by Peter over the whole Church, most fully continues and is in force.

Therefore the Roman Pontiffs, exercising the power and care of feeding the Lord's flock divinely intrusted to them by Christ Himself Our Lord in the person of Blessed Peter, have never ceased to endure all labours, to devise all counsels, in order that from the rising to the setting of the sun all peoples, and races, and nations might acknowledge the teaching of the Gospel, and, walking in the paths of truth and justice, might attain eternal life. Known unto all is the unwearied care wherewith the Roman Pontiffs have laboured to defend the deposit of faith, the discipline of the clergy and their education in sanctity and learning, and also the holiness and dignity of marriage: known also is

---

in caelis judiciorum suorum definitione (S. Leo, Serm. II). Et quoniam Ecclesiae unitas, et integritas, ejusque regimen ab eodem Christo institutum perpetuo stabile permanere debet, iccirco in Romanis Pontificibus Petri successoribus, qui in hac eadem Romana Petri Cathedra sunt collocati, ipsissima suprema Petri in omnem Ecclesiam potestas, jurisdictio, Primatus plenissime perseverat, ac viget.

Itaque Romani Pontifices omnem Dominicum gregem pascendi potestate et cura ab ipso Christo Domino in persona Beati Petri divinitus sibi commissa utentes, nunquam intermiserunt omnes perferre labores, omnia suscipere consilia, ut a solis ortu usque ad occasum omnes populi, gentes, nationes evangelicam doctrinam agnoscerent, et in veritatis, ac justitiae viis ambulantes vitam assequerentur aeternam. Omnes autem norunt quibus indefessis curis iidem Romani Pontifices fidei depositum, Cleri disciplinam, ejusque sanctam, doctamque institutionem, ac matrimonii sanctitatem dignitatemque tutari, et christianam utriusque sexus juventutis educationem quotidie magis promovere, et populorum religionem, pietatem, morumque honestatem fovere, ac justitiam de-

the care wherewith they have endeavoured to promote daily more and more the Christian education of the youth of both sexes, to cherish the religion, piety, and good morals, of the people,—to defend justice, and to consult for the tranquillity, order, prosperity, and interests, of civil society itself.

Nor have the Pontiffs omitted, when they thought it seasonable, especially in times of very grave disturbance, and of calamity to our holy religion and to civil society, to convoke General Councils; that comparing counsels and uniting strength with the Bishops of the whole Catholic world, whom *the Holy Ghost has appointed to rule the Church of God*, they might wisely and prudently establish whatsoever might conduce to the definition in an especial manner of the dogmas of the faith, to put to flight advancing errors, to defend, illustrate, and develope Catholic doctrine, to preserve and reform ecclesiastical discipline, and to correct the corrupt morals of the people.

Now, it is well known and manifest to all by how fearful a tempest the Church is at this time shaken, and what and how great are the evils with which civil society itself is afflicted. By the bitter enemies of God and men, the Catholic Church and her saving doctrine and venerable power, and the supreme authority of this Holy See, have been assailed and trodden under

---

fendere, et ipsius civilis societatis tranquillitati, ordini, prosperitati, rationibus consulere studuerint.

Neque omiserunt ipsi Pontifices, ubi opportunum existimarunt, in gravissimis praesertim temporum perturbationibus, ac sanctissimae nostrae religionis, civilisque societatis calamitatibus generalia convocare Concilia, ut cum totius catholici orbis Episcopis, quos *Spiritus Sanctus posuit regere Ecclesiam Dei*, collatis consiliis, conjunctisque viribus ea omnia provide, sapienterque constituerent, quae ad fidei potissimum dogmata definienda, ad grassantes errores profligandos, ad catholicam propugnandam, illustrandam et evolvendam doctrinam, ad ecclesiasticam tuendam ac reparandam disciplinam, ad corruptos populorum mores corrigendos possent conducere.

Jam vero omnibus compertum, exploratumque est qua orribili tempestate nunc jactetur Ecclesia, et quibus quantisque malis civilis ipsa affligatur societas. Etenim ab acerrimis Dei hominumque hostibus catholica Ecclesia, ejusque salutaris doctrina, et veneranda potestas, ac suprema hujus Apostolicae Sedis auctoritas oppugnata, proculcata, et

foot. All sacred things have been despised ; ecclesiastical possessions have been plundered; Bishops, and most excellent men devoted to the divine ministry, and men remarkable for their Catholic spirit, have been in every way harassed ; religious communities have been destroyed ; impious books of every kind, pestilential journals, and most pernicious sects of many forms have been on every side spread abroad ; and the education of unhappy youth has been almost everywhere taken away from the clergy, and, what is worse, in no few places, committed to the teachers of iniquity and error. Hence, to our own extreme grief and that of all good men, and with a loss of souls which can never be enough deplored, impiety has been so propagated, together with corruption of morals, unbridled license, and the contagion of all kinds of depraved opinions, of all vices, and crimes, and violation of Divine and human laws, that not only our most holy religion, but human society itself, is miserably disturbed and afflicted.

Amidst so great a mass therefore of calamities wherewith our heart is overwhelmed, the supreme pastoral ministry divinely intrusted to us requires that we more and more put forth our strength to repair the ruins of the Church, to procure the salvation of the whole flock of Our Lord, and to repress the deadly

---

sacra omnia despecta, et ecclesiastica bona direpta, ac Sacrorum Antistites, et spectatissimi viri divino ministerio addicti, hominesque catholicis sensibus praestantes modis omnibus divexati, et Religiosae Familiae extinctae, et impii omnis generis libri, ac pestiferae ephemerides, et multiformes perniciosissimae sectae undique diffusae, et miserae juventutis institutio ubique fere a Clero amota, et quod pejus est, non paucis in locis iniquitatis, et erroris magistris commissa. Hinc cum summo Nostro, et bonorum omnium moerore, et nunquam satis deplorando animarum damno ubique adeo propagata est impietas, morumque corruptio, et effrenata licentia, ac pravarum cujusque generis opinionum, omniumque vitiorum, et scelerum contagio, divinarum, humanarumque legum violatio, ut non solum sanctissima nostra religio, verum etiam humana societas miserandum in modum perturbetur, ae divexetur.

In tanta igitur calamitatum, quibus cor Nostrum obruitur, mole supremum Pastorale ministerium Nobis divinitus commissum exigit, ut omnes Nostras magis magisque exeramus vires ad Ecclesiae reparandas ruinas, ad universi Dominici gregis salutem curandam, ad

attacks and endeavours of those who labour to overthrow from the foundation both civil society and, if it were ever possible, the Church herself. We indeed, by God's help, from the very commencement of our supreme Pontificate, have never ceased, according to the duty of our most weighty office, to raise our voice in many consistorial Allocutions and Apostolic Letters; and unflinchingly to defend with all zeal the cause of God and of His Holy Church intrusted to us by Christ the Lord; to defend the rights of this Apostolic See, and of justice and truth; to detect the treacheries of enemies; to condemn their errors and false doctrines; to proscribe the impious sects, and to watch over and provide for the salvation of the Lord's whole flock.

But treading in the footsteps of our illustrious predecessors, we have therefore thought it opportune to collect into a General Council (as we had long wished) all our Venerable Brethren, the Bishops of the whole Catholic world, who have been called to a share of our solicitude. These Venerable Brethren indeed, inflamed as they are with singular love towards the Catholic Church, distinguished for eminent piety and loyalty towards us and this Apostolic See, anxious for the salvation of souls, excelling in wisdom, knowledge, and learning, are together with ourselves grievously

---

exitiales eorum impetus conatusque reprimendos, qui ipsam Ecclesiam, si fieri unquam posset, et civilem societatem funditus evertere connituntur. Nos quidem, Deo auxiliante, vel ab ipso supremi Nostri Pontificatus exordio nunquam pro gravissimi Nostri officii debito destitimus pluribus Nostris Consistorialibus Allocutionibus, et Apostolicis Litteris Nostram attollere vocem, ac Dei, ejusque sanctae Ecclesiae causam Nobis a Christo Domino concreditam omni studio constanter defendere, atque hujus Apostolicae Sedis, et justitiae, veritatisque jura propugnare, et inimicorum hominum insidias detegere, errores, falsasque doctrinas damnare, et impietatis sectas proscribere, ac universi Dominici gregis saluti advigilare et consulere.

Verum illustribus Praedecessorum Nostrorum vestigiis inhaerentes, opportunum propterea esse existimavimus, in Generale Concilium, quod jamdiu Nostris erat in votis, cogere omnes Venerabiles Fratres totius catholici orbis Sacrorum Antistites, qui in sollicitudinis Nostrae partem vocati sunt. Qui quidem Venerabiles Fratres singulari in catholicam Ecclesiam amore incensi, eximiaque erga Nos, et Apostoli-

afflicted at the most sad condition both of sacred and of civil affairs, they have nothing nearer at heart than to communicate to us and to combine their counsels, and apply salutary remedies to so many calamities. For in this Œcumenical Council all those things are to be most accurately weighed and determined which, particularly in these painful times, have especial regard to the greater glory of God, the integrity of the faith, the beauty of divine worship, the eternal salvation of men, the discipline as well as the salutary and solid instruction of the clergy, secular and regular; the observance of ecclesiastical laws; the reformation of morals; the Christian education of youth, and the common peace and concord of all. Every effort also must be made that, by God's good help, all evils may be removed from the Church and from civil society; that unhappy wanderers may be brought back into the straight path of truth, justice, and salvation; that, vices and errors being taken away, our august religion and its salutary doctrine may receive fresh life over all the earth, and increase daily in extent and power; and that thus piety, honour, probity, justice, charity, and all Christian virtues may abound and flourish, to the great benefit of human society. For no one can deny that the power of the Catholic Church, and of her doctrine, not only regards men's eternal salvation, but also

---

cam hanc Sedem pietate et observantia spectati, ac de animarum salute anxii, et sapientia, doctrina, eruditione praestantes, et una Nobiscum tristissimam rei cum sacrae tum publicae conditionem maxime dolentes, nihil antiquius habent, quam sua Nobiscum communicare, et conferre consilia, ac salutaria, tot calamitatibus adhibere remedia. In Oecumenico enim hoc Concilio ea omnia accuratissime examine sunt perpendenda, ac statuenda quae hisce praesertim asperrimis temporibus majorem Dei gloriam, et fidei integritatem, divinique cultus decorem, sempiternamque hominum salutem, et utriusque Cleri disciplinam, ejusque salutarem, solidamque culturam, atque ecclesiasticarum legum observantiam, morumque emendationem, et christianam juventutis institutionem, et communem omnium pacem et concordiam in primis respiciunt. Atque etiam intentissimo studio curandum est, ut, Deo bene juvante, omnia ab Ecclesia, et civili societate amoveantur mala, ut miseri errantes ad rectum veritatis, justitiae, salustisque tramitem reducantur, ut vitiis, erroribusque eliminatis, augusta nostra religio ejusque salutifera doctrina ubique terrarum reviviscat, et quotidie magis

benefits the temporal welfare of the people; and that it promotes their true prosperity, order, and tranquillity, and also the progress and solidity of human sciences, as the annals of sacred and profane history by conspicuous facts clearly show and constantly and evidently prove. And since Christ Our Lord wonderfully refreshes, recreates, and consoles us by those words, "Where two or three are gathered together in My name, there am I in the midst of them," therefore we cannot doubt but that in this Council He will vouchsafe to be at hand in the abundance of His Divine Grace, in order that we may be able to determine all those things which appertain in any way to the greater advantage of His Church. Having, therefore, in the humility of our heart, poured forth, night and day, most fervent prayers to God the Father of lights, we have judged that this Council should by all means be assembled.

Wherefore, relying and resting on the authority of Almighty God Himself, Father, Son, and Holy Ghost, and of the Blessed Apostles Peter and Paul, which we also exercise on earth, with the counsel and assent of our Venerable Brethren the Cardinals of the Holy Roman Church, by these Letters we proclaim, announce, convoke, and appoint a sacred Œcumenical and General Council to be held in this Holy City of

---

propagetur, et dominetur, atque ita pietas, honestas, probitas, justitia, caritas omnesque christianae virtutes cum maxima humanae societatis utilitate vigeant, et efflorescant. Nemo enim inficiari unquam poterit, catholicae Ecclesiae, ejusque doctrinae vim non solum aeternam hominum salutem spectare, verum etiam prodesse temporali populorum bono, eorumque verae prosperitati, ordini, ac tranquillitati, et humanarum quoque scientiarum progressui ac soliditati, veluti sacrae ac profanae historiae annales splendidissimis factis clare aperteque ostendunt, et constanter, evidenterque demonstrant. Et quoniam Christus Dominus illis verbis Nos mirifice recreat, reficit, et consolatur : *Ubi sunt duo vel tres congregati in nomine meo ibi sum in medio eorum* (Matth. c. xviii., v. 20); iccirco dubitare non possumus, quin Ipse in hoc Concilio Nobis in abundantia divinae suae gratiae praesto esse velit, quo ea omnia statuere possimus, quae ad majorem Ecclesiae suae sanctae utilitatem quovis modo pertinent. Ferventissimis igitur ad Deum luminum Patrem in humiliate cordis Nostri dies noctesque fusis precibus hoc Concilium omnino cogendum esse censuimus.

Rome, in the coming year one thousand eight hundred and sixty-nine, in the Vatican Basilica; to be begun on the eighth day of the month of December, sacred to the Immaculate Conception of the Virgin Mary, Mother of God; to be continued, and by the help of God to be completed and finished for His glory, and for the salvation of the whole Christian people. And we therefore will and command that, from every place, all our Venerable Brethren the Patriarchs, Archbishops and Bishops, our Beloved Sons the Abbots, and all others to whom by right or by privilege power has been granted of sitting in General Councils and declaring their opinions therein, shall come to this Œcumenical Council proclaimed by us. We require, exhort, admonish, and none the less enjoin and strictly command them, by force of the oath which they have taken to us and to this Holy See, and in virtue of holy obedience, and under the penalties ordinarily enacted and proposed by law or custom in the celebration of Councils against those who do not come, that they be altogether bound to be present, and to take part in this Sacred Council, unless they happen to be detained by just impediment, which nevertheless they will be obliged to prove to the Synod through their legitimate proctors.

And we are borne up by the hope that God, in

Quamobrem Dei ipsius omnipotentis Patris, et Filii, et Spiritus Sancti, ac beatorum ejus Apostolorum Petri et Pauli auctoritate, qua Nos quoque in terris fungimur, freti et innixi, de Venerabilium Fratrum Nostrorum S. R. E. Cardinalium consilio et assensu, sacrum Oecumenicum et Generale Concilium in hac alma Urbe Nostra Roma futuro anno millesimo octingentesimo sexagesimo nono, in Basilica Vaticana habendum, ac die octava mensis Decembris Immaculatae Deiparae Virginis Mariae Conceptioni sacra incipiendum, prosequendum, ac Domino adjuvante, ad ipsius gloriam, ad universi Christiani populi salutem absolvendum, et perficiendum hisce Litteris indicimus, annuntiamus, convocamus et statuimus. Ac proinde volumus, jubemus, omnes ex omnibus locis tam Venerabiles Fratres Patriarchas, Archiepiscopos, Episcopos, quam Dilectos Filios Abbates, omnesque alios, quibus jure, aut privilegio Conciliis Generalibus residendi, et sententias in eis dicendi facta est potestas, ad hoc Oecumenicum Concilium a Nobis indictum venire debere, requirentes, hortantes, admonentes, ac nihilominus eis vi jurisjurandi, quod Nobis, et huic Sanctae Sedi praestiterunt,

whose hands are the hearts of men, propitiously granting our petitions, will by His unspeakable mercy and grace bring it to pass that the supreme governors of all nations, and especially Catholic rulers, knowing daily more and more that the greatest blessings redound to human society from the Catholic Church, and that she is the firmest foundation of empires and kingdoms, not only will throw no impediment in the way of our Venerable Brethren the Bishops and others above named coming to this Council, but will even willingly favour and help, and will, as becomes Catholic princes, most studiously coöperate in all those things which may tend to the greater glory of God and the good of the said Council.

But in order that these our Letters, and all that is contained therein, may come to the knowledge of all whom they concern, and that no one may pretend ignorance of them, since perhaps not all to whom they ought to be nominally made known can be safely reached, we will and command that they shall be publicly read in a loud voice, by the Apparitors of our Court or by some public notaries, in the Lateran, Vatican, and Liberian Patriarchal Basilicas, at a time when the multitude of people is wont to come together to hear Mass; and that after the reading of

---

ac sanctae obedientiae virtute, et sub poenis jure, aut consuetudine in celebrationibus Conciliorum adversus non accedentes ferri, et proponi solitis, mandantes, arcteque praecipientes, ut ipsimet, nisi forte justo detineantur impedimento, quod tamen per legitimos procuratores Synodo probare debebunt, Sacro huic Concilio omnino adesse, et interesse teneantur.

In eam autem spem erigimus fore, ut Deus, in cujus manu sunt hominum corda, Nostris votis propitius annuens ineffabili sua misericordia et gratia efficiat, ut omnes supremi omnium populorum Principes, et Moderatores praesertim catholici quotidie magis noscentes maxima bona in humanam societatem ex catholica Ecclesia redundare, ipsamque, firmissimum esse Imperiorum, Regnorumque fundamentum, non solum minime impediant, quominus Venerabiles Fratres Sacrorum Antistites, aliique omnes supra commemorati ad hoc Concilium veniant, verum etiam ipsis libenter faveant, opemque ferant, et studiosissime, uti decet Catholicos Principes, iis cooperentur, quae in majorem Dei gloriam, ejusdemque Concilii bonum cedere queant.

the Letters they shall be affixed to the doors of the said churches, to the gates of the Apostolic Chancery, in the accustomed place in the Campus Floræ, and in other usual places: that there, in order that they may be read and known by all, they shall for some time be left exposed; and that, when they shall have been removed, copies of them shall in the same places remain affixed. For, by the aforesaid reading, publication, and affixing, we will that all and whomsoever these our Letters concern, shall, after the space of two months from the publication and affixing of the same, be obliged and bound in the same way as if the letters had been read in their presence. Also we command and decree that to copies taken by public notaries or signed by them, and stamped with the seal of any person of ecclesiastical dignity, certain and undoubted faith be given.

Let no one therefore infringe this document of our indiction, announcement, convocation, statute, decree, command, precept, and exhortation, or with rash attempt oppose it. But if any one shall attempt to do so, let him know that he will incur the indignation of Almighty God, and of the Holy Apostles Peter and Paul.

Ut vero Nostrae hae Litterae, et quae in eis continentur ad notitiam omnium, quorum oportet, perveniant, neve quis illorum ignorantiae excusationem praetendat, cum praesertim etiam non ad omnes eos, quibus nominatim illae essent intimandae, tutus forsitan pateat accessus, volumus, et mandamus, ut in Patriarchalibus Bascilicis Lateranensi, Vaticana, et Liberiana, cum ibi multitudo populi ad audiendam rem divinam congregari solita est, palam clara voce per Curiae Nostrae cursores, aut aliquos publicos notarios legantur, lectaeque in valvis dictarum Ecclesiarum, itemque Cancelleriae Apostolicae portis, et Campi Florae solito loco, et in aliis consuetis locis affigantur, ubi ad lectionem et notitiam cunctorum aliquandiu expositae pendeant, cumque inde amovebuntur, earum nihilominus exempla in ejusdem locis remaneant affixa. Nos · enim per hujusmodi lectionem, publicationem, affixionemque, omnes, et quoscumque, quos praedictae Nostrae Litterae comprehendunt, post spatium duorum mensium a die Litterarum publicationis et affixionis ita volumus obligatos esse et adstrictos, ac si ipsismet illae coram lectae et intimatae essent, transumptis quidem earum, quae manu publici notarii scripta, aut subscripta, et sigillo personae alicujus Ecclesiasticae in dignitate constitutae munita fuerint, ut fides certa, et indubitata habeatur, mandamus ac decernimus.

Given at Rome, at St. Peter's, in the year 1868 of Our Lord's Incarnation, on the third day before the calends of July, in the 23rd year of our Pontificate.

✠ I, PIUS, BISHOP OF THE CATHOLIC CHURCH.

Nulli ergo omnino hominum liceat hanc paginam Nostrae indictionis, annuntiationis, convocationis, statui, decreti, mandati, praecepti, et obsecrationis infringere, vel ei ausu temerario contraire. Si quis autem hoc attentare praesumpserit, indignationem Omnipotentis Dei, ac Beatorum Petri et Pauli Apostolorum ejus se noverit incursurum.

Datum Romae apud Sanctum Petrum Anno Incarnationis Dominicae millesimo octingentesimo sexagesimo octavo, tertio kalendas Julias. Pontificatus Nostri Anno Vicesimotertio

✠ EGO PIUS CATHOLICAE ECCLESIAE EPISCOPUS.
Loco ✠ Signi

✠ Ego Marius Episc. Ostiensis et Veliternus Card. Decanus Mattei Pro-Datarius.
✠ Ego Constantinus Episc. Portuen. et S. Rufinae Card. Patrizi.
✠ Ego Aloisius Episc. Praenestinus Card. Amat S. R. E. Vice-Cancellarius.
✠ Ego Nicolaus Episc. Tusculanus Card. Paracciani Clarelli a Secretis Brevium.
✠ Ego Camillus Episc. Albanus Card. Di Pietro.
✠ Ego Carolus Augustus Episc. Sabinensis Card. de Reisach.
✠ Ego Philippus Tit. S. Laurentii in Lucina Proto-Presb. Card. de Angelis Archiep. Firmanus, et S. R. E. Camerarius.
✠ Ego Fabius Maria Tit. S. Stephani in Monte Coelio Presb. Card. Asquini.
✠ Ego Alexander Tit. S. Susannae Presb. Card. Barnabò.
✠ Ego Joseph Tit. S. Mariae in Ara Caeli Presb. Card. Milesi.
✠ Ego Petrus Tit. S. Marci Presb. Card. de Silvestri.
✠ Ego Carolus Tit. S. Mariae de Populo Presb. Card. Sacconi.
✠ Ego Angelus Tit. SS. Andreae et Gregorii in Monte Coelio Presb. Card. Quaglia.
✠ Ego Fr. Antonius Maria Tit. SS. XII. Apost. Presb. Card. Panebianco Poenitentiarius Major.
✠ Ego Antoninus Tit. SS. Quatuor Coronator. Presb. Card. de Luca.
✠ Ego Joseph Andreas Tit. S. Hieronymi Illyricorum Presb. Card. Bizzarri.
✠ Ego Joannes Bapt. Tit. S. Callixti Presb. Card. Pitra.
✠ Ego Fr. Philippus Maria Tit. S. Xysti Presb. Card. Guidi Archiep. Bononiensis.
✠ Ego Gustavus Tit. S. Mariae in Transpontina Presb. Card. d'Hohenlohe.
✠ Ego Aloisius Tit. S. Laurentii in Pane Perna Presb. Card. Bilio.
✠ Ego Lucianus Tit. S. Pudentianae Presb. Card. Bonaparte.
✠ Ego Joseph Tit. SS. Marcellini et Petri Presb. Card. Berardi.
✠ Ego Raphael Tit. SS. Crucis in Hierusalem Presb. Card. Monaco.

On the 8th September, 1868, the Sovereign Pontiff issued a Letter of Invitation to all the Bishops of the Oriental Rite, who are not in communion with the Holy See, inviting them to attend the General Council of the Vatican. In doing this he followed the example of his predecessors, Gregory X. and Eugenius IV.; the former having invited the Oriental schismatics to assist at the Second Council of Lyons, and the latter at that of Florence. It is unnecessary after what has been said of the constituent members of a General Council to do more than point out that this Invitation was one of pure charity; that the presence of schismatical Bishops is neither in any way necessary to a General Council, nor can it possibly add any weight or power to it; for schismatical Bishops could not take any active part in such an assembly, nor be members of it at all, until they had first submitted to the Pontiff, re-entered the fold out of which they have gone, and acknowledged the Head which calls the Council together and presides over it in all its deliberations. But in this Letter of paternal entreaty the zeal for unity, the charity which forgives all things, and humbly condescends to be the first to invite a reconciliation between the separated Churches of East and West, are made abundantly conspicuous. Though the Church is one and perfect in her Divine life and organization, the Sovereign Pontiff, acting as the Good Shepherd of all who have been baptized into the Fold, has not hesitated to go into the wilderness to bring back, if they would, those erring sheep who have wandered away from the Flock which he so lovingly tends. We here subjoin the words of this Invitation, so full of Apostolic charity and of desire for unity and salvation:—

✢ Ego Jacobus S. Mariae in Via Lata Proto-Diac. Card. Antonelli.
✢ Ego Prosper S. Mariae Scalaris Diac. Card. Caterini.
✢ Ego Theodulphus S. Eustachii Diac. Card. Mertel.
✢ Ego Dominicus S. Mariae in Domnica Diac. Card. Consolini.
✢ Ego Eduardus SS. Viti et Modesti Diac. Card. Borromeo.
✢ Ego Hannibal S. Mariae in Aquiro Diac. Card. Capalti.
M. Card. MATTEI *Pro-Datarius* — N. Card. PARACCIANI CLARELLI
Loco ✢ Plumbi   Visa de Curia D. Bruti
Reg. in Secretaria Brevium   *I. Cugnionius.*

*LETTERS APOSTOLIC OF HIS HOLINESS POPE PIUS IX.
TO ALL BISHOPS OF CHURCHES OF THE EASTERN RITE NOT IN COMMUNION WITH THE APOSTOLIC SEE.

Having been established by the secret design of Divine Providence, without any merits of our own, in this lofty Chair, as heir of the most blessed Prince of the Apostles, who, *according to the prerogative granted him by God, is the most firm and solid rock on which the Saviour built His Church*, and urged by the solicitude of the burden which has been placed upon us, we most earnestly desire and endeavour to extend our cares to all those in every region of the world who are called by the Christian name, and to draw all within the embraces of our paternal charity. For we cannot, without grave danger to our soul, neglect any part of that Christian people which, having been redeemed by the most precious blood of Our Saviour, and brought by the sacred waters of baptism into Our Lord's flock, justly claims for itself all our vigilance. Therefore, since we should unintermittingly bestow all our care and thought on promoting the salvation of all who know and adore Christ Jesus, we turn our eyes and paternal mind to those Churches which were formerly united in

---

* SANCTISSIMI DOMINI NOSTRI PII DIVINA PROVIDENTIA PAPAE IX. LITTERAE APOSTOLICAE AD OMNES EPISCOPOS ECCLESIARUM RITUS ORIENTALIS COMMUNIONEM CUM APOSTOLICA SEDE NON HABENTES.

AD OMNES EPISCOPOS ECCLESIARUM RITUS ORIENTALIS, COMMUNIONEM CUM APOSTOLICA SEDE NON HABENTES.

PIUS PP. IX.

Arcano Divinae Providentiae consilio, licet sine ullis meritis Nostris, in hac sublimi Cathedra haeredes Beatissimi Apostolorum Principis constitui, qui *juxta praerogativam sibi a Deo concessam firma et solidissima petra est, super quam Salvator Ecclesiam aedificavit* (S. Greg. Nyss. *Laudatio altera S. Steph. Protomart. apud Galland*. VI. 600), impositi Nobis oneris sollicitudine urgente, ad eos omnes in qualibet terrarum Orbis regione degentes, qui christiano nomine censentur, curas Nostras extendere, omnesque ad paternae caritatis amplexus excitare vehementissime cupimus et conamur. Nec vero absque gravi animae Nostrae periculo partem ullam christiani populi negligere possumus, qui pretiosissimo Salvatoris Nostri Sanguine redemptus, et sacris baptismi aquis in Dominicum gregem adlectus, omnem sibi vigilantiam Nostram jure

the bond of unity with this Apostolic See, and flourished with so great renown of holiness and of heavenly doctrine, producing rich fruits for the glory of God and the salvation of souls. These Churches are now, to our extreme grief, through the wicked arts and machinations of him who in heaven excited the first schism, separated and divided from the communion of the Holy Roman Church which is spread throughout the world.

On this account, at the very beginning of our supreme Pontificate, we spoke to you with full affection of heart words of peace and charity. And although these words did not obtain their most desired result, the hope has never left us that our humble and fervent prayers will be heard by the most merciful and most benign Author of salvation and peace, Who *wrought salvation in the midst of the earth, and Who, the Orient on high, manifestly showed forth peace as pleasing to Him and to be accepted by all, and announced it at His rising by the ministry of angels to men of good-will, and while dwelling among men both taught it by word and preached it by example.*

But at this time when, with the advice of our Venerable Brethren the Cardinals of the Holy Roman Church, we have lately proclaimed and convoked an

---

deposcit. Itaque cum in omnium procurandam salutem, qui Christum Jesum agnoscunt et adorant, studia omnia, cogitationesque Nostros indesinenter conferre debeamus, oculos Nostros ac paternum animum ad istas convertimus Ecclesias, quae olim unitatis vinculo cum hac Apostolica Sede conglutinatae tanta sanctitatis, caelestisque doctrinae laude florebant, uberesque divinae gloriae et animarum salutis fructus edebant, nunc vero per nefarias illius artes ac machinationes, qui primum schisma excitavit in caelo, a communione Sanctae Romanae Ecclesiae, quae toto orbe diffusa est, sejunctae ac divisae cum summo Nostro moerore existunt.

Hac sane de causa jam ab ipso Supremi Nostri Pontificatus exordio Vobis pacis caritatisque verba toto cordis affectu locuti sumus (Epist. ad Orient. *In suprema*, die 6 Januarii an. 1848). Etsi vero haec Nostra verba optatissimum minime obtinuerint exitum, tamen nunquam Nos deseruit spes fore ut humiles aeque ac ferventes Nostras preces propitius exaudire dignetur clementissimus ac benignissimus salutis pacisque Auctor, *qui operatus est in medio terrae salutem, quique oriens ex alto pacem sibi acceptam et ab omnibus acceptandam evidenter ostendens, eam in ortu suo Angelorum ministerio bonae voluntatis hominibus nunciavit,*

Œcumenical Synod to be celebrated next year in Rome, and to begin on the eighth day of the month of December, which is sacred to the Immaculate Conception of the Virgin Mary, Mother of God, we again direct our voice to you; and with the greatest possible earnestness of soul we beseech, admonish, and pressingly exhort you to come to the said General Synod, as your ancestors came to the Second Council of Lyons held by our predecessor blessed Gregory X. of venerable memory, and to the Council of Florence held by Eugenius IX. of happy memory, also our predecessor; in order that the conditions of our former love may be renewed, and the peace of our fathers (that heavenly and salutary gift of Christ which by lapse of time has withered) may be once more recalled to vigour, after the long-continued cloud of grief and the dark and deplorable night of long-continued dissension, and so the light of desired union may shine brightly upon all.

And may this be the most happy fruit of benediction wherewith Christ Jesus, the Lord and Saviour of us all, may console His immaculate and most beloved spouse the Catholic Church, and dry up and wipe away her tears in this bitter time: that all division being removed, voices hitherto at variance may, with

---

et inter homines conversatus verbo docuit, praedicavit exemplo (Epist. B. Gregorii X. ad Michaelem Palaeologum, Graec. Imper. die 24 Octobris an. 1272).

Jam vero cum nuper de Venerabilium Fratrum Nostrorum S. R. E. Cardinalium consilio Oecumenicam Synodum futuro anno Romae celebrandam, ac die octavo mensis Decembris Immaculatae Deiparae Virginis Mariae Conceptioni sacro incipiendam indixerimus et convocaverimus, vocem Nostram ad Vos rursus dirigimus, et majore, qua possumus, animi Nostri contentione Vos obsecramus, monemus et obtestamur ut ad eamdem generalem Synodum convenire velitis, quemadmodum Majores Vestri convenerunt ad Concilium Lugdunense II., a recol. mem. B. Gregorio X. Praedecessore Nostro habitum, et ad Florentinum Concilium a fel. record. Eugenio IV., item Decessore Nostro celebratum, ut dilectionis antiquae legibus renovatis, et Patrum pace, caelesti illo ac salutari Christi dono quod tempore exaruit, ad vigorem iterum revocata (Epist. LXX., al. CCXX. S. Basilii Magni ad S. Damasum Papam), post longam moeroris nebulam et dissidii diuturni atram ingratamque caliginem serenum omnibus unionis optatae jubar illucescat (Defin. S. Oecum. Synodi Florent. in Bulla Eugenii IV.: *Laetentur Caeli*).

perfect unity of spirit, join together in the praise of God, Who desires not that schism may be among us, but has commanded by the voice of the Apostle that we should all speak and think alike. Thus may continual thanksgivings be ever offered up to the Father of Mercies by all His Saints, and especially by those most glorious ancient Fathers and Doctors of the Eastern Churches, when from heaven they look down on the restoration and renewal of that union with the Apostolic See, the centre of Catholic truth and unity, which they whilst living upon earth laboured with every effort and with unwearied toil to cherish, and daily to forward more and more both by teaching and example,—through the love which, diffused in their hearts by the Holy Ghost, they had for Him Who broke down the wall of division, and who through His Blood reconciled all things and brought them into peace; Who willed that the proof of being His disciples should consist in unity; and Whose prayer went forth to His Father, "I pray that all may be one, as We are One."

Given at Rome, at St. Peter's, on the 8th day of September in the year 1868, the twenty-third year of our Pontificate.

Atque hic sit jucundissimus benedictionis fructus, quo Christus Jesus nostrum omnium Dominus et Redemptor immaculatam ac dilectissimam Sponsam suam catholicam Ecclesiam consoletur, ejusque temperet et abstergat lacrimas in hac asperitate temporum, ut, omni divisione penitus sublata, voces antea discrepantes perfecta spiritus unanimitate collaudent Deum, qui non vult schismata esse in nobis, sed ut idem omnes dicamus et sentiamus Apostoli voce praecepit; immortalesque misericordiarum Patri semper agantur gratiae ab omnibus Sanctis suis, ac praesertim a gloriosissimis illis Ecclesiarum Orientalium antiquis Patribus et Doctoribus, cum de caelo prospiciant instauratam ac redintegratam cum hac Apostolica Sede catholicae veritatis et unitatis centro conjuctionem, quam ipsi in terris viventes omnibus studiis atque indefessis laboribus fovere et magis in dies promovere tum doctrina, tum exemplo curarunt, diffusa in eorum cordibus per Spiritum Sanctum caritate Illius, qui medium maceriae parietem solvit, ac per Sanguinem suum omnia conciliavit et pacavit, qui signum discipulorum suorum in unitate esse voluit, et cujus Oratio, ad Patrem porrecta, est: Rogo ut omnes unum sint, sicut et Nos unum sumus.

Datum Romae apud S. Petrum, die 8 Septembris Anno 1868.
Pontificatus Nostri Anno Vicesimotertio.

On the 13th of September, 1868, the Sovereign Pontiff issued another Letter of Invitation to "all Protestants and other non-Catholics." Every person who has received the Baptism of Christ is thereby made a member of that One Church of Christ over which His Vicar presides upon earth. He remains within the fold of that Church, no matter from whose hands he may have received the Sacrament of Baptism, until by some act he practically leaves that fold by either rejecting its authority or by associating himself with some form of error. Still, though he may have forsaken the one faith, or Church of Christ, into which by the One Baptism he had been admitted, he can never cease to be the subject of that Church, however much he may rebel against it, or abjure its authority. The fact is irrefragable; if he has received Baptism, he was baptized into the Church of Christ. The expression of the Apostle, "One Lord, one Faith, and one Baptism," speaks of a radical and essential union between God and His Church and His Baptism. This Sacrament is the one door of admission into the Church, as the Church is the divinely-appointed ark of salvation built and governed by the Lord.

The Sovereign Pontiff, then, addressing all those baptized persons who are actually separated from him either by wilfulness or by the accident of ignorance, paternally and affectionately calls them back to the obligation they contracted in their Baptism. They are still subject to his authority as Vicar of Christ and Head of the Church into which they have been once admitted; and the Pontiff urges, as one of his motives for addressing them, that he fears to have one day to render account to Him Who is our Judge if he does not show them, as far as it is in his power to do so, the way to attain Eternal Salvation. He says, "We address these Letters to all Christians separated from us, and we again and again exhort and conjure them quickly to return to the one fold of Christ." The whole of the Letter is an argument and a prayer for unity among all Christians. The Pope has not addressed himself in any Letter to heathens, atheists, or to the unbaptized. His jurisdiction does not extend over them. His Letters have been written to those to whom he can speak by right and with authority, that is, schismatics and heretics, whether formal or material—in other words, to all baptized non-Catholics.

The Sovereign Pontiff has, therefore, hereby discharged his duty of charity towards those Christians who have separated from his communion. We may confidently appeal to the tenor of his Letters as to whether he could have used words more full of gentleness, charity, and condescension. He has called them; it will not be his fault if they do not hear, or if hearing they forbear to come.

In the sixteenth century Luther formally appealed from the Bull of Leo X. to a General Council, and many of his colleagues invoked the same authority. The preamble to the Confession of Augsburg appealed to it. But it was then thought that it would be next to impossible to assemble a General Council. When the Council, however, was finally determined upon and convoked, Luther, with his followers, treated its pretensions and power with ridicule and contempt, and in presence of all the protestations and reiterated appeals to a Council made by him, his abettors, and his Diets, Melancthon declared, "They never had a real intention to abide by a Council." It remains now to be seen how far the Protestants of the nineteenth century, who have again and again appealed to a General Council, resemble their brethren in the sixteenth. The following is the Papal document addressed to "all Protestants and other non-Catholics":—

*LETTERS APOSTOLIC OF HIS HOLINESS POPE - PIUS IX.

TO ALL PROTESTANTS AND OTHER NON-CATHOLICS.

You already know that we having been raised,

---

* SANCTISSIMI DOMINI NOSTRI PII DIVINA PROVIDENTIA PAPAE IX. LITTERAE APOSTOLICAE AD OMNES PROTESTANTES, ALIOSQUE ACATHOLICOS.

AD OMNES PROTESTANTES, ALIOSQUE ACATHOLICOS.

PIUS PP. IX.

Jam vos omnes noveritis, Nos licet immerentes ad hanc Petri Cathe-

notwithstanding our unworthiness, to this Chair of Peter, and therefore invested by Christ Our Lord with the supreme government and guardianship of the whole Catholic Church, have judged it seasonable to call unto us our Venerable Brethren the Bishops of the whole earth, and to unite them together for the celebration next year of an Œcumenical Council. We have done so in order that, in concert with these our Venerable Brethren who are called to share in our cares, we may take those steps which may be opportune and necessary, both for dispelling the darkness of the many noxious errors which, to the great loss of souls, everywhere and daily prevail, and for establishing and increasing daily more and more amongst the Christian people entrusted to our watchfulness, the kingdom of true Faith, Justice, and the Peace of God. Confidently relying on the close ties and most loving union, which, in so marked a way, unite to ourselves and to this Holy See these our Venerable Brethren, who, through all the time of our Supreme Pontificate, have never failed to give to ourselves and this Holy See the clearest tokens of their love and veneration, we have a firm hope that this Œcumenical Council, summoned by us at this time, will produce, by the inspirations of Divine Grace, as other General Councils in past ages

---

dram evectos, et idcirco supremo universae catholicae Ecclesiae regimini et curae ab ipso Christo Domino Nobis divinitus commissae praepositos opportunum existimasse, omnes Venerabiles Fratres totius orbis Episcopos apud Nos vocare, et in Oecumenicum Concilium futuro anno concelebrandum cogere, ut cum eisdem Venerabilibus Fratribus in sollicitudinis Nostrae partem vocatis ea omnia consilia suscipere possimus, quae magis opportuna, ac necessaria sint, tum ad dissipandas tot pestiferorum errorum tenebras, qui cum summo animarum damno ubique in dies dominantur et debacchantur, tum ad quotidie magis constituendum, et amplificandum in christianis populis vigilantiae Nostrae concreditis verae fidei, justitiae veraeque Dei pacis regnum. Ac vehementer confisi arctissimo et amantissimo conjunctionis foedere, quo Nobis, et Apostolicae huic Sedi iidem Venerabiles Fratres mirifice obstricti sunt, qui nunquam intermiserunt omni supremi Nostri Pontificatus tempore splendidissima erga Nos, et eamdem Sedem fidei, amoris, et observantiae testimonia praebere, ea profecto spe nitimur fore ut veluti praeteritis saeculis alia generalia Concilia, ita etiam praesenti saeculo Concilium hoc Oecumenicum a Nobis indictum uberes, laetissimosque,

have done, abundant fruits of benediction, to the greater glory of God and the eternal salvation of men.

Sustained by this hope, and roused and urged by the charity of our Lord Jesus Christ, Who gave His life for the whole human race, we cannot restrain ourselves, on the occasion of the future Council, from addressing our Apostolic and paternal words to all those who, whilst they know the same Jesus Christ as the Redeemer, and glory in the name of Christian, yet do not profess the true faith of Christ, nor hold to and follow the communion of the Catholic Church. And this we do in order to admonish, and conjure, and beseech them, with all the warmth of our zeal and in all charity, to consider and seriously examine whether they follow the path marked out for them by Jesus Christ Our Lord, which leads to eternal salvation. No one can deny or doubt that Jesus Christ Himself, in order to apply the fruits of His redemption to all generations of men, built His only Church in this world on Peter, that is to say, the Church, One, Holy, Catholic, and Apostolic; and that He gave him all the power necessary to preserve the deposit of Faith whole and inviolate, and to teach the same Faith to all kindreds, and peoples, and

---

divina adspirante gratia, fructus emittat, pro majore Dei gloria, ac sempiterna hominum salute.

Itaque in hanc spem erecti, ac Domini Nostri Jesu Christi, qui pro universi humani generis salute traditi animam suam, caritate excitati, et compulsi, haud possumus, quin futuri Concilii occasione eos omnes Apostolicis, ac paternis Nostris verbis alloquamur, qui etiamsi eumdem Christum Jesum veluti Redemptorem agnoscant, et in christiano nomine glorientur, tamen veram Christi fidem haud profitentur, neque catholicae Ecclesiae communionem sequuntur. Atque id agimus, ut omni studio et caritate eos vel maxime moneamus, exhortemur, et obsecremur, ut serio considerare et animadvertere velint, num ipsi viam ab eodem Christo Domino praescriptam sectentur, quae ad aeternam perducit salutem. Et quidem nemo inficiari, ac dubitare potest, ipsum Christum Jesum, ut humanis omnibus generationibus redemptionis suae fructus applicaret, suam hic in terris supra Petrum unicam aedificasse Ecclesiam, idest unam, sanctam, catholicam, apostolicam, eique necessariam omnem contulisse potestatem, ut integrum inviolatumque custodiretur fidei depositum, ac eadem fides omnibus populis, gentibus, nationibus traderetur, ut per baptisma omnes in mysticum suum corpus

nations; so that all men might through baptism become members of His mystical Body; that the new life of grace, without which no one can ever attain to life eternal, might always be preserved and perfected in them; and that this Church, which is His mystical Body, might always in its own nature remain firm and immoveable to the consummation of ages, that it might flourish, and supply to all its children all the means of salvation.

Now, whoever will carefully examine and reflect upon the condition of the various religious societies which are divided amongst themselves, and separated from the Catholic Church, which from the days of Our Lord Jesus Christ and his Apostles has ever exercised, by its lawful pastors, and still does exercise, the divine power committed to it by this same Lord, will easily satisfy himself that none of these societies, either singly or altogether, in any way form, or are, that one Catholic Church which Our Lord founded and built, and which He chose should be in the world; and that he cannot by any means say that these societies are members or parts of that Church, since they are visibly separated from Catholic unity.

For such-like societies, being destitute of that living authority established by God, which especially teaches

---

cooptarentur homines, et in ipsis semper servaretur, ac perficeretur illa nova vita gratiae, sine qua nemo potest unquam aeternam mereri et assequi vitam, utque eadem Ecclesia, quae mysticum suum constituit corpus, in sua propria natura semper stabilis et immota usque ad consummationem saeculi permaneret, vigeret, et omnibus filiis suis omnia salutis praesidia suppeditaret. Nunc vero qui accurate consideret, ac meditetur conditionem, in qua versantur variae, et inter se discrepantes religiosae societates sejunctae a catholica Ecclesia, quae a Christo Domino, ejusque Apostolis sine intermissione per legitimos sacros suos Pastores semper exercuit, et in praesentia etiam exercet divinam potestatem sibi ab ipso Domino traditam, vel facile sibi persuadere debebit, neque aliquam peculiarem, neque omnes simul conjunctas ex eisdem societatibus ullo modo constituere, et esse illam unam et catholicam Ecclesiam, quam Christus Dominus aedificavit, constituit, et esse voluit, neque membrum, aut partem ejusdem Ecclesiae ullo modo dici posse, quandoquidem sunt a catholica unitate visibiliter divisae. Cum enim ejusmodi societates careant viva illa, et a Deo constituta auctoritate, qua homines, res fidei, morumque disciplinam praesertim docet, eosque dirigit, ac moderatur in iis omnibus, quae ad

men the things of faith and the rule of morals, and which guides them in everything that relates to eternal life, are always varying in their doctrines; and this change and instability are increasing. Every one can easily understand, and clearly and evidently see, that this is distinctly opposite to the Church instituted by Our Lord Jesus Christ, in which truth must always continue firm and inaccessible to change, as a deposit given to the Church to be guarded in its integrity, and for the guardianship of which the presence and aid of the Holy Ghost have been promised to her for ever. Every one also knows that from these divergent doctrines and opinions, social schisms have had their birth, and that these again have generated sects and communions without number, which are continually spreading, to the great injury of Christian and civil society.

Indeed, whoever observes that religion is the foundation of human society, must perceive and acknowledge the great influence which this division of principles, this opposition, this strife of religious societies amongst themselves, must have on civil society; and with what force the denial of the authority established by God, for ruling the persuasions of the human mind and directing the actions of men as well in private as

---

aeternam salutem pertinent, tum societates ipsae in suis doctrinis continenter variarunt, et haec mobilitas ac instabilitas apud easdem societates nunquam cessat. Quisque vel facile intelligit, et clare aperteque noscit, id vel maxime adversari Ecclesiae a Christo Domino institutae, in qua veritas semper stabilis, nullique unquam immutationi obnoxia persistere debet, veluti depositum eidem Ecclesiae traditum integerrime custodiendum, pro cujus custodia Spiritus Sancti praesentia, auxiliumque ipsi Ecclesiae fuit perpetuo promissum. Nemo autem ignorat, ex hisce doctrinarum, et opinionum dissidiis socialia quoque oriri schismata, atque ex his originem habere innumerabiles communiones, et sectas, quae cum summo christianae, civilisque reipublicae damno magis in dies propagantur.

Enimvero quicumque religionem veluti humanae societatis fundamentum cognoscit, non poterit non agnoscere, et fateri quantam in civilem societatem vim ejusmodi principiorum, ac religiosarum societatum inter se pugnantium divisio, ac discrepantia exercuerit, et quam vehementer negatio auctoritatis a Deo constitutae ad humani intellectus persuasiones regendas, atque ad hominum tum in privata, tum in sociali vita actiones dirigendas excitaverit, promoverit, et aluerit hos in-

in social life, has fostered, spread, and supported those deplorable changes of times and circumstances, and those troubles which at this day overwhelm and afflict almost all nations.

Let all those, then, who do not profess the *unity and truth of the Catholic Church* avail themselves of the opportunity of this Council, in which the Catholic Church, to which their forefathers belonged, affords a new proof of her close unity and her invincible vitality ; and let them satisfy the longings of their hearts, and liberate themselves from that state in which they cannot be assured of their own salvation. Let them unceasingly offer fervent prayers to the God of Mercy, that He will throw down the wall of separation, that He will scatter the darkness of error, and that He will lead them back to the bosom of our Holy Mother the Church, in whom their fathers found the salutary pastures of life, in whom alone the whole doctrine of Jesus Christ is preserved and handed down, and the mysteries of heavenly grace dispensed.

For ourself, to whom the same Christ our Lord has entrusted the charge of the supreme Apostolic ministry, and who must, therefore, fulfil with the greatest zeal all the functions of a good Pastor, and love with a paternal love and embrace in our charity all men

---

felicissimos rerum, ac temporum motus, et perturbationes, quibus omnes fere populi miserandum in modum agitantur, et affliguntur.

Quamobrem ii omnes, *qui Ecclesiae Catholicae unitatem et veritatem* non tenent (S. August. ep. LXI., al. CCXXIII.), occasionem amplectantur hujus Concilii, quo Ecclesia Catholica, cui eorum Majores adscripti erant, novum intimae unitatis, et inexpugnabilis vitalis sui roboris exhibet argumentum, ac indigentiis eorum cordis respondentes ab eo statu se eripere studeant, in quo de sua propria salute securi esse non possunt. Nec desinant ferventissimas Miserationum Domino offerre preces, ut divisionis murum disjiciat, errorum caliginem depellat, eosque ad sinum Sanctae Matris Ecclesiae reducat, in qua eorum majores salutaria vitae pascua habuere, et in qua solum integra Christi Jesu doctrina servatur, traditur, et caelestis gratiae dispensantur mysteria.

Nos quidem cum ex supremi Apostolici Nostri ministerii officio Nobis ab ipso Christo Domino commisso omnes boni pastoris partes studiosissime explere, et omnes universi terrarum orbis homines paterna caritate prosequi, et amplecti debeamus, tum has Nostras ad omnes christianos a Nobis sejunctos Litteras damus, quibus eos etiam, atque etiam hortamur et obsecramur, ut ad unicum Christi ovile redire fes-

wherever dispersed over the earth, we address these Letters to all Christians separated from us, and we again and again exhort and conjure them to return quickly to the one fold of Christ.

For we ardently desire their salvation in Jesus Christ; and we fear to have one day to render account to Him Who is our Judge, if we do not show them and prepare for them, as far as is in our power, the way to attain to eternal salvation. In all our prayers and supplications and thanksgiving, we cease not day nor night to ask earnestly and humbly for them, of the Eternal Pastor of souls, the abundance of light and heavenly grace. And since, notwithstanding our unworthiness, we hold the office of His Vicar upon earth, with outstretched hands we wait in the most ardent desire the return of our erring sons to the Catholic Church, so that we may receive them most lovingly into the House of our Heavenly Father, and may enrich them with His inexhaustible treasures. On this longed-for return to the truth and unity of the Catholic Church depends the salvation not only of individuals, but still more of the whole Christian society; and the whole world cannot enjoy true peace, unless there shall be one fold and one shepherd.

Given at St. Peter's in Rome, the 13th day of September, 1868, in the twenty-third year of our Pontificate.

---

tinent; quandoquidem eorum in Christo Jesu salutem ex animo summopere optamus, ac timemus ne eidem Nostro Judici ratio a Nobis aliquando sit reddenda, nisi, quantum in Nobis est, ipsis ostendamus, et muniamus viam ad eamdem aeternam assequendam salutem. In omni certe oratione, et obsecratione, cum gratiarum actione nunquam desistimus dies noctesque pro ipsis caelestium luminum, et gratiarum abundantiam ab aeterno animarum Pastore humiliter, enixeque exposcere. Et quoniam vicariam Ejus hic in terris licet immerito gerimus operam, idcirco errantium filiorum ad catholicae Ecclesiae reversionem expansis manibus ardentissime expectamus, ut eos in caelestis Patris domum amantissime excipere, et inexhaustis ejus thesauris ditare possimus. Etenim ex hoc optatissimo ad veritatis, et communionis cum catholica Ecclesia reditu non solum singulorum, sed totius etiam christianae societatis salus maxime pendet, et universus mundus vera pace perfrui non potest, nisi fiat unum ovile, et unus pastor.

Datum Romae apud S. Petrum, die 13 Septembris, 1868.
Pontificatus Nostri Anno Vicesimotertio.

Chapter VII.

VISIT OF THE ABATE CARLO TESTA TO THE GREEK AND ARMENIAN PATRIARCHS.—FREEDOM OF ACTION OF THE GREEK BISHOPS AT THE COUNCIL OF FLORENCE.—DYING TESTIMONY OF JOHN, PATRIARCH OF CONSTANTINOPLE AT THAT TIME.—SUBSERVIENCE OF THE GREEK BISHOPS TO THEIR PATRIARCH.—THEIR FUTILE OBJECTIONS TO THE COUNCIL.—THESE OBJECTIONS REFUTED.—TWO BISHOPS HONOURABLY DISTINGUISHED FROM THE REST.—DESPOTISM OF THE PATRIARCH.—HUMILIATION INFLICTED UPON HIM BY THE OTTOMAN GOVERNMENT.—PROPOSED SEPARATION OF GREEK AND BULGARIAN CHURCHES.—THE PATRIARCH PROPOSES TO CALL A COUNCIL.—OBJECTIONS TO THIS ON THE PART OF BOTH TURKS AND GREEKS.

THE announcement to the Catholic world was followed, on the 8th of September, as we have already said, by an invitation from the august Pontiff to all the Bishops of the Oriental Rite who are not in communion with the See of Rome, to attend the Vatican Council. In the absence of Monsignor Paolo Brunoni, the Vicar Apostolic of Constantinople, his Vicar General, the Abate Carlo Testa, was appointed by the Pope to be the bearer of his letters to all the Oriental Archbishops and Bishops of whatever rite, not in communion with Rome, resident within the limits of his vicariate. He accordingly began to accomplish his mission in the middle of October, 1868.

Having caused his intended visit to be previously announced by two of his priests, the Abate Testa proceeded on the appointed day, the 15th of October, first to the Greek Patriarch and afterwards to the Armenian, accompanied by his Chancellor and two other ecclesiastics. On arriving at the Fanar, where the Greek Patriarch resides, they were shown into the apartment of the Protosyncellos, a personage filling an office similar to that of our Vicars-General, who received them with the usual Oriental forms. The deputation was then admitted to the presence of his superior, who behaved in the first instance with ordinary civility, addressing to its members a few friendly words. The whole scene had been evidently preconcerted and prepared. Such politeness as was shown was entirely extra-official, and what followed was designed to mark that no consideration was intended to be expressed by the Patriarch towards his visitor in the capacity of Papal delegate. The Encyclical, handsomely bound in red morocco, and bearing these words on its frontispiece : "*Sanctissimo Patriarchæ Novæ Romæ Græci Ritus de mandato Beatissimi Domini Nostri Pii Papæ IX. pro Revmo Archiepiscopo Vicario ac Delegato Apostolico C. Testa V. G.,*" was now presented. The Patriarch did not touch it, but made a sign that the document should be laid on the divan, and commenced at once delivering himself of a speech in Greek, which the Protosyncellos translated in lengthened form into French. This harangue appeared a few days later in the public journals, with still more copious amplifications.

The substance of what the Patriarch was understood to say was as follows :—" It is useless for me to attend a Council where discussions so frequently renewed without effect will, by their resumption, only issue in dividing minds still more widely. The Oriental Church will never depart from the doctrine which it holds from the Apostles, and which was transmitted to it by the Holy Fathers and by the Œcumenical Councils. It is true that a union was brought about at the Council of Florence; but this was a resolution imposed by hard political circumstances, and the whole Eastern Church protested against it. Our conscience is quite tranquil on the subject." The Protosyncellos, besides paraphrasing the expressions of his superior at considerable length, added certain insulting observations of his own, to the effect that the Greek Church cannot recognize either the monarchy which the Pope of Rome assumes over the Universal Church, his infallibility, or his superiority over Œcumenical Councils. When these speeches were concluded, the Patriarch signed to the Protosyncellos, who, already acquainted with the part he had to perform, gave back the Encyclical of his Holiness to the Latin Vicar, who now took his leave with the usual interchange of formal civilities. In future ages, when the acts of the Vatican Council shall have become matter of history, men will judge whether of the two was animated by that charity and zeal for union which is according to the will and the Heart of Jesus, by comparing the Encyclical of Pius IX. with the speech of the Patriarch Gregory, and by contrasting the behaviour of him who sent a deputation to present letters of invitation with that of him who not only refused to receive those letters, but seemed to dread to contaminate himself by so much as touching or looking at them.

It is undeniable that the schismatic Patriarch made upon this occasion but a poor show either of ecclesiastical erudition or theological science, not to speak of that common urbanity which might have been expected of him under any circumstances. As regards the pretended compulsion under which the Greek Bishops acted at Florence, when they agreed to the union, none other existed but such as truth must ever exercise over the will when ignorance and misunderstanding have been removed, and passion and prejudice are not allowed to interfere. The Oriental Bishops professed themselves fully satisfied by the answers which the Latins gave to their objections, and peace was accordingly concluded with every evidence of joy. The Bull of Union, written in Greek and Latin, was signed by all the Bishops of the respective Churches, Mark of Ephesus alone excepted, who obstinately persevered in his schism. A circumstance which occurred twenty days before the subscription of the Bull of Union is worthy of remembrance. John, the Patriarch of Constantinople, suddenly died. At this unexpected news the Fathers hastened to his dwelling, and were told by his servants that in the evening he had sat down to write, but that an attack of trembling seized him while engaged in the act, and he shortly after breathed his last. All were eager to read the Patriarch's last recorded thoughts, which he had doubtless committed to paper because he felt the near approach of death. And such indeed had been the case. These were the words in which he expressed his adherence to Catholic unity:—" John, by the Divine mercy Archbishop of Constantinople, the new Rome, and Œcumenical Patriarch. Finding myself at the close of my life, I desire, through God's goodness, to declare in this letter my decision to my beloved sons, and thereby to fulfil the duty of my office. All those things which the Church of ancient Rome, the Church of our Lord Jesus Christ, the Church Catholic and Apostolic, believes and teaches, I also profess to hold and to believe, and to all of them do I give the fullest assent. I profess that the Most Blessed Father of Fathers, the Sovereign Pontiff and Pope of ancient Rome, is the Vicar of Jesus Christ our Lord, and I admit that there is a purgatory for the souls of the departed. Given at Florence the 8th of June, 1439." "Hard political circumstances" had certainly no share in prompting this solemn and cordial confession of the dying Patriarch of the Eastern Church. All these facts are recorded in history, the Greeks cannot deny them, the Bishops who unanimously gave their adhesion at the Council never attempted to deny them. When, with a few exceptions, they joined Mark of Ephesus and relapsed into schism after their return to their own country, all they attempted to allege was that they had betrayed their faith at Florence, and yielded to the violence of the Latins. Men who can thus proclaim their infidelity and inconstancy, avow with their own lips that they are persons unworthy of credence. Their testimony, by their own confession, is good for nothing.

The Greek Church, which still persists in a state of schism, and refuses to recognize the infallibility of the Roman Pontiff and his superiority over the Universal Church and Œcumenical Councils, ought, in order to be consistent, to separate itself also from that multitude of Fathers and Doctors who lived and died in the East in the early centuries, and illustrated it by their sanctity and the excellency of their doctrine. Suffice it to allude to the 730 Bishops of the Council of Chalcedon, who with one united voice exclaimed, *Petrus per Leonem locutus est.* East and West alike in those days called the Roman Pontiff their Head and Father, and themselves his subjects and his children. The slightest acquaintance with history, or with the records and tradition of their own Church, might be sufficient, therefore, to create uneasiness in consciences not wrapped in the imperturbable slumber which the present schismatic Patriarch of Constantinople mistakes for peace. It is the peace of men such as those to whom Jeremiah alludes, of men who cry Peace, peace, when there is no peace—"*dicentes Pax, pax, et non erat pax.*"

Very different was the welcome which the Pontifical deputation received from the Armenian Patriarch. Two prelates, with veils on their heads, were at the door of the Patriarchal residence to meet the Latin priests, and to escort them at once, instead of allowing them to wait in an antechamber, to the Patriarch's presence. When about to kiss his hand he would not suffer them to do so, but imprinted on the Latin Vicar's forehead the fraternal kiss of peace. He took the Pope's letter in his own hand, asked several questions concerning its contents and form, as well as with reference to the persons who had brought it, appearing well satisfied with all the answers given. He then said, "Formerly the enemies of Christianity were the Gentiles ; now they are bad Christians and unbelievers. It is indeed time for all the differences which separate us to be removed, that we may all, united in the same bond, oppose a barrier to the impiety which is assailing the Church of Jesus Christ." As for the letter, which he willingly received, he replied that it did not rest with him whether or no he should act upon the invitation, but with the Catholicos of Echmiadzin, to whom he exhorted the Fathers to transmit a copy of the Pontifical letters. He then invited the Latin priests to visit his church, to which act of courtesy they considered it their duty to condescend. They were then escorted as before to their carriage door.

Copies of the Encyclical were also sent to all the Bishops and Archbishops of the two Patriarchates. There is good reason for believing that the Greek Patriarch sent express orders to the Bishops subject to him to reject and send back the Letters Apostolic, as he had done. The subjection in which he holds them appears from his own words in the prolix discourse reported or put into his mouth by his Protosyncellos. In it he says, "The Church of my nation is entirely represented by me"; a national Church, let it be remembered, which numbers more than eighty Archbishops, each of whom has some two, three, or even as many as five suffragans. From the state of subserviency to which they are reduced, it might be anticipated that their answers, generally speaking, would be mere echoes of their Patriarch's dictum, the mere repetition of the order transmitted from head-quarters. The Metropolitan of Chalcedon sent the Pope's letters back, with this laconic reply written upon it: *Epistrephete*; that is, "Let it be rejected." The Bishop of Varna declared himself unable to receive them, as they had been rejected by his Patriarch. The Bishop of Salonica also returned the Apostolic letters, but vouchsafed to give five detailed reasons, which are worth mentioning for their very futility. 1. "If I accept the invitation and go to the Council, my Patriarch may reprove and punish me"; a reason suggested by that bad adviser, fear. 2. "An Œcumenical Council at Rome! And why not in any other city? Have not eight General Councils been held in the East?" We might reply by reversing the question, for in whatsoever city the Council was summoned to meet, you might always say, Why not elsewhere? If Councils are always to meet in the same place, you must beg the Sultan to raise again the ruins of Isnik, the ancient Nicæa, now a poor scattered village, chiefly inhabited by Jews. So foolish an objection is hardly worthy a serious reply. But why, indeed, should the Council be called in the East rather than in the West, particularly since its primary object does not regard the East? 3. "The Pope wants to get us to Rome, that he may have us under his hand, and domineer over us." The Holy Father has in his Encyclical expressed his reason for wishing to have the Greek and other schismatical Easterns at Rome. "Come," he says, "to renew by means of this Council that union with the Apostolic See and that concord which your most glorious ancient Fathers and Doctors laboured to maintain by their strenuous and unwearied exertions, and evermore to strengthen by their doctrine and example. At the renewal of this concord the thick darkness which now surrounds you will be dissipated, and the heavenly and salutary gift of Christ, which has dried up within you through the guilt of schism, will flourish anew." With the light and life which reunion with the head will restore to these members, liberty of action, of which they are now deprived, will also be regained. The Pope is therefore seeking the freedom not the enslavement of the Oriental schismatics. 4. "The Pope is a king and bears a sword, which is contrary to the Gospel. Let him lay aside his sword, and dismiss his army, and then we will join him." The Pope's small but valiant army does not so much depend on the Pope's will as upon the very nature of the office he holds as Pastor of the Universal Church. The temporal dominion, and the army, without which that dominion cannot be maintained, are most necessary, especially in these unhappy times, to the free exercise of the pastoral office of the Roman Pontiff. This is not the Holy Father's judgment alone. It is shared by Catholics throughout the world, who are persuaded that this dominion and this army are the indispensable conditions of free communication with their spiritual head; which free communication they have the right to seek, uphold, and defend, in the name of liberty of conscience understood in its rightful sense. To have this army dismissed, then, the Bishop must not address himself only to the Pope, he must cry out to the four winds of heaven and get himself attended to if he can. Moreover, we may add that, supposing even it were a fault in the Pope to maintain an army, that would not remove from the Orientals the guilt of schism.

But let us follow this Bishop's argument upon his own ground, and sift the Scripture text which Protestants have often urged against the temporal power. Is the Pope forbidden by the Gospel to carry a sword? Let us keep to the letter, as the Bishop of Salonica does, or professes to do. We answer, certainly not. On the contrary, we find Christ allowing his Apostles to carry two actual swords; nay, He had said to them, "*Qui non habet, vendat tunicam suam, et emat gladium*—He that hath not, let him sell his coat, and buy a sword." The Apostles replying that they had two, Christ said, "*Satis est*—It is enough."

Now, whatever that *Satis est* may have meant, we know, at any rate, that the Apostles kept the swords, and carried them, and that Christ did not interfere to hinder them from so doing. Peter also, we know, used one of them against Malchus, and although Christ reproved him for having used it, we do not read that He blamed him for having carried it. He did not say, "Cast away thy sword," but bade him put up his sword into its scabbard: *Mitte gladium tuum in vaginam*. There is, then, a sword of sharp steel which Christ actually called Peter's sword: gladium *tuum*; and this sword he bade him sheath. But, it will be urged, He at any rate reproved Peter for using it, for it was then that Jesus uttered that famous menace, that "all who take the sword shall perish with the sword." To this we reply that this threat, as all the doctors of the Church agree, and as natural reason would also suggest, meant that all who rashly, and against the command of God, draw the sword, deserve to perish by the sword. If the meaning were that all who take the sword *ipso facto* violate God's commands, it is clear that the sentence must have a general application, and consequently include also secular princes and rulers. Now, St. Paul says that the temporal ruler bears not the sword in vain; that is, he bears it to use on just and lawful occasions, and no question is raised by any one as to this right of the temporal ruler. Our obvious conclusion, then, must be that Peter, when he wounded Malchus, was rebuked by Christ because, having only asked but not obtained his Lord's permission, he had drawn and used his sword. Besides, at the time when Peter was guilty of this error and received this reproof, the supreme Pontificate had as yet only been promised, not conferred upon the Apostle. The argument, therefore, which has been drawn from our Lord's words is inapplicable to the case in point, and consequently worthless.

5. "The Roman Church has added the *Filioque* to the creed. Let that addition be removed, and the Greeks will join the Latins." We reply, In the form of union subscribed at Florence by all the Bishops, Greek as well as Latin, not only was it solemnly

defined as a dogma of faith that the Holy Ghost proceeds eternally from the Father and from the Son, as from one principle and by one spiration, but it was also defined that, in order to render clear this truth of faith, it was lawfully and with good reason explained in the creed by the addition of the word *Filioque*. The Greeks, on subscribing these articles, declared themselves fully convinced by the arguments of the Latins; all their difficulties being removed, and their minds perfectly satisfied by the evidence laid before them of the falsification, through heretical fraud, of all those passages in ancient Fathers and codices of Councils by which the Greek Church had justified itself in adhering to its error concerning the Procession of the Holy Ghost. The Eastern Bishops, although by relapsing into schism they again adopted their old error, have never brought forward any argument to subvert or even controvert the irrefragable evidence to which they had yielded their own willing assent at the Council of Florence; an assent confirmed by them in the most solemn manner. Let the Bishop of Salonica ponder this fact, and consider with what reason he or his co-religionists can make the demand here set forth.

There have not been wanting, however, some consoling exceptions even amongst the schismatical Bishops of the Greek Patriarchate. The Bishop of Trebizond, a man of venerable age, received the Encyclical of the Holy Father with signs of the deepest respect and even affection. He pressed it to his bosom; he kissed it; he laid it against his forehead; he eagerly inspected it, admiring the form of the Latin characters, although he did not understand their meaning, from time to time exclaiming:—
"O Rome, O Rome! O St. Peter, O St. Peter!" Nevertheless, not a word of promise could be extracted from him that he would attend the Council, though neither did he refuse. May God give him grace to lay to heart those words of Christ: "Not every one that saith to me Lord, Lord, but he that doeth the will of my Father shall enter into the kingdom of heaven." The Bishop of Adrianople sent back the Apostolic letters, but

said, "I wish to reflect upon the subject for myself, and decide for myself." These are very hopeful words; it were much to be wished that there were more amongst his body with the courage to think and act for themselves. Were it so, the Holy Father's Encyclical would have met with a very different reception. These Bishops for the most part, as well as the inferior clergy generally, deplore their separation from the Western Church, and those alone are utterly insensible to so great a calamity who belong to an unfortunately increasing class within the bosom of the so-called *orthodox* communion. These are virtually Protestants and Rationalists, who have mostly studied in the Universities of Germany. We know on good authority that many of the schismatic Greek Bishops, although not bold enough to give an independent reply similar to that by which the Bishop of Adrianople has so honourably distinguished himself, have at least dared openly to blame their Patriarch for his discourteous refusal, as well as those amongst their brethren who have imitated his behaviour. Their flocks join in loudly expressing the same sentiments. "Our Episcopate," they say, "by refusing to attend the Œcumenical Council, would incline us to think that it feels itself unequal to sustain a discussion with the Latin Episcopate."

It is true that now, as ever, there are mischievous and interested persons who are continually filling the ears of the Greeks with the same old declamations against what they call the spiritual tyranny of Rome. But it is inconceivable that they should continue to be deceived by such language. The demeanour of their own Patriarch must, it may be hoped, go far to open their eyes as to the real bondage under which their own Church is groaning. The gravest of questions, the most solemn of propositions, no less than an invitation from the Pope to attend a General Council, which has been ever recognized in the Church of Christ as the sovereign means for maintaining or renewing the bond of union, is laid before him, and he resolves the matter on his own single authority. Does he, then, arrogate to himself that infallibility which he dares to deny to the Roman Pontiff? With what right does he assume a superiority over the consciences and opinions of his eighty Archbishops, with their hundred and seventy suffragans, and of his entire flock, thus disposing of their eternal salvation without so much as consulting his synod? Does history, we may ask the Greeks—and we trust they will lay the question to heart—record the example of any one single Pope who ever acted after the despotic manner of the present schismatical Patriarch of Constantinople?

It pleased God to make use of the Ottoman Government to inflict a severe humiliation on the schismatic Patriarch of Constantinople upon the very day when he contemptuously rejected the overtures of the Sovereign Pontiff; and perhaps God so ordained it in order that this haughty prelate might read therein, if so be, the chastisement of his inordinate pride. Unhappily he has not understood the warning, but, while smarting under the very mortification which ought to have opened his eyes, he has conceived the idea of an act which, we may say, sets the crown on the insolence of his assumption. Is he not the Œcumenical Patriarch? then he, too, will hold a Council, which, from the title he bears, shall also be styled Œcumenical. The contemptible, not to say ridiculous, character of this pretension will be set in a still stronger light when we have briefly indicated the character of the humiliation to which he has been subjected by the Sublime Porte. It had its origin in the question of the Bulgarian Church, of which we shall by-and-by have to speak more fully. From the ninth century, when Pope Nicolas I. brought the Bulgarians into the fold of Christ, down to the present time, the schismatic Greeks have never ceased to employ every means in their power to seduce or force this people out of the unity of the Church. The sacrilegious frauds by the help of which successive Patriarchs have pursued and accomplished this end, have been but the repetition of those adopted by the arch-schismatic Photius in the days of Pope Nicolas. It is in the memory of all how the Bulgarians desired to return to the obedience of Rome, and how our august Pontiff stretched forth his pastoral arms so lovingly to them, and with his own hands consecrated the Archimandrite Sokolsky, whom he sent to them as Vicar Apostolic; and how this unfortunate prelate was carried off from Constantinople by the Russians, and imprisoned in a monastery of Kief, where, if not dead (as reported), he probably still remains. This act, although successful in hindering the reunion of this people to the Catholic Church, failed of its full effect; for the Bulgarians abhor the tyrannical yoke of the Constantinopolitan schismatic, who, to rivet this yoke upon their shoulders, avails himself of Russian help. To shake it off the Bulgarians had recourse to the Sublime Porte, which decided the question in their favour. Accordingly, on the very day (as we have said) that the Patriarch rejected the letters of the Holy Father, he was compelled to receive the missive of the Ottoman Government, which, through Fuad Pasha, its Minister of Foreign Affairs, intimated to the unhappy Gregory the separation which it had decreed between the Greek and Bulgarian Churches. It suggested two modes of effecting this end, leaving to the Patriarch the permission to choose between them, or to suggest any other which might prove acceptable to both the contending Churches. The Patriarch was too worldly wise to close with either of these propositions. The separation would be ruinous to his Patriarchate; for, of the little over five millions which his flock numbers, the Bulgarian Church furnishes above four millions. Their secession would therefore leave this so-called universal head of the Church with a bare million of subjects. To accept either of the proposals of the Turkish Government was to allow himself to be pushed down the precipice; to make one of his own was to cast himself down. In this dilemma he threw himself on the Sultan's clemency, and addressed a petition to him, which, long as it is, may be reduced to two heads: his reasons for considering that the Bulgarians ought not to be granted their desire, and his own proposal to summon an Œcumenical Council of the Orthodox Church, which he regards as the only means of settling the question. The main reason which he gives to induce the Ottoman Government not to yield to the prayers of the Bulgarians is, that their separation would prove the ruin of the Orthodox Church; a matter not likely to appear of any great consequence to a Turk, or to move him to much compassion. The proposal of the Œcumenical Council, on the other hand, is unacceptable. The Turk has at this moment his differences to settle with the Greek Government, and would ill brook the additional inconvenience which the holding of this Council in his capital would entail. Besides, the object of the Council is to rob the Bulgarians of that which they so deeply prize, independence, and for which, having now obtained it from the Sublime Porte, they are already singing *Te Deums*, mingled with prayers for the Sultan's prosperity, and are preparing with every testimony of joy to celebrate the new era of their national Church. Finally, the Greeks themselves are adverse to the Council. They point to the Œcumenical Council summoned to meet at the Vatican, and which the whole Catholic world is preparing to celebrate, and say, " If our Patriarch's pretensions to keep the Bulgarians united to him are just, and his reasons for keeping us all disunited from Rome are good, why does he refuse to go to Rome, there to produce and support those reasons at the Vatican Council ? "

Chapter VIII.

Sentiments of the Catholicos of Echmiadzin.—Origin of his See and of its Title.—Its lapse into Schism, pretensions to dominion, and jealousy of the Armenian Patriarchate.—Apprehensions of the Catholicos with reference to the General Council.—His attempt to establish a Nuncio at Constantinople, and refusal of the Ottoman Government.—Proceedings of the Unionist and anti-Unionist party in the Armenian Church.—Intimidation of the Patriarch and his resignation.—Separation of the Bulgarians from the Greek Church and their contest with the Patriarch. — Consequent disturbances. — Reception of the Papal letter by the Coptic Patriarch of Alexandria.

THE courteous reception which the schismatic Armenian Patriarch of Constantinople gave to the Holy Father's deputation, and his acceptance of the Apostolical Letters, were the cause of much displeasure to Kévork IV., another schismatic Armenian Patriarch, who resides in the monastery of Echmiadzin, about three leagues distant from Erivan. Both that city and the monastery were, up to the year 1827, in the alternate possession of Persians and Turks; but, at that date, they were occupied by the Russians, to whom they still belong. This Patriarch arrogates to himself the lofty title of Catholicos, in virtue of which he makes pretensions akin to those of the so-called Œcumenicos of Constantinople, asserting his right to universal jurisdiction, not only over all the Armenian Christians subject to the Russian Emperor, but over all those who are scattered throughout Persia and Turkey. Accordingly, when he heard of the Pope's invitation to the Orientals, he felt as if his throne was shaken. Like the Greek Patriarch, however, he had no resource but to turn to the infidel in his distress, and to make humble suit to the Sultan. These unhappy schismatics, whose pride and love of dominion make them scorn the obedience of Rome, and reject that yoke which, like the Saviour's, gives rest and true freedom to those who submit to it, have to bow to Mussulman dictation and to "entreat the face" of the enemy of their Lord and of their faith,—of men who esteem and call them "dogs." But it will be well, before speaking of this letter and the reply it elicited, to give a few words to the Armenian Churches and to the Patriarchs of Echmiadzin, which will help to a better understanding of the situation. The monastery was built in the year 650 by Nierse III., an Armenian Patriarch of holy memory. The name Echmiadzin, which signifies "The Descent of the Only Begotten"—Descensus Unigeniti—took its origin from an ancient tradition, according to which, on the spot where now stands the great church of the monastery, dwelt St. Gregory surnamed the Illuminator, who was the first Catholicos, that is, the first Supreme Patriarch of all the Armenians. The tradition goes on to relate how in the same place Jesus Christ appeared to the saint and foretold to him the fortunes of the different Churches he had founded; for he had baptized a very great number of the heathen, many of whom, however, had relapsed into idolatry. There is another tradition regarding St. Gregory the Illuminator, from which the present schismatic Patriarch might do well to take a lesson. Having baptized Tiridatus, king of Armenia, the queen, and the whole court, ordained priests, built churches and monasteries, decreed laws for the maintenance of ecclesiastical discipline, and prescribed the rites to be observed in the sacred functions, he undertook a journey to Rome, and induced the King to accompany him. Pope Silvester I. occupied at that time the Pontifical throne, and the visit of Gregory and Tiridatus, who in their persons might be said to represent all Christian Armenia, was a splendid homage paid to the rights and prerogatives of the Holy See. Pope Silvester approved all that Gregory had done, and confirmed to him the title of Catholicos, with the permission of transmitting it to his successors. And to this very day in the Church of Echmiadzin, upon certain solemn occasions, an ancient hymn is sung, in which God is entreated to preserve the Patriarch in these words: " Preserve, O Lord, the son of Thy servant Gregory, who was exalted by the See of Rome, where the foundation-stone of the Church is laid." But the present son of Gregory has forgotten "the rock whence he was hewn," or, rather, he disowns and exalts himself against it, with these very words of his own ritual ringing in his ears.

The Armenian schism began when the heresy of Eutyches arose. Many remained united to the Catholic Church, others separated themselves from the obedience of Leo I., and refused to recognize the Council of Chalcedon. The Armenians as a nation have never been very obstinate in their schism, and have more than once been on the point of renouncing it, or have even temporarily been reconciled to Rome; the most memorable of these reunions being that effected at the Council of Florence. The obstacle has not, in fact, come from the people themselves, but from their Patriarchs, amongst whom those of Echmiadzin have been foremost in making the most strenuous exertions to perpetuate a state of separation which flattered their love of dominion. However, by God's just judgment, they have reaped bitter fruits from their revolt against the Chair of Peter, and have had Bishops amongst their own suffragans who refused obedience to their Patriarch, and even disputed with him his title of Catholicos. After the conquest of Constantinople by the Turks in 1453, a more powerful rival sprang up, for Mahomet II., who had invited many Armenian families to settle in Constantinople, set John, the schismatic Bishop of Bursa, the ancient Bithynian capital, as Patriarch over them. Such was the origin of the Armenian Patriarchs of Constantinople, always regarded with a jealous eye by the Catholicos of Echmiadzin, who has dreaded that they might avail themselves of the favour of the Ottoman Court to entrench on his own assumed universal jurisdiction.

It may be readily imagined, then, what a storm was raised in the bosom of Kévork IV. when he heard of the gracious reception of the Sovereign Pontiff's Letters by his brother Patriarch. He seemed therein to read the impending fall of his own See. He had already taken measures to provide against the danger which he apprehended from the Œcumenical Council, even before the schismatical Bishops had been invited, and when as yet rumour only asserted that they were about to be so. For on the ninth of July he had despatched Serkis Cialalian, one of his Bishops, to the shores of the Bosphorus with a letter which he was commissioned to remit to Safvet Pasha, for his superior, Fuad Pasha. The purport of it was to commend to the good offices of the Sultan's Government, and obtain the recognition of this individual as his legate for Turkey, where dwell the greater part of those Armenians who, to use the Patriarch's expressions, "enjoy the gentle protection of the empire." He took care to set forth his own claim to authority as Supreme Patriarch over the whole nation, and referred to precedents of a similar conduct on the part of some of his predecessors, who from time to time had sent legates to divers cities in Europe as well as Asia, to inform themselves of the moral needs of the Armenians residing in them, as well as to rectify abuses occasioned by the indigenous Bishops, Archimandrites, and other prelates. These legates, he said, had always obtained the Sultan's favour, thanks to the prayers of the Catholicos, and had received aid from the public authorities in all their affairs. But notwithstanding these precedents, and the confidence expressed, if not felt, by the petitioner in the "generous protection of the glorious kingdom of Turkey," the present Sultan exhibited no disposition to imitate the alleged favour of his predecessors, nor did Serkis Cialalian meet with the desired countenance; for the Catholicos had hoped that he would be at once recognized in his office of legate, and would be able to establish himself openly at Constantinople with that title. No reply, however, proceeded from the foreign office, and, accordingly, when the Pope's deputation reached Constantinople, and the delegate of the Catholicos learnt how it had been received by the Armenian Patriarch, he pressed Safvet Pasha on the subject of his mission once more, who rid himself of further importunity by giving him a final answer in the form of a letter to his Patriarch Kévork. In it, after politely thanking him for the letter of recommendation he had addressed to Fuad Pasha for Mgr. Serkis Cialalian, and after prefacing the unwelcome substance of his reply with other courteous words, he reminded him of the fulness of liberty accorded to all religions by the Turkish Government; a fact with which no one could be better acquainted than his holiness, as he had himself for several years occupied the Armenian Patriarchal See, and had certainly at that time yielded to none in the desire to maintain his dignity and prerogatives, in which the Imperial Government had entirely coincided. This might suffice to show his holiness how the presence of a legate from the Catholicos of Echmiadzin was in no way reconcileable with the functions of the Patriarch of Constantinople, to whose office it appertains to watch over the spiritual interests of the Turkish Armenians. It would besides be a novelty, no precedent having existed of a stationary legate of the kind in Constantinople. Delegates bearing the holy oil*

---

* Amongst other privileges which the Patriarchs of Echmiadzin claim to have inherited from S. Gregory the Illuminator, is that of consecrating the holy chrism for all the Armenian Churches.

had come from time to time, yet were never suffered to tarry, but were sent on their road to Russia as soon as their commission was accomplished. Even this short stay had proved inconvenient, and the communities desiring the oil had begged that it might in future be simply sent to them with the blessing of the successor of St. Gregory the Illuminator. " Faithful to its traditions "—one might almost imagine here an indirect reproach aimed at St. Gregory's faithless successor—the Sublime Porte declared that it must decline recognizing any official mission in the person of Mgr. Cialalian, since the ministry of the Armenian Church was exclusively in the hands of the Patriarch of Constantinople ; and what other office did the Catholicos's letter design for its bearer save the sacred mission with which that Patriarch was already invested ? May the Patriarch Kévork derive more benefit from the humiliation he has received at the hands of the Turk than the Greek Patriarch has hitherto reaped from the repulse he met with in the same quarter. The envoy of the Catholicos remained, however, in the Ottoman capital, in order, no doubt, to make what profit he could out of circumstances.

Many of the Armenian schismatic Bishops of the Constantinopolitan Patriarchate imitated the example of their head in receiving the Pope's Letters with marks of courtesy and even good-will. In fact, there exists among them a strong party desirous of reconciliation with Rome. This party has gained fresh life, and developed into systematic action since the announcement of the coming Council and the reception of the Pope's Letters. The "Unionists"—the name given to these Bishops—had no sooner received these letters of invitation than they began to hold secret consultations upon the means to be adopted for the furtherance of their end. Notwithstanding the caution with which they acted, their proceedings could not escape the watchful eye of their colleagues, and a strong opposition party was immediately organized to defeat their endeavours. From all that appears, the notions of the Armenian Unionists with respect to the contemplated terms of reunion with

Rome would require some rectification. There is one point upon which they feel very strongly, and that is the sound orthodoxy of their body. Dogmatic errors, they say, have been attributed to them by ignorant or malicious persons; their Church neither holds nor ever did hold these errors. Accordingly, as a preliminary step, they would have the Holy See declare that the Armenian Church is not heretical. Another condition upon which they also insist is the maintenance of the ecclesiastical autonomy of their Church. The bond of union ought, according to them, to consist only in the commemoration of the Roman Pontiff by the Bishops in the divine office, and in the collation of their Patriarch by reception of the pallium from Rome. In matters of faith, however, they would be willing to recognize the infallibility of the See of Rome, and would even be disposed to allow a right of appeal thereto. There is evidently too much of making conditions and debating terms of agreement between, as it were, independent contracting parties to render this programme quite satisfactory. They have been developed to a certain extent in a long article published in an Armenian journal of Constantinople, written by Mgr. Nerses, one of the most eminent of the Armenian schismatic Bishops for science and eloquence. While demonstrating that the Armenian Church ought to seek religious alliance with Rome, and accord it the pre-eminence, he maintains that this ought only to be upon the condition of preserving their own autonomy and independence intact. We may confidently look to the acts of the General Council itself for producing a decided effect in enlightening the minds and removing the prejudices of all men of good-will and sincerity of purpose; amongst whom we would willingly number these "Unionists." A meeting of them took place, in December, at the residence of the Patriarch of Constantinople, to discuss the Holy Father's invitation to the Vatican Council. The result of the deliberation was favourable, as was manifested by their having immediately forwarded the Apostolic Letters to the other Patriarch, the Catholicos of Echmiadzin, along with the minutes of their consultation. Preparations also were set on foot for holding a synod, in which the prelates might come to an agreement with reference to the proposals to be made to the Vatican Council on the part of the Armenians. Thirty-six priests, divided into two Commissions, have been chosen to make the preparatory studies, and one of the chief points which they strive to place in the clearest light is the falseness of that accusation which the opposition party brings against the See of Rome, of an intention to Latinize either the Armenian or any other Oriental Church. The Armenian Catholics of Constantinople are not idle spectators of this hopeful movement, but actively co-operate by every means at their disposal.

The desire for reunion is far from being limited to the Episcopate. A large body of the laity, and amongst them men of great worth and eminence, as well as some holding official rank, earnestly desire to see their nation restored to the bosom of the Catholic Church. The Armenian Patriarch of Cilicia having caused the Pope's Encyclical to be translated into Armenian, and exerted himself by means of the press to disperse copies of it throughout the whole Ottoman Empire, much may be hoped for in the way of promotion of the movement by the general perusal of a document breathing in every word the spirit of evangelical charity. It is a curious fact that Mgr. Serkis Cialalian, who, as we observed, lingered on in Constantinople after he had been informed, in November, by the Turkish Ministers that his assumption of the position of Nuncio would be viewed as intolerable, in the month of January exhibited symptoms of favouring the party and objects of the Unionists, and even of desiring to join their number. Meanwhile the opposition, who enjoy of course the strong support of Russia, were taking active measures, and seven Bishops of that party loudly remonstrated with their Patriarch for his favourable reception of the Encyclical. So violent was their demeanour that they succeeded so far in intimidating the Patriarch as to lead him to insert a species of official apology for his conduct in the public journals, in which he endeavoured to reduce the import of his reception of the Pope's Letters to a mere act of courtesy and urbanity. As for the acceptance or non-acceptance of the invitation to the Vatican Council, he left the decision to the Patriarch of Echmiadzin; the interpretations put upon his conduct and published in foreign papers were therefore false and groundless. Courage and fortitude to face persecution are hardly to be expected from those who are themselves irresolute, and have as yet no firm grasp of a principle. From the behaviour of Mgr. Boghoz, the Armenian Patriarch, at his reception of the Supreme Pontiff's Letters, favourable sentiments indeed might be inferred; but no immediate decisive step could have been anticipated on his part. Having now become, along with the Unionists, the object of the most violent attacks in the press of Constantinople, directed against them by the anti-Unionist, or Philo-russ party, as it is called, his heart failed him, and he would willingly, if possible, have retreated into a safer position, sheltering his responsibility under that of the Patriarch of Echmiadzin. Catholicism was of course also fiercely assailed in these journals, and the engine which Russia has always so effectively used to retain the Orientals in schism was most energetically employed in order to turn away the Armenian nation from a desire of re-union with the Catholic Church, viz., the assertion that Rome seeks to Latinize their Church and destroy its autonomy. Appeal was thus made to a national sentiment which is always strong, and at the same time to one of the strongest, if not *the* strongest, of the passions—fear. It is, at any rate, that by which the popular mind can most readily be excited.

The schismatic spirit has always been prone to exhibit itself in acts of violence, and it has not on this occasion belied its character. The unhappy Patriarch who had ventured to manifest the leanings of his heart towards the Catholic Apostolic and Roman Church had now to dread even personal violence from his own flock. Excited by the anti-Unionist Bishops, chiefly through the press, the Armenian populace began with the opening year to break out into open tumults, noisily interrupting the divine office in many of the churches, and specially in that where the

Patriarch was officiating, at the moment when, according to custom, a momento of him is made, crying out that the Patriarch was unworthy of being commemorated. The memento had accordingly to be omitted. The Sultan's Government, which, it must be observed, has throughout these transactions given its support to Catholic interests, endeavoured to repress the persecution directed against the Armenian Patriarch, a persecution originating manifestly with the Russo-Armenian party, and put forth a manifesto condemning the disturbances, and threatening punishment in case of their renewal. The Minister of Police also summoned to his presence the principal disturbers of the peace, and reprimanded them severely. More than this, the Ottoman Government has in every way endeavoured to second the efforts of Catholics, and in particular it has sought to check the great source of mischief, the press, by giving a kind of semi-official *avertissement* to one of the most prominent organs of the Philo-russ party. Good hopes were also entertained that it would lend its support to a Catholic journal, if it should be found possible to establish one. That the Turkish Government should have every reason to discountenance the promoters of Russian interests can be readily understood; nevertheless, we cannot but think that it has also the sagacity to discern that Catholicism is the best safeguard of political order, and the surest guarantee of public peace. Tumults and outrages against the Patriarch still, however, continued to occur, and increased in violence on the vigil and on the feast of the Epiphany, when the services were interrupted by still louder clamours and in a greater number of churches. Cries for the Patriarch's deposition now mingled with those which were raised to prohibit his commemoration; and so alarming was the confusion in the church where that Prelate officiated, that he fainted away from the distress it occasioned him. Alarmed and perplexed, and feeling himself quite unequal to cope with the appalling difficulties of his position, his great desire was now to withdraw from the conflict. Thrice he offered his resignation of office to the Government, which finally accepted it, and the Armenian Bishop of Scutari was appointed to fill his place until another Patriarch should be elected.

The tumults caused by the Russo-Armenian party in Constantinople were not the sole disturbances which occurred in that city at the commencement of the present year. Others took place originating in the dispute between the schismatic Greek Patriarch and his rebellious Bulgarian subjects. The present state of the Bulgarians is calculated to raise very painful reflections in the minds of Catholics. So lately reconciled to the Church, then by Russian artifice deprived of their spiritual head, and again lapsing into their schism, they are now in all the first exultation of their deliverance from the yoke of the Greek Patriarch of Constantinople, without showing the slightest disposition to turn their eyes once more towards Rome, or manifesting the faintest aspiration after Catholic unity. This behaviour leads necessarily to the belief that it was chiefly, if not wholly, fear of Russia and detestation of their bondage under the Greek schismatic Church, which made them hold out their arms to their true mother. Be this as it may, their attitude is very unsatisfactory, and no good can be anticipated from the present movement. Schism with them is simply running the usual course which it entails; beginning with division, it issues in division and subdivision.

The Sublime Porte having decreed the separation which the Bulgarians so ardently desired, they began forthwith, without waiting even for its official announcement, to take possession of the churches and drive out the Greek priests. The Patriarch of Constantinople, however, did not give in, and continued to protest that the matter was strictly religious, and that the Ottoman Government was not competent to give judgment on a question which it appertained to a Council to decide—an Œcumenical Council, since he, the Œcumenical Patriarch, was to summon it. But the Bulgarians have disregarded all his arguments, and contented themselves as their sole reply with pointing to a precedent which occurred about a century ago, in order to prove that the good pleasure of the Sultan was quite sufficient to effect a separation without the intervention of a Council, and that for the very cogent reason that it had been considered sufficient to sanction a union. It seems that in 1767 the two Bulgarian Patriarchs of Ocridas and Ipek, desiring to submit their sees to Samuel, the schismatic Greek Patriarch of Constantinople, had recourse to the Sultan Mustapha, who promulgated a law decreeing the desired union and submission. The Patriarch Samuel made no difficulty as to the mode in which the transaction was brought about. He considered all to be done holily and excellently well, as appears from an authentic document of his, still to be found amongst the archives of his Patriarchate. The Bulgarians have dragged it to light, and given it full publicity. As an *argumentum ad hominem* it is certainly a powerful weapon. It begins by a most solemn profession of faith in the right of the State to do the very sort of thing which the present schismatic occupant of the Constantinopolitan See declares that the Turkish Government does not possess. But then it must be remembered that Mustapha had ruled the case in Samuel's favour, whereas Abdul Azis has given judgment against Gregory. This makes all the difference. "To those who legally and truly reign it is given to make laws by means of *hatti-cherifs*, or decrees. Thus acts the most powerful, and eternally august, our victorious master and king, the Sultan; may he reign for ever!" Such is the exordium of a document worth studying by those who would wish to know what is the essentially Erastian spirit of the schismatic Greek Church. The end is in keeping with the commencement. God is solemnly thanked for having inspired their powerful sovereign to pass such a decree, which truly merits the appellation of a royal law, seeing that it is favourable to the interests of the Churches in question, and emanates from him who is their legitimate sovereign, and bears the sceptre by right of inheritance. The Bulgarians take their stand on this precedent. "What," they ask, "was the motive alleged for abolishing the autonomy of those two Bulgarian sees? The bad government of their Archbishops. And what was the authority which decreed its abolition? According to the Patriarch

G

Samuel, it was the authority, not of a Council, but of the Sultan Mustapha. Now, we set the Patriarch Samuel against the Patriarch Gregory. We have demanded the restoration of our old autonomy on account of the execrable government of the Greek Pastors. Sultan Abdul Azis has granted us the separation we sought, and he is no less legitimate and hereditary a sovereign than in his day was Mustapha. The Patriarch Samuel did not ask for a Council, why then should the Patriarch Gregory?" This cogent reasoning has all appeared in the Constantinopolitan journals, and the *Courier d'Orient* in particular has published an address of four Bulgarian Bishops to the Patriarch of Constantinople, laying bare the details of the struggle of which Bulgaria has been the theatre for eight years past through its repugnance to its Greek rulers. Hence dioceses without bishops, flocks without pastors, churches deserted, sacraments neglected, and ecclesiastical discipline fallen into utter ruin. No remedy, they say, remained but separation, and upon this separation they had conscientiously resolved. What they were unable to obtain as a boon from the Patriarch, the State has now accorded, and the Patriarch must by this time be aware that he spoke to the winds when he proposed to summon an *Œcumenical* Council of the whole Orthodox Church to decide the Bulgarian question, or, rather, to hinder the Bulgarian Church from throwing off his authority. The separation not only has been already effected on the Bulgarian territory, but is taking place in whatever part of the Turkish empire Christians of that nation are to be found. This has led to no slight disturbances in Constantinople. Bulgarian priests began in January last going round to the houses of their co-religionists for the purpose of bestowing certain customary benedictions. Hitherto these ceremonies have been performed by Greek priests. Hence a conflict; the Patriarch Gregory having taken measures to support his own clergy in the exercise of their functions, and to maintain what he calls his authority against these rebel Bulgarian priests.

In Egypt schismatics belonging to all the different rites are to be met with, but the only two rites which have Bishops of their own are the Greeks and the Copts. The Copts have a Patriarch who takes his title from Alexandria, where he resides; he has fourteen Bishops under him, whereof nine are in Upper Egypt, one in Soudan, one in Abyssinia, one in Cairo, and two in Lower Egypt. To Mgr. Luigi Ciurcia, Archbishop of Trenopolis *in partibus*, Vicar Apostolic for the Latins in Egypt, and Apostolic Delegate for the Oriental Catholics of Egypt and Arabia, was committed the office of delivering the Pope's Encyclical to the Coptic schismatics. His first thought was to have a good and faithful translation made into Arabic, to accompany the Latin text. He then requested Mgr. Abrano Bsciai, Bishop of Clariobolus *in partibus* and Apostolic Vicar of the Catholic Copts of Egypt, to transmit his Holiness's Letters to the nine Bishops of Upper Egypt, and availed himself of the help of the missionaries in Lower Egypt to perform a like office to the Coptic Bishops in those parts. He reserved to himself the charge of presenting the Encylical to Mgr. Demetrius, the Coptic schismatic Patriarch of Alexandria. The manner in which that prelate received it is worthy of the highest praise. He displayed the greatest satisfaction in perusing the Arabic translation, and entered into long and friendly discussion with the Latin Delegate, accompanying him to the very foot of his palace stairs with demonstrations of courtesy of a truly affectionate character. The discussion chiefly turned upon some historical points connected with the early Œcumenical Councils celebrated in the East, and upon those erroneous dogmas in which the Coptic schismatics have followed the Greeks. The Patriarch seemed to be interested by Mgr. Ciurcia's appropriate replies, and to desire to renew the discussion at more leisure on some future occasion. The Coptic schismatic Bishops have a great horror of the Protestants, who endeavour to pervert their flocks, regarding them as the plague of Christendom, especially on account of the false maxims by which they labour to extinguish devotion to the Blessed Virgin in the hearts of Christians. This was one of the subjects upon which the conversation frequently turned at the delivering of the Encyclical to the

Bishops. They listened with pleasure and attention to the account given them of the constant combat which the Catholic Church has never ceased to wage against Protestantism, and expressed their joy at hearing that many Protestants, among whom were men remarkable for learning and virtue, had abjured the errors of their sect and submitted to the obedience of the Roman Pontiff.

CHAPTER IX.

BENEFITS WHICH MAY BE ANTICIPATED FROM THE COUNCIL IN RESPECT TO THE SCHISMATIC BODIES.—BLINDNESS OF CATHOLIC RULERS TO THEIR TRUE INTERESTS.—BEHAVIOUR OF THE FRENCH GOVERNMENT.—ITS RESERVATIONS IN REGARD TO THE APPROACHING COUNCIL.—DISPOSITIONS OF THE FRENCH EPISCOPATE.—DESUETUDE OF CANON LAW IN FRANCE.—ITS CAUSES AND INCONVENIENCES.—THE SENTIMENTS OF LIBERAL CATHOLICS AND OF CATHOLICS PURE AND SIMPLE.—FEELING AND ATTITUDE OF THE NON-CATHOLIC BODY.—ASPIRATIONS AND EXPECTATIONS OF CATHOLICS RESPECTING DOGMATIC DECISIONS.

NOTWITHSTANDING the existence of some discouraging circumstances, and the evil activity of those who are interested in maintaining the separation, the fairest hopes, we conceive, may be cherished of the approaching restoration of the schismatic nations of the East to Catholic unity. These unhappy nations must be led to perceive that, along with the loss of union with Rome, they lost all which formerly rendered them illustrious. Where are the successors of the Chrysostoms, the Gregorys, the Cyrils, the Basils, the Athanasiuses? The sun of science which of old irradiated those Eastern lands, and thence illuminated the West itself, is gone down. The profoundest ignorance reigns in those regions, and if some religious practices are still kept up amongst the people, it is more through the tenacity with which they have clung to old habits, than owing to any instruction which they have received from their pastors. Knowledge of Scripture, theological science, eloquence, and all that mental and literary culture which adorn the Catholic clergy, are perished from amongst them. The priest's lips no longer keep knowledge. Neither have they less degenerated in virtue. Where are their saints and great servants of God, their martyrs, their apostles of the faith? Who has ever heard of a schismatic nation manifesting that zeal for the conversion of the heathen which is the peculiar note of the true Church? If they reflect and compare they cannot but see that as regards science they are sunk in the grossest darkness, and as regards virtue they are fallen into a state of utter languor, while as respects that vitality which is the essential property of the Church of Jesus Christ they are oppressed with a mortal lethargy. And now when that Church stretches forth her hand to them, may we not hope that they will accept the invitation, recognize the truth, and surrender themselves to it? In the present state of the world these schismatic peoples cannot much longer remain isolated, but will be drawn into constant intercourse with the Western nations: and what will be the consequence? One or other of these alternatives will be their lot; they will either be built firmly up on the immoveable rock of Peter, and will then be able to guard intact the principles of the Christian religion, and become truly civilized; or they will remain as they now are, resting on sand, and must go to ruin, borne away by the hurricane of impiety. They will not pass over to Protestantism, which, as a religion, has evidently lived out its day; but will be submerged at once in that gulf of Indifferentism, Naturalism, Deism, Atheism, to which Protestantism naturally leads. We must look to the time as near at hand when two classes of men alone will exist in the world, Catholics and Atheists. This is the final goal to which things are tending, as has long been foreseen, both by ungodly men who have been preparing the way, and by good men who have been watchful observers of the current of events. The future prospects of these nations, then, for good in this world, as in the next, hang upon their reunion with Rome; and it is to be hoped that their rulers, secular as well as ecclesiastical, will be enlightened to perceive this truth. Specially may we hope that their Bishops, were it but from that natural instinct which prompts every one to wish to raise himself out of a state of degradation and contempt, may see wherein their true interests lie, and listen to the benignant invitation which has been so paternally addressed to them. Rome, which has everything to bestow, desires not to take anything from them, and never has desired to do so, as they might easily convince themselves. Language, liturgy, ceremonies, rites, privileges of which they are so proud and so tenacious,—of not one of these things does the Catholic Church purpose or wish to rob them. If they will but consent to renew the bond of unity with their head, and give in their adhesion to those few articles which their Fathers subscribed at Florence, the Church will at once open her arms wide to receive them, and press them as dear children to her heart.

If it is difficult to imagine that the rulers, whether spiritual or temporal, of the schismatic nations, can fail to see that safety and prosperity alike are only to be sought in Catholic unity, it is still harder to imagine how Catholic rulers should be so blind to the dictates of mere human prudence as, surrounded as they are by their deadly foes, to be suspicious and fearful of the Church's influence and of the authority of the Vicar of Christ, seeing that there they would find their surest—may we not say, their sole ?—protection at the present crisis. No monarch can find his account in having a people whom it is impossible to govern, yet where is the sanction of the principles of order, authority, and subordination to be found save in the teaching of the Church and in obedience to her voice ? Those principles which held society together are perishing from the minds of men ; communism, socialism, anarchy, barbarism, threaten it from the seething depths below. Force alone keeps it from dissolution, the iron band of force.

At this juncture the Father of Christendom summons a General Council, where those principles which are the world's salvation, and on which the well-being and very existence of civil society and respect to lawful authority depend, will be re-asserted and proclaimed. Sovereigns, it might reasonably be expected, would hail with gladness this auspicious event, if it were only from the instinct of self-preservation ; but we have had too lamentable an experience of the blindness of governments as to their best interests for our hopes to rise above an abstention from interference on their part. We shall be content if they do not try to thwart what, by every means at their disposal, they ought to favour and promote.

The behaviour of the French Government towards the future Council deserves the first consideration, inasmuch as in the present condition of European affairs it is the State whose conduct, more than that of any other, can most directly affect its material security. And of this it is quite aware. It observed, however, perfect silence on the subject, and caused its official organs to practise the same reserve, until the 10th of July, 1868, when the Minister of Justice and of Worship made some important declarations before the Legislative Body. From the speech of M. Baroche it appeared that the Government did not purpose to place any obstacle in the way of the meeting of the Council; that as yet it was uncertain as respected sending ambassadors, but that it was considering the question and collecting historical precedents; that it was disposed to interpret the omission of any special invitation to the sovereign in a favourable sense; and that it rejected the idea of separation of the Church from the State. These four so far favourable dispositions had their counterpart in several others of by no means so pleasant a character. The Minister declared that the Government repudiated the doctrine of the Syllabus, "which contains," he said, "certain propositions at variance with the principles upon which the constitution of the Empire is based." He also asserted that "the infallibility of the Pope alone is not admitted by an immense majority of the French clergy and Episcopate," and said that, in its relations with the Church, the Government took the Concordat for its basis, and the Organic Articles, "which," he added, "I place in the same category." He reserved to the Government full liberty of action in an affair which, he observed, "would be replete with difficulties and perhaps, which might God avert, perils." In conclusion, he said :—
' We are armed, as the French Government has heretofore been, both now and under the *ancien régime*, with the Concordat. It is clear that after the Council

a great question will come before the Government. Are the decisions of the Council to be admitted in whole or in part? This is a question still more strictly reserved than others." The spirit manifested by the Imperial Government in M. Baroche's speech was also subsequently exhibited in the eagerness with which the official journals patronized Monseigneur Maret, a prelate considered to be the champion of Gallican ideas.

The French Government's fears may then be summed up under three heads. It is afraid—1. That the future Council will proclaim the doctrine of the Syllabus. 2. That it will declare the dogmatic infallibility of the Sovereign Pontiff. 3. That it will annul the Organic Articles. In this triple dread the Government and the Opposition are entirely agreed. The Government is politically opposed to the Syllabus on the ground that it is irreconcileable with the principles of the Imperial constitution. It is evident that the interpretation put by it upon the Syllabus is both arbitrary and exaggerated, and that it is founded, to a considerable extent, upon a misunderstanding of its import. Be this, however, as it may, and whatever be the discrepancy between the principles laid down by the Holy Father in the Syllabus and those which the Imperial Government is pleased to adopt and patronize, its refusal to allow it to be promulgated from the pulpit has not prevented that document from becoming known to all French Catholics, and from being received by them with no less respect than a rule of faith. So that this precaution has had no other result than to mark a divergence between the Holy See and the French Government, a circumstance by no means to the advantage of the latter, since it is manifest that it ought to be one of the most cherished objects of the Emperor to conciliate the sympathy of Catholics for his dynasty, which sympathy, except in the case of a few party men, would be entirely secured to him if he had only shown himself sincerely devoted to the Holy See and to the Church. He has not had the prudence so to act. The dogmatic infallibility of the Pope, as well as the Syllabus, is a sort of scarecrow in his eyes, and he accordingly takes his stand on the declaration of 1682, and arms himself with the Organic Articles against any ulterior decisions of the Council.

He has certainly got an arsenal of anti-Papal weapons in these same Organic Articles, which, we need scarcely observe, have always been repudiated by the Holy See. The very 1st of them forbids the publication or execution in France of any bull, brief, rescript, decree, mandate, from the Court of Rome without the previous authorization of the French Government; and the 3rd makes special mention of the decrees of foreign synods, General Councils included, as forbidden to be published in France until the Government has examined their form, and ascertained their conformity to the laws, rights, and franchises of the State. Then there is the 10th, abolishing every privilege whatsoever which confers exemption from Episcopal jurisdiction or attributes jurisdiction to any other authority. The next suppresses all ecclesiastical institutions except cathedral chapters and seminaries. Another article prescribes as of obligation the teaching of the doctrine of the Declaration of 1682—a glaring inconsistency by the way, since the Declaration of 1682 at any rate recognizes the supremacy without appeal of a truly Œcumenical Council. Another prohibits priests from giving the nuptial benediction to such persons as cannot prove in due form that they have already contracted a civil marriage before the magistrate. In this repertory Napoleon III. cannot fail of finding a text and a precedent to support him in any opposition he may think good to offer to the decrees of the Council. He must, however, be well aware that, in spite of the official character of the Organic Articles, as a law of the State, and of the Declaration of 1682, as embodying its governing code of theology, an overwhelming majority of the French clergy does not believe one word of the statements of the famous Declaration; and as for the Organic Articles the greater part of their provisions remains a dead letter. Obstinately, therefore, to persevere in pretending to impose them, is but to nourish a permanent state of mistrust and contention between the State and the Church, and to constitute them in an abiding attitude of opposition to each other. To add to the folly of such a policy, there is the flagrant contradiction of its adoption in the name of a constitution which proclaims universal liberty of conscience. The Imperial Government ought to know that all the dislike and even resistance it may offer to the decrees of the coming Œcumenical Council will never hinder its Catholic subjects from accepting them. Instead, then, of assuming a suspicious and antagonistic attitude, calculated vitally to damage his interests with those whose attachment it would be most essential to secure, how is it that the French Emperor does not perceive that, if he had at once proclaimed himself the protector of the future Council, he would have placed himself in a position at once more glorious and more advantageous ? He has not the greatness of mind to rise to the part of a Constantine, a Theodosius, or a Charlemagne.

The behaviour of the Government had, no doubt, a certain effect in keeping the French Bishops comparatively silent, for, with the exception of Mgr. Dupanloup's well-known letter, and a few Episcopal "mandements," nothing calling for any special notice has emanated from that venerable body on the subject of the General Council. Every one, however, is well aware that the French Episcopate holds, with reference to the Syllabus and Papal infallibility, the same doctrine as all other Catholic Bishops. As respects discipline, the Church of France does not resemble that of other Catholic countries, and perhaps there is none other which looks to profit more largely by the decisions of the coming Council. The state of the French clergy ever since the Concordat with Napoleon I., in 1802, has been altogether exceptional, not only in their relations with a government which has taken the Organic Articles as its rule, but as respects internal discipline. Canon law is practically non-existent in France. Some canonists, indeed, there are,—perhaps a dozen, possibly twenty,—but, speaking generally, the science as well as the practice has disappeared. This is a state of things which it is well to face, without exaggerating its inconveniences, but at the same time without concealing them. The abolition of all benefices, the confiscation of Ecclesiastical property, the assignment in compensation of a salary paid by the State to the clergy — such have been the chief causes of the oblivion into which the study of canon law has fallen in France. The study declined from the moment that the law itself ceased to be practically applicable. On the other hand, the administration of Episcopal authority over the clergy is almost exclusively effected by means of decisions *ex informata conscientia*. The numerous appeals to Rome of late years bear witness to this fact; and on many of these occasions the proper canonical forms had been omitted simply from ignorance of them. That in the present state of France there should be a disposition to avoid—as, for instance, in the case of any scandal, or of refractory conduct on·the part of any member of the clergy—a legal judgment involving a certain amount of publicity, however restricted, we can easily understand. The affair would at once be taken up by all the irreligious journals, to be blazoned abroad and misrepresented, as a matter of course, in order to satisfy the greedy curiosity of a million of readers. The decision *ex informata conscientia* here presents itself as a resource possessing obvious advantages. It is certain, however, that it excites mistrust amongst the inferior clergy, and opens the door to multiplied recriminations. The same may be said of the removeability of those priests who in France are called *Desservants* or *Succursalistes*, and who can be transferred from one place to another *ad nutum Episcopi*. Complaints from this cause are no less frequent. What may be anticipated with respect to the decision of the Council regarding the canon law? Will it reinforce the disciplinary decrees of the Council of Trent? or will it introduce, and, if so, to what extent, modifications adapted to present circumstances? These questions, we believe, form a very special subject of the consideration and study of the French Bishops, who, it must be observed, as well as the clergy of the second order, deeply lament the neglect into which the study of canon law has fallen in France.

Every one knows that in France Catholics are unfortunately split into two parties: the one party consists of those who are simply and purely Catholics; the other party of those who are called "liberal Catholics." Among the rural population this distinction does not exist. Catholic liberals, as a matter of course, are the object of Government predilections, from which, however, we must not conclude that the majority of the Catholic liberals are favourable to the Government. Quite the reverse is notoriously the case. Nevertheless, on the subject of the General Council, they have certain sympathies in common. For these liberal Catholics, who are always desirous to reconcile as best they may their political creed, embodied in the principles of '89, with the Church's doctrine, have their fears and misgivings with respect to the Syllabus, which they apprehend may be proclaimed by the Vatican Council; fears which are, however, tempered by the hope that it may modify or interpret certain of its propositions in a sense more favourable to their ideas. The Catholics, pure and simple, who constitute the great majority of the faithful, join heartily with their brethren throughout the world in looking forward with confident hope to the meeting of the Council, and submit beforehand with both mind and heart to its infallible decisions. They are not like the former class, men who seem more anxious that the Church should agree with them, than to place themselves in agreement with the Church, and who are, therefore, eagerly solicitous as to whether or not her decisions may run counter to certain personal opinions of their own, to which they cling as to a second religion. Those Catholics who, as Catholics, set up no party banner, having no other desire but to learn with docility from the Church, with whose teaching their minds are in perfect harmony, are unanimous in hailing as most opportune the convening of a General Council at a time when it has become so needful to recall and reassert those immutable truths upon which society rests, and to draw closer the ties of unity in the flock of Jesus Christ. They admire the courage with which this great assembly of the Church has been summoned to meet amidst the storms of revolution which are raging around, and daily pour forth their supplications before the Most High that He will stretch forth His arm to protect her from all the perils which surround and menace her.

The non-Catholic portion of the French nation, in which we include rationalists and unbelievers, with those who, like the Protestants, profess some form of Christianity, are as a body hostile to the future Council. But they do not all adopt the same language with respect to it. Serious-minded men, to whatever sect or school of thought they belong, speak with gravity and decorum of an event which they cannot but regard as truly extraordinary. The recent words of an illustrious Protestant on the subject, M. Guizot, are known to all; and the recollection of the applause with which M. Emile Olivier's words were greeted in the Chamber is fresh in men's minds. "It is now three centuries," he said, "since so important an event has taken place in the Catholic world. I discern in the language of the Pope a boldness which imposes upon me; it strikes me with respect and admiration; because I love those powers which display strength and manifest with a frank energy the confidence which animates them and the faith which inspires them." But while grave, sensible, and conscientious men amongst non-Catholics are expressing these and such-like sentiments, the mouth-pieces of infidelity are publishing abroad that the Council is the feeble effort of a Church at its last gasp, and that it is calling it to meet over its own grave already dug. Others, assuming a different tone, represent the Council as a meeting eminently hostile to what they call the progress of the human intellect, to national liberty, and to the existence of modern society. Such are the general tactics of the enemies of religion. The Protestants on the whole seem disturbed and anxious about the future Council, but speak of it in terms of moderation which strikingly contrast with those which their ancestors used about the Council of Trent. Their ministers in particular seem very desirous to dissuade their co-religionists from going to Rome during its session. Such is the scope of a circular addressed by the Company of Pastors of Geneva to all the French Synods, and reproduced in the journal entitled *Le Protestant Liberal.* This precautionary measure is in itself an index to the Protestant state of mind, and betokens a certain movement in the body. Some, indeed, have already declared their intention of repairing to Rome during the sitting of the Council, and their example will no doubt be followed, if only from motives of curiosity, by a certain number of rationalists, unbelievers, and indifferentists. The approaching elections in France have, however, engrossed so large an amount of attention, that as yet the subject of the General Council has not come so prominently before the public mind as it may be expected to do when they are over.

We have spoken of the hopes which Catholics entertain of seeing the doctrine of the Syllabus promulgated by the Council, and on the other hand of those which are fostered by liberal Catholics that its propositions will be modified so as better to accord with the modern theories they have embraced. That the Council will *modify* any doctrine of the Syllabus we can confidently pronounce as a chimerical expectation; but it is very possible that, while enunciating its propositions formally and with their needful developements, it may thus indirectly indicate what those propositions do not but are erroneously taken by some to mean, and in so doing may remove the misunderstanding existing, not only in governmental spheres, but also in a large number of individual minds, cultivated in other respects, but not familiar with theological language, and hence liable to misinterpret it. Be this as it may, time will serve to dissipate prejudice, eyes will get used to the light, and truth, being immortal, will triumph by its own inherent strength. The Catholics of France would joyfully welcome a proclamation by the future Council of the Pope's infallibility. It would thus by implication annul the famous Declaration of 1682, without any need of a special discussion of those wretched "Four Articles" which so long formed the life of Gallicanism. It is impossible, however, not to feel that the Sovereign Pontiff, whom such a decision would personally regard, is likely from sentiments of reserve to be reluctant to take upon himself the initiative of a proposition of this character. But it is hoped that the Holy Spirit may by the mouth of the assembled Fathers affirm it by unanimous acclamation. As regards discipline, the wants of the Church of France are (as we have said) very numerous, and would need a much fuller exposition than has here been given.

We cannot for the present leave the subject of the state of religious opinion in France without some allusion to the press, so mighty an engine for evil as for good, though much more, we fear, for evil than for good, in the present day. As respects religion—the only matter with which we are here concerned—the French press may be generally divided into four classes: the revolutionary press; the parliamentary press; the religious liberal press; and the religious Roman press. The revolutionary press, as being inimical to all revealed religion, is of course specially hostile to the Council, which is the boldest assertion of the power and reality of the true faith: hitherto, however, it has not occupied itself very much with the subject; but whenever it has alluded to it, it is almost superfluous to add, that it has been in terms of depreciation and ridicule. The parliamentary press, to which category the *Liberté*, the *Presse*, and the *Journal des Débats* belong, as well as the *Patrie*, the *Constitutionel*, and the *Etendard*, all political journals, have not taken much notice of the coming Council; but when they have spoken, they have always adopted the line to which the State adheres, and have defended its old administrative traditions, and the pretensions of the temporal power in relation to those spiritual questions which appertain to the Church's competence. The religious liberal press, as the *France*, the *Gazette de France*, the *Français*, the *Villes et Campagnes*, is favourable to the Council, and speaks of it in very proper terms; we may observe, however, a certain predilection for the doctrines of the old French clergy, and a certain disposition to dwell upon and magnify the power of Bishops. Perhaps, however, nothing would be more difficult than precisely to characterize the views and feelings of the French Catholic liberals, of which the press is the great public exponent. Liberalism in them has various shades and degrees, and in a very large proportion of their number is combined with the most sincere and loyal devotion to the Holy See, certain suspicious or unsound notions which they are known to favour, being, we have good reason to think, errors of intellect rather than of heart or will, and in great measure the result of the difficult political circumstances under which they have been reared. Of men like these, who number in their ranks some devoted champions of the Church (so different in *animus* from many of those who in other Catholic lands are known as "liberal Catholics," and who are, in fact, Catholics undergoing a process of deterioration and decomposition), we would speak with all tenderness, esteem, and respect. The leading organs of the religious Roman press, to which the designation of Ultramontane has been affixed by its opponents, are the *Monde* and the *Univers*. These journals are daily occupied with the subject of the Council, and manifest, we need scarcely add, the most unexceptionable spirit in its regard. They labour to predispose the faithful to accept with filial submission the decisions of this august assembly, and to keep alive in their hearts the hopes of the benefits which will accrue from it to Christendom.

We cannot be silent on a discussion which has arisen between the *Civiltà Cattolica* and some organs of the liberal school of Catholics in France. The *Civiltà* published two months ago an account of the state of feeling manifested in France towards the General Council by Catholics and by others. This account was written by a person who had the means and the right to form an opinion. It erred by being in parts too true to be palatable, and it raised a storm. An elaborate answer was published in the *Français*, which, though written by M. Besloy, has been attributed to the Bishop of Orleans. It is well-known that the spirit of Gallicanism and nationalism abundantly survives in the French nation, and is carefully kept alive by the Government, which is interested in having it to play off against the purity of Catholic policy and doctrine. The sensitiveness and self-love of a school in France were wounded, as anything short of praise is apt to wound those who so pride themselves upon their nationality as to raise it to the dignity of a kind of *culte*. It is not surprising therefore that journals, which declare that the definition of the infallibility of the Pope would be an outrage to the France of Louis XIV. and of Napoleon III., should be a little impatient of the pure Catholic traditions which are put forward by the *Civiltà Cattolica*. We congratulate the *Civiltà*, however, upon the effect which its words have produced. A little stimulant, mingled as it was with honey, has not been thrown away. The defence given in the number of the *Civiltà* for the 17th of April has left nothing to be desired, either in tender consideration for the sensitiveness of the French liberal school, or in justification of its own correspondence.

Chapter X.

The Pope's conduct towards the Bishops of the Eastern Schism.—Their condition.—Necessity of their submission to the Holy See.

Quæ enim semper una vocatur, et est, nunquam dividitur aut secatur; quæ semper perfecta, hoc est, plena, nunquam minuitur aut evacuatur; quæ semper immaculata, nunquam corrumpitur aut maculatur. Quoniam etsi nonnunquam ab ea plerique ita exeunt, ut non revertantur, non tamen ejus unitas inde discinditur, aut perfectio minoratur, seu virginitas violatur.—*S. Leo IX. Ep. ad Michael. Const.* § 3.

THE SOVEREIGN PONTIFF having summoned a General Council of Holy Church, like his predecessors under like circumstances, turned his eyes to those whom he would not summon, because disobedient children, and admonished them of their erroneous way. He warns and beseeches them to take advantage of his offer to them, in the Indiction of the Council. As only those who are subject to him, and own his salutary rule, can sit in the great congregation, so he calls upon those bishops—it is all he can do for them—who are unhappily not in the fold of Christ to come to Rome in order to their return into the fold from which they are now by their sins excluded.

It is observable that the Vicar of God has addressed no Bishops in the West as aliens from the Kingdom of Christ. Those to whom he wrote are Bishops of the Eastern Rite not in the communion of the Holy See. There are then no such Bishops of any rite in the West, otherwise the Holy Father would have directed his words also to them. The West has no Bishops not in the communion of the Church, none disobedient to the voice of the great Shepherd of the Sheep. But it is not so in the East; in that land once so blessed of God, but now trodden down by the heathen, are many Bishops and many priests who minister valid sacraments, but illegally, and who are, notwithstanding the gift of order, living at best in material sacrilege, for they have set altar against altar, and, unmindful of Our Lord's words, offer up the great gifts unreconciled to their brother.

The condition of the Bishops of the Eastern Rite is one of the most deplorable on the face of the earth : so near the truth, and at the same time so far from it; in the light and yet not seeing.* They are bound by their position and the obligations belonging to it, to know the law, for they are teachers of others, and they are only the blind guides of a blinded people! They have voluntarily undertaken duties which they cannot discharge; they have possessed themselves unlawfully of the most mysterious powers, and by their ignorance or blindness use them unlawfully always, except in their case who are in danger of death. They are in the spiritual world what in the material world would be an army struck with lunacy; a terrible danger to all within their reach.

The Pope in the beginning of his reign made an earnest effort to bring the Eastern nations back to the unity

---

* "No saint upon the altars of the Church has ever spoken one consoling word of the dreary darkness of those who are without. Sad enough are the words of theologians, but sadder far the words of saints—sad, indeed, and weighty with the wisdom of their spiritual discernment. Even the sunshine of the gentle saint of Sales is gloom, when he thinks of those who are not of the fold, and his sweet words turn bitter as he characterizes the lot of those who are not children of the Church."—*F. Faber, Blessed Sacrament*, bk. I., pp. 63–64, 3rd. ed.

of the Church; he makes another now at its close, in a more solemn way and on a more solemn occasion. As General Councils are not necessary for the administration of the Church, nor provided for by any law, it is a serious matter for the Eastern heretics, for they may never again hear the voice of the Shepherd, they may exhaust the patience of the Most Merciful, and it may happen to them as it did to the Jews, who, by refusing to receive the gospel from the Apostles, made way for the overflow of the heathens, and left themselves outcasts from the kingdom of grace.

Ever since the schism, the Popes have been unwearied in their efforts to recover again for the Church the ravaged provinces of the East; they have never spared themselves, and they have toiled in the face of difficulties, which only they would meet, and even when their efforts were sure to be thwarted and their offers of forgiveness and of grace misinterpreted and scorned, still persevered. His Holiness now reigning, invites the Oriental schismatics to Rome, during the sessions of the Council of the Vatican; and though the earnest exhortation addressed to them in the beginning of his reign did not result in the end he most desired, he never ceased to hope that God would hear his prayers for the recovery of these lost sheep, and that the Most Merciful, "who wrought salvation in the midst of the earth," would have compassion on so many souls for whom He shed His blood.

The Pope reminds them, also, of what their forefathers did in times past, when they came, with peace on their lips at least, to the Councils of Lyons and Florence, and there made profession of the one saving faith, and were for a moment restored to the bosom of the Church, their mother, longing to receive them back. But, as a generous and forgiving father, he does not remind them of their ancient perfidy, if not hypocrisy; he would gladly believe them honest and true, for it would be a relief to his compassion if he could think that they were sinning from ignorance, not from malice. The Church can live without them, the dignity of the Holy See is not diminished by their rebellion, nor is the unity of the faith forfeited even if millions fell away and disowned the sovereign authority of the Pope. It is not for his own sake that he wishes them to return, though it is necessary for him to invite them back, because that is a duty of his office; it is not to be laid at his door that they have gone into the ways of error, or that they continue to walk in them, notwithstanding his fatherly cry warning them of the evil to come. The Eastern heretics have been most tenderly treated at all times, their very prejudices respected, and no burdens laid on them which the profession of the faith did not necessarily involve. It was not the fault of the Popes that they fell again, and, like dogs, returned to their vomit, and now again in the nineteenth century compel the Shepherd to go out into the wilderness in quest of the straying sheep.

If the prelates of the Eastern Rites, now aliens from the city of God, came to Rome, they would receive, as the former prelates did, the most generous welcome, and be the objects of the most tender love. They would be strangers certainly, but still Rome is their true home, and the fatted calf would be killed for them, as it was for the prodigal child before them. The Sovereign Pontiff's arms are open to receive them, and in his heart there is always room for them.

His Holiness speaks clearly on this point. The schismatics are not invited to the Council as members of it, and the equals of the prelates who have not tarnished their honour by schism. They are invited in the same way, and to the same purpose, as their forefathers were in the thirteenth and fifteenth centuries. The Pope's words are plain. *Vocem nostram ad vos rursus dirigimus, ut majore, qua possumus, animi Nostri contentione vos obsecramus, monemus et obtestamur, ut ad eandem Generalem Synodum convenire velitis,* QUEMADMODUM *majores vestri convenerunt ad Concilium Lugdunense II. a recolendæ memoriæ B. Gregorio X. prædecessore Nostro habitum, et ad Florentinum Concilium a felicis recondationis Eugenio IV., item Decessore Nostro, celebratum.* That is, the Oriental Bishops are invited to come as their predecessors came, and on the same conditions. The Sovereign Pontiff has not two measures. There is only one door into the Church; there must be absolute submission of the understanding and the will. Bishops cannot take counsel in common, nor deliberate in the charity of Christ if they are not true sheep of the one Shepherd. The Sovereign Pontiff is the teacher of the Church, he goes before his sheep, and they follow him because they know his voice; they could not follow him if they did not know him, and Bishops in schism neither know his voice nor follow him into the salutary pastures wherein he feeds the sheep and the lambs.

Chapter XI.

ELECTION OF GREGORY X. TO THE PONTIFICATE.—HE INVITES THE EMPEROR TO THE COUNCIL OF LYONS.—THE EMPEROR PROFESSES THE ROMAN FAITH.—THE OPENING OF THE COUNCIL.—SERMON OF ST. BONAVENTURE.—ARRIVAL AND SUBMISSION OF THE EASTERN DEPUTIES.—THE EMPEROR (BY PROXY) AND THE DEPUTIES ABJURE THE SCHISM.—DEATH OF ST. THOMAS AND OF ST. BONAVENTURE.—INSINCERITY OF THE EASTERNS.—EXCOMMUNICATION OF MICHAEL PALÆOLOGUS.

Non defuit summorum Pontificum cura, ut gens illa ad Catholicam veritatem rediret, ut cum reliquis orthodoxis in unius Petri simul collecta gremio, de Matris Ecclesiæ utero fluenta doctrinæ salutaris hauriret; id enim egerunt nedum tot salutiferis constitutionibus eam ad unitatem invitantibus, sed conciliorum coadunatione, pecuniæ profusione, vigiliis, ac laboribus ; et eo magis Romanorum Pontificum charitas eluxit, quod licet a Græcis tam impiè neglecti semper eorum salutem anxius perquisiverint.—*Card. Petra, ad Const. XIV. Innocent IV.*

GREGORY X. was in the Holy Land when the Cardinals in Viterbo elected him to be the successor of St. Peter, after an interregnum of two years and nine months. Having seen with his own eyes the miserable condition of the East, and knowing how schism stood in the way of all change for the better, he resolutely directed all his energies towards the accomplishment of three things, the succour of Christians in Palestine, the restoration of the Greeks to the Church out of which they had gone, and the amendment of ecclesiastical discipline which had become lax. The supreme remedy for the evils he desired to correct was the convocation of a General Council, and this he summoned immediately after he had established peace between neighbours who were quarrelling, and whose contentions might have made it more difficult for the Council to assemble.

He began his work by sending legates to Constantinople, waiting, however, for some tidings first of the effect of the letters of his predecessor Clement IV. At last John the Franciscan came back with good news, and then the Pope invited the Emperor to the General Council to be held in Lyons, May 1, 1274. There were hopes entertained by many that the Greeks were in earnest, and that the Emperor, who had been begging the King of France to befriend him in his attempt to make his peace with the Church, seriously purposed to renounce his heresies, and submit himself with his people to the supreme authority of the Roman Church. It may be that St. Louis knew the Emperor of the Greeks too well to trust him, but be that as it may, he was not able to do anything more for him than recommend him to the Pope. He told the Emperor plainly that he would not take upon himself such a matter, and that he would confine himself to writing a letter giving the Pope an account of the Emperor's prayer, and recommending him earnestly to his Holiness. It was not in his power to do more, for he could not absolve him from his sins. The death of St. Louis and the vacancy of the Holy See prevented the further progress of this affair, but Gregory X. undertook it, and summoned the Bishops to the General Council at Lyons, and soon after invited the Greek Bishops also to attend it.

The Pope had grave misgivings, and wrote again to the Emperor to impress upon him the gravity of the matter he had undertaken, and the necessity of being honest and true. He tells him that many persons of high rank and dignity were not afraid to say that the Greeks were not in earnest, and that time was wasted; he hoped, nevertheless, that the good work begun would be happily ended, and that the Emperor would remove every hesitation from his mind—for the Pope admits that he had doubts—and not suffer such a stain to lie on the Imperial name.

His Holiness required at once the acceptance of the terms proposed by his predecessor, Clement IV., and those were the confession of the Catholic Faith as taught in Rome. The Emperor was to hold and believe that the Holy Ghost proceeds from the Father and the Son, and to admit the supremacy of the Holy See. If he did this he might attend the Council of Lyons; if not, he could not be received. The words of the Pope are clear enough : *Præmissis primitus adimpletis, ad memoratam Synodum, cui una cum Catholicis principibus te decebit, et nos desideramus et petimus, interesse.* The Emperor accepted the conditions, professed in the most public manner the Roman faith, and sealed the act of profession with the Imperial seal.

The Sovereign Pontiff did not treat with the Eastern schismatics as with persons who had any rights, or who were on an equality with him. He asked them to come to the Council, but not in the way he asked, or rather summoned, the Bishops who were obedient to the Holy See. These latter were his acknowledged subjects, and they were not only invited but charged to come. They could not absent themselves without sin, unless they had good cause to show. It was not so with the Eastern prelates who were in schism. Their duty was, of course, to attend Councils, when the Pope assembled them, but the Orientals were in sin and could not be summoned with their brethren. Yet as their baptism and their ordination had placed them under the jurisdiction of the Pope, they had a claim on his charity, though he alone, and not they, seemed to be aware of it. He does what in him lies to bring them back to the one fold, and accordingly he invites them to the Council. They probably knew as well as the Pope that they could never sit in the great congregation of the Church, if they were not members of her, dwelling in unity with their brethren.

All discussions were to be over before the Eastern prelates could take their seats, for the Council was not to be sullied by disputes, and it would be impossible to allow it to open, if members of it were not of one mind about the faith : for how could the profession of that faith be made if it were not held ?

The Pope is most clear in his language to the Emperor, and leaves no room for mistakes. The Greeks were not invited to dispute about the faith, for they were to profess and hold it before they could be received within the Council. The doctrines which the Greeks denied had been already settled, and his Holiness neither would, nor could, suffer them to be discussed. The Greeks might ask for explanations or instruction and they would receive all they required, but the discussion of settled doctrines of the faith, or a new definition of the faith, the Pope would not hear of.*

The Council of Lyons was opened on the 7th day of May, 1274, after a fast of three days, which the Pope had ordered to be kept five days before. The second session was held on the 18th, but before the third session the Pope had received letters from the Franciscan Friars whom his Holiness had sent to Constantinople, and the news thus brought to him filled his soul with gladness. He called all the prelates together at once in the great church of Lyons, and there the great Franciscan doctor, St. Bonaventure, Cardinal Bishop of Albano, preached a sermon on the words of the prophet Baruch: *Exurge, Jerusalem, et sta in excelso; et circumspice ad orientem, et vide collectos filios tuos ab oriente sole usque ad occidentem, in verbo sancti gaudentes Dei memoria.* v. 5. When the preacher had finished, the letters of the friars were read in the hearing of the whole assembly.

The third session of the Council was on the 7th of June, and a Dominican friar preached, who was once the Archbishop of Lyons, but now Cardinal Bishop of Ostia, and afterwards the Pope Innocent V. His Holiness then caused some of the canons already drawn up to be read, and dismissed the prelates without appointing a day for the next session, because the Greek deputies had not arrived, and because it could not be known when they might come.

On the 24th June the expected deputies entered Lyons, many prelates went out to meet them, the

---

* Non ad prædictæ discussionem vel novam diffinitionem fidei, quam tanquam innumeris sacræ paginæ auctoritatibus, numerosis sanctorum patrum sententiis, et Romanorum Pontificum stabili diffinitione firmatam, nec ipse [Clemens IV.] voluit, nec Nos intendimus, sicut nec decet nec foret expediens, in dubium, novo ipsam exponendo examini, revocare.—*Greg. X. P.P. Ep. ad Michael. Palæolog.*

Pope sent the Chamberlain and the Vice-Chancellor of Holy Church to receive them. They were brought into the Pope's palace, where he was surrounded by his Cardinals, waiting for them. They were admitted to the kiss of peace, and then produced their letters: the letter of the Emperor with its golden seal, and letters from the Eastern prelates. These being presented, the deputies declared that they were come to show themselves in all things obedient to the Roman Church, acknowledging its supremacy and confessing its faith.* The submission was complete, and the Pope dismissed them to their lodgings for the night.

Before the next session of the Council, on the feast of St. Peter and St. Paul, the Sovereign Pontiff sung Mass in the great church of Lyons, and St. Bonaventure, who had now reached within three weeks the end of all his labours, preached again; the epistle and gospel were sung both in Latin and in Greek; when the creed had been sung by the Cardinals and the Canons of Lyons, the Greek deputies, at the head of whom stood the Latin Patriarch of Constantinople, with the Greek Bishops of Calabria, sung it again in Greek, and when they came to the words "proceedeth from the Father and the Son," they sang them three times, *solemniter et devote*. The Greeks were now reconciled to the Church from which they had strayed, and though the reconciliation was not sincere on the part of many, yet there were no reasons to suspect fraud; the Pope certainly, whatever suspicions he may have had, showed no misgivings, and on the 3rd day of July announced to the Council that the next Session would be held on Friday, July 6.

On the day appointed the Prelates met in Council; and for the first time there sat among them the deputies of the Greeks, behind the Cardinals on the right hand of the Pope. His Holiness then announced to the Council the fact that the Eastern Schism was over, that the Greeks had of their own free will returned

---

* Dixerunt in præsentia Domini Papæ quod veniebant ad omnimodam obedientiam sanctæ Romanæ ecclesiæ et ad recognitionem fidei quam ipsa ecclesia tenet, et primatum ipsius.—*Brev. not. ap. Colet. Concil. Magn.*, Tom xiv. col. 503.

into the obedience of the Roman Church, professing its faith and acknowledging its supremacy; the deputies of that nation were there present with the Calabrian Bishops of the Greek rite, testifying to the extinction of the Schism.

At Lyons the Greeks were not admitted into the Council as the equals of the Catholic Bishops before they had professed the faith. They could not sit in that assembly without first submitting themselves to the jurisdiction of the Pope, and accepting his supremacy.

The Imperial Logothete in the name of his master, and, as he said, by the Emperor's command, abjured the Schism, *omne schisma prorsus abjuro*, so also did the deputies of the Prelates; both the Logothete and the deputies promising for themselves, and for those whom they said they represented, to preserve the faith inviolate, and to persevere in the obedience of the Roman See.

On his way to the Council St. Thomas, the great Dominican Doctor, died; and early on Sunday morning, July 15, the Franciscan Saint went to his rest—the two friends were not long divided—and on the very day of his death, was buried in the Franciscan Church in Lyons. The Pope and all the Prelates in the Council were present, and the Cardinal Bishop of Ostia, who was to be the next Pope, and the first of his Order raised to that dignity, preached the sermon from the words of David, *Doleo super te, frater mi, Jonatha*, 2 Regg. i. 26. Many were the tears shed at the time, for *quicumque eum videbant, ipsius amore incontinenti capiebantur ex corde*. The next morning, Monday, July 16, the canons then made were read in the fifth session of the Council, and that done the Pope addressed the assembled Fathers on the great loss to the Church caused by the death of the Friar Bonaventure, Bishop of Albano, and ordered all the Prelates and all Priests throughout the world to say, or have said, one Mass for his soul, and another for the souls of those who died on their way to, their stay in, or their return from, the Council. The next day the sixth and last Session was held, and the General Council of Lyons was dissolved July 17, 1274.

But the solemn promise of Michael Palæologus, the Greek Emperor, was not wholly sincere, nor wholly insincere. He did not keep it altogether, nor yet utterly break it at once. Some reverence was shown to the Pope, and the Greek Patriarch, an inveterate heretic, who had not come in person to the Council, was deposed, because he refused to ratify what his agents had promised in his name, and another Patriarch was set up in his place, who hated the schism. The Emperor had not formally under his own hand and seal personally renounced the schism ; neither had the Logothete produced his authority for making that renunciation in the Emperor's name, and many things were left undone which gave no comfort to the Pope Innocent V., who laboured hard to make good what his predecessor Gregory X. had begun. In his instructions to the Franciscan Friars sent to Constantinople is a clause requiring them to obtain from the Emperor his abjuration of the schism in due form : for that had not yet been obtained in any other way than by proxy.* Innocent V. did not live to see the work done, and Nicholas III., elected in November 1277, was not more successful. He complains of the Greeks generally that none of them had applied to be released from the censures they had incurred by the schism, and that, indifferent to the irregularity, they ministered the sacraments and other rites of the Church. But the conduct of the new Patriarch is the most inexcusable, for he, professing the faith and acknowledging the supremacy of the Holy See, had not applied to the Pope for the confirmation of his dignity. He had been consecrated in the beginning of June, 1275, and the Pope Nicholas III., who was not elected till February, 1276, had not received any application from him for the necessary Bulls.† The reconciliation

---

* Licet Logotheta nomine ipsius Imperatoris abjuraverit schisma in concilio Lugdunensi : quia tamen Logotheta super hoc mandatum ejus non ostendit, petatur ab ipso Imperatore quod illud personaliter abjuret. —*Martene et Durand, Ampl. Collect.*, Tom. vii. col. 254.

† Ecclesia Romana miratur, quod prælati et alii non curaverunt adhuc statui suo ex consideratione prateriti temporis providere. Cum enim ratione schismatis in quo erant, multoties latæ sint sententiæ contra eos, mirandum occurrit, quod ipsi quoad relaxationem sententiarum ipsarum tam prælati quam alii clerici et personæ ecclesiasticæ

in Lyons was probably not more sincere then the next made at Florence ; and that may explain why it never went beyond the *forum externum*, and was never perfected by the individual submission of the Greek prelates in *foro interno*. Martin IV., therefore, in the first year of his Pontificate, solemnly excommunicated the prevaricating Emperor, Michael Palæologus, and the Greeks continued in their sins.

CHAPTER XII.

PRESENT ASPECT OF AFFAIRS.—THE GREAT VICE OF THE ORIENTAL MIND.—USURPATION ON THE PART OF THE BISHOP OF CONSTANTINOPLE.—EUGENIUS IV. AND THE COUNCIL OF BASLE.—RECEPTION OF THE PATRIARCH OF CONSTANTINOPLE BY THE POPE. — MEETING OF THE COUNCIL AT FERRARA.—ITS ADJOURNMENT TO FLORENCE.—MEETING IN SEPARATE SYNODS OF THE LATINS AND GREEKS.

Quare sicut quilibet in sua ecclesia episcopus origo est, atque centrum unitatis, quatenus fideles communi consensione adhærendo illi, in unum coadunantur, atque ex unione, gregis cum pastore illa ecclesia evadit una ; ita in universali ecclesia unus Summus Sacerdos et Pastor, sanctus Petrus, Romanusque Pontifex, successor ejus, Catholicæ unitatis origo, atque centrum est, et unitatem totius Catholicæ ecclesiæ continet, quatenus omnes tum episcopi, tum pastores inferiores, cæterique fideles illi adhærent, atque ita ex pluribus peculiaribus gregibus uni Supremo Sacerdoti, atque Pastori adhærentibus, unus grex et una ecclesia universalis coalescit.—*Cerboni, de Jur. et Leg. Discipl.*, lib. xxv. cap. 2.

WHAT God in His mercy may have reserved for His Holiness now reigning, in the inscrutable decrees of His Providence, none may tell; it may be that he will fail as his predecessors, or he may prosper in his great work. At this moment everything seems against him, but with God nothing is impossible, and the greater the human difficulties the nearer the victory. The Photian schismatics generally have turned, as far as

super irregularitate, quam ex consequentia incurrerunt, se immiscendo divinis nullum adhuc petierunt remedium adhiberi. Item miratur ecclesia quod Patriarcha et alii prælati post confessionem fidei factam, recognitum et susceptum primatum ecclesiæ Romanæ, ac obedientiam promissam eidem, super confirmatione status sui nullam provisionem petere curaverunt.—*Martene et Durand, ibid.*, col. 272.

we know, a deaf ear to the voice of the Great Shepherd of the fold of Christ. The Sovereign Pontiff is preparing his great supper, and his servants have carried his invitations to the uttermost parts of the earth. It may be that at the last moment the Greek prelates may remember their first beginnings, and repent, or they may refuse, and make the miserable excuses which were made before, and which are continually made, unhappily, to the daily ruin of silly souls.

The great vice of the Oriental mind seems to be its abject worship of the civil power, and an incapacity to recognize the government of the Church as a divine institution. Constantine withdrew from Rome when his eyes were opened in baptism to see the majesty that had already taken possession of the city,* and set up his throne in Constantinople. At that time the city had not obtained that name, and the Bishop of it was subject to the metropolitan of Heraclea. But the presence of the court, and the prevalence of heresy among some of its bishops, made the clergy ambitious of ecclesiastical honours, and without any shadow of right the Bishops set the metropolitan at defiance, and called themselves Archbishops, and in the second general Council, held in Constantinople itself, A.D. 381, a canon was made to the effect that the Bishop of Constantinople should rank next to the Pope, on the ground that he was Bishop of the new Rome. In the Council of Chalcedon the Greeks went further; in the absence of the Papal Legate, they published a canon by which Constantinople is raised to a rank equal with that of Rome, and the reason assigned is that the powers of the Holy See were given it by the Councils, because it was the Imperial city. Thus the Clergy of Constantinople raised their Church above the Patriarchal Sees of Alexandria and Antioch, and then made it the rival of Rome. The canons, however, were not allowed by the Popes, and of course are of no effect, but the evil spirit working in the East has always used them, and at last brought about the Schism, which, to justify itself, set up a heresy concerning the most Blessed Trinity.

---

* Cap. *Fundamenta* in vi. to. Non absque miraculo factum esse concipitur.

The failure of Gregory X. did not discourage his successors, and in the dark days of the Councils of Constance and of Bâsle the Sovereign Pontiff never forgot the unhappy Orientals lost in heresy and schism. Even when nearly all Europe rose in rebellion against the Holy See, and the faithful Bishops were few in number, and when anarchy in the Church was preached by men who said they were learned, and was the staple of academical discussions, the Popes never quailed, but sat on their thrones in peace, waiting for the visitation of God. While the unhappy prelates and priests who had gathered together at Bâsle, and called themselves a general council, were in rebellion against the Pope, the Pope was labouring to bring over the Greeks to the unity of the faith, and his adversaries were the members of that council. Eugenius IV. commanded the prelates at Bâsle to leave that place and attend him at Ferrara, but they disobeyed him, and the Council of Ferrara was opened by his Legate Jan. 8, 1438. To this Council the Greek prelates had been invited to come, and they had promised to come, with the Emperor at their head, but only at the expense of the Pope. His Holiness undertook to send his galleys to Constantinople for them, to bring them over to Italy, and maintain them there during the sessions of the Council, and to send them home again at his own expense, even if they refused to enter the fold of the Church.* The Emperor and his Bishops did not arrive in time to be present at the opening of the Council, and reached Ferrara in the beginning of March. The Patriarch as he drew near to the Vicar of Christ became uneasy about his reception. He told a friend of the Pope that if the Pope was older than he, he would treat him as a father; if of his own age, as his equal; if younger, as a son. He

---

* Item, si hæc unio—quod Deus avertat—non sequeretur, nec ad optatum finem procederet, prædicti imperator et patriarcha, et alii superius nominati, nostris sumptibus et galeis, sine longitudine temporis, ac omni impedimento cessante, cum honore suo, bona voluntate nostra, quemadmodum ad prædictam catholicam futuram Synodum venerunt, ita Constantinopolim redeant, sive unio in dicta synodo secuta fuerit, sive non.—*Eugenii S.P., Salvus Conductus, ap. Coleti,* Tom. xviii. col. 865.

was in some trouble, for if he really believed the Patriarch of Constantinople, appointed by the Emperor, to be the equal of the Pope according to the theory of the East, he need not have been uneasy, for he might have claimed the recognition of his rank as a simple debt.

The Patriarch, or, perhaps, more correctly, the men about him, caused it to be made known to the Pope that he would not show him certain signs of reverence when he came into his presence. His Holiness replied that he regretted the fact; nevertheless, as he was desirous of seeing the Eastern nations brought back into the unity of the Church, he would waive certain things, but in that case the public reception of the Patriarch could not take place. The reception, therefore, was private, and the Patriarch asked his Holiness, when the audience was over, for permission to say Mass. The Pope gave it, but a little later, when the Patriarch wished to have a church assigned him, that he might therein celebrate Easter, according to the Eastern Rite, he made application to the Pope for one of the monasteries of Ferrara. The Pope said the application must be made to the bishop of the city, and when it was made, the Bishop simply declined to give him one. The Patriarch complained, and the ministers of his Holiness told him that it had never been agreed upon in the arrangements for the Council that a Catholic church should be at his disposal.*

The Greeks went to see how the seats for the bishops were arranged in the church; and were dissatisfied. At last the Catholics yielded to their pretensions, and gave them the aisle of the church on the Epistle side. The throne of the Pope was near the altar, and below it a seat, vacant, for the Emperor of Germany, precisely opposite to which on the other side of the church was the seat of the Emperor of Constantinople, then that of the Patriarch, with the proxies of the other Patriarchs and the rest of the Greek prelacy. The seat of the Greek Patriarch corresponded with that of the first Cardinal on the Gospel side of the church. Thus the Council of Ferrara was really composed only

---

* *Histor. Unionis*, pp., 98, 109.

of the Catholic Bishops, for the Greeks did not sit in it nor form any part whatever of it.

On the 9th April, 1438, Eugenius IV., with the Catholic prelacy entered the church, and having sung the Mass of the Holy Ghost, and recited the prayers usually said on such occasions, waited for the arrival of the Greeks. The Eastern prelates were not present at the Catholic rites ; perhaps they could not have been permitted to witness them, before they had renounced their heresy. When the Greeks, with the Emperor at their head, had taken their places, an Eastern priest stood up and made excuses for the absence of the Patriarch, who was ill, and therefore unable to attend. Then, by order of the Pope, was read, first in Latin, then in Greek, a Bull, dated that very day, announcing his earnest desires for the reconciliation of the Greeks. That done, the prelates on both sides left the church. *

In this session of the Council, if it was a conciliar session at all, the Greeks did nothing, and, indeed, could do nothing, for they were not yet members of the Church. They were not admitted into the Council, nor did they sit among the Catholic Bishops. They were there for the purpose of being instructed, not for that of counsel and deliberation ; and all the following assemblies from the day of the opening in Ferrara till the 6th day of July, 1439, in Florence, to which place the Council had been removed by the Pope, were in reality conferences, wherein men disputed on either side, for the purpose of showing the Greeks how erroneous were the opinions which they so obstinately held.

The Council of Florence, till that 6th day of July, was composed exclusively of Bishops who acknowledged the supremacy of the Pope, and of none other, but there was also present another assembly, or

---

* *Sguropul*, p. 110. The proclamation attributed to the Patriarch in the Greek account of the Council is regarded as a forgery, and is inconsistent with the facts. If it was really read it must have been read only in Greek, and to the Greeks, for the Pope would never have consented that the General Council was to begin, or be proclaimed, on that day, when it had already been long ago proclaimed by him, and had already held its first session. Sguropulus says nothing of such a paper, and he certainly would hardly have omitted it, if it had been read.

Council, composed of men who were not members of the Holy Church, but whose conversion the Pope was very anxiously promoting, and this assembly was called and addressed as the Eastern Synod, both by the Catholics and themselves. All deliberations that took place among these two assemblies were not deliberations in common, for the two assemblies never formed one whole. The Latins deliberated among themselves, and no Greek was present; while the Easterns deliberated among themselves, without the presence of any Latin Bishops, and under the direction of the Emperor of Constantinople. So clear was the division, so complete the separation, that though the disputants appointed on both sides met in the church, and saluted each other, they said their prayers each side by itself; there was an absolute *non communicatio in sacris.**

During the 13th Conference the Ambassadors of the Duke of Burgundy were introduced, who made the customary reverence to the Pope, but never heeded the Emperor and the Greek Bishops, who were present in the same church.† The letters they brought with them were read, but only in Latin, and the Greeks were not informed even of their contents. The Greeks held their own Synod for deliberation apart from the Latins, and they called it the Eastern Synod; the Pope himself regarded them as sitting in an assembly over which he did not preside. On one occasion, during the 25th Conference, Greek deputies came to him with an answer from the Emperor and his Bishops to a proposition which his Holiness had made to the former. The Pope listens, and says he will send Cardinals to the Eastern Synod.‡ Again, after the death of the Patriarch, when the Pope sent for the three Bishops of Russia, Nice, and Mitylene, and urged them to hasten to the desired end, they replied that they had

---

* See Sguropulus, p. 116.

† Concilio Œcumenico solemnem orationem fecerant, et imperatori Græcorum nil dixerant in publico. Coleti, xviii. col. 995.

‡ Cardinales mittam ad Orientalem Synodum, ut enarrent omnia, præsente quoque Imperatore.—Coleti, xviii. col. 399.

no authority from the Eastern Synod to speak,* they would, therefore, speak as private persons. The Emperor, too, in Florence, called together the whole Eastern Synod.† The Pope also speaks in the same way, and on one occasion says he will consult his own Synod.‡ The Latin and the Greek accounts agree in this; nor is there anything recorded of the Council of Florence to show that the Greeks were treated there in a different way from that in which they were treated at Lyons before. They had been invited to the Council, not as members of it, but as erring children whom the Pope was ready to receive again into his house. In both places they were received, for they promised to keep the laws of the Church, but they never kept their promise, and they are again to-day, where they were before the Councils of Lyons and Florence.§ They are in most grievous error, for they think the one Church can be divided, and that the Patriarch of Constantinople is equal in rank and power to the successor of S. Peter. They think that bishops can be bishops, though not in communion with the Holy See, and that men can be in the Church, and partakers of lawful sacraments, who obey bishops in schism, bishops who have never received authority to govern Christian men. The Holy See is patient and forbearing, forgiving seventy times seven, and has once more called on the poor Oriental schismatics groaning under a double oppression to consider their ways, and come back to the salutary pastures which only Rome can give them.

---

* Nos respondendi facultatem non habemus ab Orientali Synodo. Coleti, ut sup. col. 507.

† Universam Orientalem Synodum. Coleti, ibid. col. 507.

‡ Papa vero dixit se cum sua Synodo consilium initurum. Coleti, ibid. col. 514.

§ Postea vero ad schisma reversi ac proinde excommunicati permansere, excommunicatione majori, qua omnes schismatici in Bulla cænæ Domini feriuntur. Et ideo ab ecclesia Latina et Catholica divisi in statu damnationis æternæ versantur.—*Thom. a Jesu, De Convers. Gentium procuranda,* lib. vi. cap. 8.

Chapter XIII.

The Pope's Address to Protestants.—Differences between the Greeks and Protestants.—Heretics never summoned to a Council.—Conduct of the Protestant Princes when invited by Paul III.—Impossibility of Discussion between Catholics and Heretics.

Exacerbastis enim eum qui fecit vos, Deum æternum, immolantes dæmoniis, et non Deo; obliti enim estis Deum qui nutrivit vos, et contristastis nutricem vestram, Jerusalem.—*Bar.* iv., 7.

THE SOVEREIGN PONTIFF having summoned the prelates who obey him to assemble together in Rome on the Feast of the Immaculate Conception of this year, and having invited the Eastern Bishops who are lost in heresy and schism to present themselves before him at the same time, turns his eyes to another class of people still further sunk in the depths of ignorance and sin, sheep without shepherds even in name; having no guides with even a colourable title to guide them; with nothing to rely on but their own judgment weakened and perverted by disobedience. The Pope addresses himself to those nations who have driven out the "priests of the Lord," and who have given up His service and worship, who deny the faith and reject the sacraments, but who have not yet ceased to baptize their children, and who, therefore, retain the distinction of Christians. The Greeks and the Oriental sects have kept the sacraments and the priesthood; their priests are true priests, and their bishops true bishops, for these have received validly, but not lawfully, the sacrament of Order. They present a semblance of the Church, and pretend to have claims for consideration; the Pope, therefore, deals with them according to their demands, and addresses himself to their prelates, whom he invites to the General Council, not, however, as members of it, for that they cannot be while they are aliens from the faith.

There is a great difference between the Eastern and the Western sheep who have gone astray. The former may receive in the article of death the full forgiveness of their sins, if they are penitent, for at that time the most merciful provisions of Holy Church take effect, and all censures and prohibitions cease, so that the schismatical and heretical priests may as validly minister as any priest in Christendom to the souls of the dying. But in the West there is no such help for perishing souls; men have put it out of their reach, and in a manner secured their own destruction, for they have got rid of priests and sacraments. There is in the West no person who has authority, even in name, over others; there are none who stand in the position of the Eastern Bishops, so the Pope, looking over the wild waste of the waters of heresy, saw nobody to whom he could in particular direct his words. He has invited none to Rome, for there is nobody with a pretence to authority among them; but he has most tenderly told them of the perilous course they have taken, and of the certain ruin at the end.

Heretics and schismatics are never summoned to a Council, nor are they even invited to attend as members of it, for they are not members of the Church. But the Popes invited them to appear in his presence when they held Councils; so did Gregory X., and Eugenius IV., and so in the beginning of the Western heresy did Paul III., when he summoned a Council to be held in Mantua; he invited the Princes of the Empire, who were encouraging heresy, not however as members, for they were laymen, but to hear the voice of the Church. It was found afterwards impossible to hold the Council, and the Princes already corrupted denounced it in coarse and scurrilous language.* The Pope was patient, and sent Thomas, Bishop of Feltre, to Worms, in 1540, where Catholics and Heretics, eleven on each side, were to meet for the discussion and settlement of the doctrines disputed by the latter. Paul III. said, that though the assembly was called together without his sanction, he might therefore not only disapprove of it, but even condemn it, yet, remembering whom he represented on earth, he forgave the slight and the insult, and directed the Bishop to treat

---

* Sleidan, Hist. Reform. Bk. xi., p. 226.

the heretics with every consideration, and to let them know how ready he was, provided they showed themselves obedient, to receive them into the Church out of which they had gone. But at the same time the Bishop was to watch these deputies, among whom, the Pope had been told that some Catholics were to be found, who were not right-minded, *non bono in hanc Sedem nostram animo sint affecti*, * as indeed was the case everywhere then throughout the West, for the Reformation could never have been made without the help of Catholics, who were not Papal.

The Western heresy is in one respect singular, it is the only heresy that has been able to deny its own name; and call itself by another that enabled it to elude the penalties and the dishonour which the common sense of Christendom, as well as the teaching of the Church had always attached to the profession of any opinion at variance with the faith. † The secular princes who supported heresy, because of the worldly gains it brought them, were well aware that if the name of heretic once clung to them, they were in danger of losing not only what they had stolen, but what they held before they became thieves. They called themselves Protestants, a term that need not mean heresy, but which in the end was found to include all heresies, and issue in the unbelief of paganism. ‡

The new sectaries, though occasionally, when it served their interests, affecting a reverence they did not feel for Councils, never made a serious attempt to return into the Church whose lands and possessions they so shamelessly stole. They carried on their foreheads the brand of heresy from the first, and, filled with the spirit of unwisdom, refused to listen to any voice but their own. They were the true children of Luther, mocking and unclean; and whenever they

---

* Hoffman. Collect. i., p. 594.

† Unde et Protestantium nomen sibi ipsis gloriose nec minus subdole arrogarunt, quo veteris infamiam nominis, quod ab hæresi sua sibi merito comparaverant, abolerent, ut jam non hæretici sicut prius jure, sed Protestantes injuria vocentur. *Ambros. Catharini Politi Oratio habita Bononiæ, ap. Martene et Durand. Coll. Ampl. viii. col.* 1147.

‡ Peccatum igitur paganitatis incurrit, quisquis, dum Christianum se asserit, Sedi Apostolicæ obedire contemnit. *Words of St. Gregory VII., cited by Gerhous Reicshpergensis, in comment. in Ps. x.* 3.

found themselves unexpectedly caught and brought as it were before the judge, they instantly refused the trial they had courted, or insisted on impossible conditions. Luther appealed from the Papal Legate to the Pope, then from the Pope to a General Council, yet nobody imagines Luther to have been serious. He saved his person from penalties by the first appeal, and that was probably all he meant by it, and the second appeal to a General Council was simply to insult the Pope, and to fill the taverns of Germany with disorderly priests who were ready for the reign of licentiousness.

The Protestant princes, when required to appear before the Council convoked by Paul III., knew they must excuse themselves in some form or other, for however careless they may have been, and however weak their faith, they were not yet strong enough to defy the power of the Church and break the laws of the Empire—that would have been too much for them—if they had not observed some sort of respect for the laws which they were about to cast away for ever. They had grown up in the Church, and knew her strength, so they were cautious in their public language, and affected a zeal for truth, for they would have been glad, if it were possible, to fight the Church with her own weapons. They professed to reverence Councils, and undertook to prove that they not only hated false doctrine and heresy, but also that they were free from all obstinacy and pride.* Nevertheless, they would not appear before the Council; they rejected it and refused to be judged by the Pope; that is, they would not be judged at all; they had made up their minds to accept the heresy, with its worldly profits, and risk their souls for the lands of the Church, which they had stolen, and would not restore. The doctrines which had become too common in the Council of Constance, and which grave men, who might have known better, had so ruthlessly propagated in the interest of their miserable factions, by this time

---

* Ostendemus enim nos non solum ab hæresibus et impiis dogmatibus abhorrere, sed etiam alienissimos esse ab arrogantia et pertinacia. *Causa quare Synodum recusarint Principes, ap. Le Plat. Monument. Col. ii.,* 576.

had borne fruit, and the fruit it bore was ripe. The protesting princes had the hardihood to say, that the Sovereign Pontiff, was only a party to the dispute, that he could not be the judge of the controversy because he was not impartial, and so they asked for a Council in which the Pope was not judge. *Synodus pia et libera, in qua non committatur cognitio doctrinæ Romano Pontifici.** Thus, from the very beginning, the Protestant heresy seems to have attained to the fulness of its strength, and the perfection of its unreason.

When the Council at last was held in Trent, hopes were still cherished that the heretics would submit; the assembled Fathers granted a safe conduct to as many as chose to come, but none came in the disposition the Council desired. The dukes of Wurtemberg and of Saxony, compelled by the Emperor, sent their agents to the Council in January, 1552, with a treatise on heresy, which the Fathers allowed to be read in their hearing. It was one of the confessions of the new religion, and for the time as accurately made as it was possible. The Fathers and the deputies of the two dukes, did not discuss it; the former listened, that was all, and when the reading was over, the answer of the Council was, "the holy and Œcumenical Synod has heard your words and will give them due considerations."

There could be no discussion between the Catholics and the heretics, because there was nothing in common between them. They could not find a ground whereon to stand, nor a point wherefrom to start; there were no first principles admitted by both sides; the heretics had gone so far and so fast that they were now beyond the reach of argument. They had discarded the principles they had always held, and were now under the influence of opinions that were nothing else but the scattered ruins of human reason. Men do not reason with lunatics, neither do they argue with criminals. Some first principles must be sacred, or the world must perish in the confusion, and thus, when the orators of the two dukes recited their extravagances be-

---

* Ibid p. 579.

fore the Council, the Fathers could but reply as they did, for they could not admit that the Christian faith was to be submitted anew for the discussion of heretics, nor suffer the very first principle of it to be called in question, as if it needed proof, in the sixteenth century.

Chapter XIV.

DIFFERENCE BETWEEN THE MOTIVES OF THE GREEKS AT FLORENCE—AND THAT OF THE PROTESTANTS AT TRENT.—INSTRUCTIONS OF JULIUS III. TOUCHING THE LATTER.—DEFINED DOCTRINES CANNOT AGAIN BE DISCUSSED.—THEREFORE THE PROTESTANTS ABSTAINED FROM THE COUNCIL OF TRENT.—END OF THAT COUNCIL.

Dividuntur vestimenta Christi, Sacramenta Ecclesiæ scinduntur: sed integra manet tunica inconsutilis, desuper contexta per totum. Tunica hæc unitas est Ecclesiæ, quæ scissuram ignorat, divisionem non recipit. Quod enim desuper contextum est, quod a Spiritu Sancto compactum est, non dissolvetur ab hominibus. Cum hæretici exacuerunt linguam suam sicut serpentes, cum omnes aculeos ingenii sui excusserunt, ut pacem Ecclesiæ conturbent; tamen quoniam portæ inferi sunt, non prævalebunt adversus eam—S. Bernard. Ep. ad Guidonem Pisanum.

THE Eastern Prelates when they came to the Council of Florence, seem, at first sight, to have been more favourably received, than were the deputies of the Western heretics at Trent. The difference in the two cases arose from the conditions of the persons who came to the Council. The Greeks came for a definite purpose, that of being restored to the unity of the Church; but as they had certain doubts or difficulties which stood between them and union, they required these doubts to be solved. That was done in several private conferences, and when the difficulties were all removed, the Greeks yielded, and confessed the faith. Then again the Greeks held not only many doctrines of the faith, but also maintained certain principles in common with the Church: they respected the authority of their Bishops; held the ancient traditions, and with them the Church had little to do beyond showing them the true application of the principles they maintained.

The Western heretics went to the Council without

the slightest intention of learning anything ; they were inaccessible to reason, having made up their minds that they only were in the right, and everybody who differed from them in the wrong. They did not even admit that they could by any possibility have made a mistake, though they had for many, and those the purest, years of their lives believed and taught what the Fathers of the Council still believed and taught. It was therefore not possible to enter upon a disputation with them, because they rejected the first principles of the faith, still less to instruct them, for they came in their vanity to instruct a Council of Holy Church. These men had not the excuse which the Greeks had in the long possession of their heresy, for they had been all instructed in the true Faith, had lived in the Church, and acknowledged the supremacy of the Holy See. Besides, they knew the fearful issues of heresy, and that the laws of the States in which they lived were more or less Christianized, and, consequently, a perpetual menace of the loss of their earthly possessions.

The Fathers of Trent were not there to dispute with contumacious heretics, but to pronounce sentence upon errors lately scattered among the faithful. They were ready to hear anybody who had a word to say, but they neither would nor could dispute with men who denied the first principles of revealed truth. His Holiness the Pope, Julius III., sent definite instructions to the Council concerning the manner in which the heretics were to be received. He repeats what Gregory X. had said to the Greeks in the thirteenth century : settled doctrines could not be discussed. The principles of the Catholic religion must be accepted, for God has not given them, as He has given the world, to the disputation of men.* Those who came to Trent were to submit to the court and the judge ; to confess that there was but one Church, with one head, the Vicar of Christ, whom the word of Christ had made. If they refused to acknowledge these doctrines, they were to be dealt with as if they had made open profession of heresy and schism, for

---

* Mundum tradidit disputationi eorum.—*Eccles.* iii., 11.

he who doubts does not hold the faith. Thus the Council was not a school where men might dispute; it was, on the contrary, an extraordinary high court of justice of the Church, with settled precedents and clear rules of procedure. The Protestants had disturbed the public peace, thrown Germany into confusion, and the Council had to establish order not only by hearing the defence of the criminals, but by pronouncing sentence anyhow, even if they did not appear to defend themselves.*

The safe conduct offered by the prelates assembled in Trent is, as may be expected, to the same purport. The Council promised perfect freedom to all who might come, not liberty of person only, but liberty of speech also. The heretics were to be allowed to "treat, examine, and discuss," to produce their own statements, and to prove them, either in writing or by word of mouth, but in language sober and becoming, free from reproaches and insults. Though the Council required decorous language to be used by those whom it admitted, it could not obtain it, and the prelates sat and listened more than once to the foulest and grossest calumnies which the evil spirit, working in the children of disbelief, poured forth so recklessly in those calamitous times as well as in these. And, in addition to the sober language, they were required, according to the instructions of the Pope, to accept the teaching and traditions of the Church as the rule and test of their opinions.†

The Church must have ceased to be the Church if a different rule had been adopted. The Supreme Pon-

---

* Antequam quidquam cum hæreticis tractetur aut disputetur, illud omnino servandum—quod et divini et humani juris est—ut primum conveniant de judicio ac judice, et confiteantur unam esse ecclesiam Christi toto orbe terrarum diffusam, unumque esse ipsius ecclesiæ caput Christi Vicarium, Ipsiusque Christi verbo constitutum. . . . Quod si hæc inficientur, non debent quovis modo audiri super quoquam contendentes, cum se declarent apertissime schismaticos et hæreticos; nam is qui dubitat, non habet principia fidei, et articulum Catholicæ ecclesiæ convincitur non recipere.—*Monita PP. ap. Le Plat. Monum. Coll.* iv., p. 417.

† Opprobriis, conviciis ac contumeliis penitus semotis; et signanter, quod causæ controversæ secundum sacram scripturam, et Apostolorum traditiones, probata Concilia, Catholicæ Ecclesiæ consensum, et sanctorum Patrum auctoritates in prædicto Concilio Tridentino tractentur.—*Salv. Conduct. Sess.* 18.

tiff appointed by Our Lord to govern His Church could not allow his right to be questioned, nor his authority discussed, by men who denied the former and were rebels from the latter. He is the Sovereign judge, but by no human institution, so he cannot suffer his dignity to become the object of insulting discussions, nor accept it as a concession of human reason. He is what he is by the act of God, and our duty is to admit it and obey. The old truths of the faith, long ago defined, and by many generations held, must be secured against profane curiosity; they were taught in, and by, an infallible Church; none of them could be laid aside, and none ever had been;* they might be increased in the fulness of the light which the Holy Ghost supplies to the Great Teacher of the Church, but not one of them could ever be forgotten or denied.

The heretics themselves knew and confessed that the Church could not allow them to discuss doctrines already defined; it was one of their complaints that definitions once made could not be reviewed, still less changed. They went out of the Church, not so much for doctrine as for the right to question and doubt everything. They were taking leave for ever of fixed principles, and in doing so admitted that the Church held unchanging principles which it is not lawful for men to dispute. The safe conduct and the invitation to the Council did not satisfy their desires, and so they never went. They did not mean to submit themselves to the authority of the Church, and having once tasted of the liberty of the flesh, they made up their minds, knowing the issues, to persist in the errors they had invented. The electors and princes of Germany had reasons of their own for not presenting themselves before the assembled prelates of Trent, some of which they published, that they might not seem, at least, to be unable to defend an indefensible position, and one of them is certainly true, namely, that the

---

* Quamvis in Ecclesia nunc quædam credantur explicite, quæ olim, utpote nondum definita, pro articulis fidei, tantum credebantur implicite; nullum tamen ab adversariis fidei dogma in medium proferri unquam potuisse, quod in Ecclesia Catholica olim creditum, nunc vero abolitum sit; nam hoc esset errare, non autem illud. *Pichler, August, Confess. Art viii., v. 2.*

Council was not summoned for the discussion of doctrine, but for the rooting out of heresy.*

Thus, in the very beginning of the great Western heresy, the whole matter was clearly understood. Those who went out of the Church knew that there was but one way by which they could return, and that the Sovereign Pontiff would make no concessions. He is the guardian and the keeper of the faith, and has not the power given him to destroy it. The heretics, it is true, made offers, but offers which they knew would not be accepted, for they admitted that the Pope would not tolerate the discussion of settled principles. Besides, the terms they proposed were so utterly unreasonable that it may well be doubted whether they were serious when they made them. They wanted a Council, over which the Pope should have no authority; they wanted the Sovereign Pontiff to release the Bishops from the obligations of obedience; they wanted all questions to be decided by the written word, and to have all the decrees then made in Trent to be annulled and declared of non-effect, and, moreover, that no question should be determined by plurality of voices in the Council.† Though their terms are foolish in themselves, they are nevertheless consistent with their heresy, for they would, if by impossibility they had been accepted, end in nothing but disorder and wandering from the truth.

The Council was dissolved at last, but no heretic came, and the assembled Fathers, on the 4th day of December, 1563, confessed that they had then no

---

* Ex bullis quoque indictionum concilii Pontificii manifeste constat, concilia ab ipsis non eo indicta esse, ut piorum et eruditorum virorum disputatione ac collatione lux evangelii illustretur, vel quod Pontifices conciliorum decretis se subjicere, atque emendationem ullam ferre velint sed ideo potius, ut Augustana confessio damnetur, eaque condemnatio executioni mandetur, atque adeo ut status ei confessioni adhærentes et opprimantur et funditus deleantur.—*Le Plat. Monum. Amplissima Collect.* v. pp., 54 55.

† Ac primo quidem, ad indicendam piam synodum maxime necessarium esse ducunt, ut omnia ea decreta, quæ in synodis Tridentinis facta sunt, prorsus e medio tollantur, aboleantur, et irrita esse publice denuntientur. Deinde ut concilium . . . . convocetur, non a Romano Episcopo, qui etiam gubernator, præses ac judex synodi esse non permittatur. . . . . Tertio, ut sola vox divina, tradita scriptis propheticis et Apostolicis, norma sit secundum quam in concilio judicetur. —*Le Plat. ut supr: p.* 74.

hope whatever that the heretics, so long expected, would come.* That great Council did a great work—a work that will last for ever—but it did not do that which the world expected from it, and which it also did all it could to hinder. As in Lyons and in Florence, so in Trent, the Sovereign Pontiff's rights, immunities, and prerogatives, were not submitted for discussion. Heretics were treated as heretics, kindly and mercifully, but as heretics and aliens from the fold of Christ, till they made their submission to the one Shepherd to whom Our Lord has given the care of His sheep and His lambs.

Chapter XV.

The Sovereign Pontiff the only possible Convener of a Council.—His sanction necessary to its Decrees.—The Council not superior to the Pope.—Supposed case of a Pope dying during the Session; the case of Antipopes.—Council of Pisa.—Conduct of the Cardinals.—Mutual relations between the Pope and a Council.—The Pope cannot be accused of Heresy.—Prejudices of certain Canonists.

Ex his ergo deducitur concilio ecclesiasticam potestatem supremam non convenire. Nam suprema potestas non potest ab alia regi et regulari, sed debet moderari omnes alias. Potestas enim quæ errare potest, et quæ errat, ab alia regi et regulari debet. Non est igitur suprema, sed superiorem habeat a qua regitur et regulatur. Concilium itaque errare potest, et sæpe erravit ; ergo supremam non habet auctoritatem, sed est alia potestas concilio superior, a qua concilium regi debet, ne a veritate deflectat. Summus vero Pontifex in iis, quæ fidei sunt, errare non potest, ergo ab hoc concilium dependet, et hujus auctóritate regi debet, ne a veritate recedat. Inter omnes Catholicos et hereticos convenit aliqua concilia errasse.—*Fabulotti, de concilio,* c. viii.

AS the Convocation of a General Council must be the act of the Pope, so also must the dissolution of it be. In former times men disputed many of the prerogatives of the Pontiffs, but time, in this as in other questions, brings wisdom, and there are hardly any men now living, including even heretics, who would seriously maintain that the Catholic Episcopate

---

* Nec ulla spes restet, hereticos, toties fide etiam publica, quam desiderarunt, invitatos et tamdiu expectatos huc amplius adventuros.—*Conc. Trident. sess.* 25. *Cont.*

could be brought together in a General Council by any other summons than that of the Supreme Pontiff. When the greater part of the known world acknowledged the civil superiority and rank of the Emperor, there were men, dazzled by the splendours of secular dominion, who said that the Emperor might convoke a General Council. Time has answered this: for the Emperor has disappeared as a power in the world, while the successor of the fisherman is, if it be lawful to say so, more powerful than ever. His power, it is true, is not greater, but it is more readily admitted. The great Roman Empire that once measured its strength with the kingdom of Christ has vanished; the Emperor of the West sunk into the Emperor of Germany; the Emperor of Germany into the Emperor of Austria; and now the Empire of Austria is in trouble, for it has been an undutiful child of the Church. The Sovereign Pontiff who fought with weapons not of this world against the Empire of old Rome, and with the powers of Europe since, stands still in his place; the most marvellous authority, for he is a perpetual miracle; the most strange elective Monarch, for each election is the direct work of the Holy Ghost, and the power of the Pope is derived to him immediately from our Lord.*

It may be asked, What is the meaning then of the discussions, deliberations, and conferences of the Prelates, and above all of their decisive voice, in a General Council, when the whole matter is resolvable into the will and decision of the Sovereign Pontiff? It is a question more easily asked than answered, and one that must be left for those who are able to reconcile without difficulty the foreknowledge of God with the free will of man. What is certain on both sides is this: the Prelates of Holy Church are summoned to a Council, and in Council they may discuss and determine the questions proposed to them; they have always done so; on the

---

* Quod enim educitur ex illa electione sacri senatus cardinalium, est simplex indicium et signum personæ quam Christus Dominus ecclesiæ suæ præesse voluit, et omnis potestas immediate ab Ipso Christo in talem personam designatam derivat.—*Vinc. de Justis, De Dispensat. Matrim.* lib. ii, c. 2. n. 24.

other hand their decisions are of no effect except when sanctioned by the Supreme Pontiff. Many learned men have at different times laboured hard to escape this conclusion, and to find some grounds whereon to rest the claims which they would gladly set up on behalf of the authority of General Councils; but the General Councils themselves refused the treacherous support of their learning. No Council has ventured, no Council has even wished, to raise up its own power above the Pope. And it was immediately after the calamities of Pisa, Constance, and Basle that the prelates of Holy Church, assembled in Florence, declared with one consent that the Pope was not only the Head of the Church as a whole, but also the father and teacher of each Christian man. The teacher is not the taught, and the Pope is, therefore, not bound by the decrees of any assembly, or by the opinions of any man however learned.

The canonist, commonly called the Abbot, and his master, the Cardinal Zabarella, both involved in schism, have been always regarded as the pillars of the opinion which attributes to General Councils a power to judge the Pope. S. Antoninus of Florence in the third part of his *Summa* having quoted the former at length, has been occasionally referred to as not unfavourable to what is called the Gallican opinion, but the real teaching of the Archbishop of Florence is not to be found where he quotes Panormitan, but in the fourth part of the *Summa*,* where he says that even if the Pope might as a private person fall into error, yet in all that relates to the faith he is always true, and that we are therefore to abide by his decision rather

---

* *Tit. viii. c.* 3. *Col.* 450. Et licet Papa in particulari errare possit, ut in judicialibus, in quibus proceditur per informationem, alias in his quæ pertinent ad fidem, errare non potest, scilicet ut Papa, in determinando, etiamsi ut particularis et privata persona possit. Unde magis standum est sententiæ Papæ de pertinentibus ad fidem quam in judicio perferret quam opinioni quorumque sapientum, quum et Caiphas, licet malus, prophetaverit inscius.—It was lately said that, "throughout the middle ages and down to the time of the Reformation . . . the modern Ultramontane view was not held. The distinction between the Pope *ex-cathedrâ* and the Pope as private doctor was never heard of." S. Antoninus, to whom the distinction seems to have been familiar, was born in 1389. The latter part of the extract is taken almost literally from S. Thomas, *Quodlibet.* 9, *art.* 16.

than by the opinions of learned men. Muzzarelli speaks the same language in modern times, and is not afraid to say that he would obey the Pope, though the whole Church, if that were possible, taught what the Pope condemned.*

But this is nothing more than the common opinion current among the canonists from the beginning, admitted always in peaceful times, and disputed only when the passions of men had burst all bounds.† Even Panormitan and Zabarella may be cited as really holding the absolute supremacy of the Pope, though in general they are regarded as the doctors of the Gallican school. They lived in evil times, took the wrong side, and were driven more by the necessity of their position than by their convictions, to magnify the powers of a Council and to assail the rights of the Pope. In their day the opinion was new and there was therefore the charm of novelty to resist, which is so often too powerful even for wise and aged men. The ancient gloss in Gratian‡ was known to them, and besides they knew very well that it had become the common possession of the canonists, before they ventured to break in on the immemorial tradition of the Church. The necessities of their false position made them enemies of the Pope, and hence their authority, notwithstanding their learning, has ever been less than it would otherwise have been.

Among theologians, Gerson, the most famous of the doctors who wrote in his haste against

---

* *De Auctorit. R. Pontificis.* c. 18. *sec.* 2, *p.* 467. Posita definitione Concilii Florentini, scilicet, quod Romanus Pontifex est Doctor omnium Christianorum, ut Pastor Universalis Ecclesiæ cum plena potestate pascendi illam ; etiam si possibile fieret, ut Ecclesia Universalis staret contra eum in doctrina fidei, ego constanter parêre tenebor potius Romano Pontifici, qui datus est Pastor cum plena potestate a Christo Domino Ecclesiæ Universali, quam ecclesiæ universali quæ tradita est pascenda plenæ potestati Romani Pontificis. Et si Papa doceret aliquod dogma, et universitas episcoporum doceret contrarium, nos omnes fideles adhærebimus potius Romano Pontifici quam universo collegio episcoporum.

† Denique, ut cætera omittam, ad annum usque 1395 nemini in mentem venit, Pontificem Maximum generali concilio subesse.—*Card. Soglia, Inst. Juris Publ. Eccles. Prænot.* c. 2. *sec.* 38.

‡ *Caus.* 9. *Q.* 3. *cap.* Nemo. Concilium non potest Papam judicare, unde si totus mundus sententiaret in aliquo negotio contra Papam, videtur quod sententiæ Papæ standum esset.

the sovereign rights of the Holy See, has himself confessed * that he was maintaining an opinion which was so much at variance with the tradition of the Church before the Council of Constance, that any one who held it would have been branded as a heretic. What was obscured in the Councils of Pisa, Constance, and Basle, was made clear at Florence, and put beyond all doubt in Trent, where the bishops admitted with one voice, when they supplicated for the confirmation of the Council, that the Pope alone could teach the Church. "A General Council is like no other Parliament, for its decisions on points of doctrine become infallible when approved by the Sovereign Pontiff. Yet the gift is in him, not in the Council, nor is a Council needed to its use. The judgment is in him alone, irreformable, irrefragable, indivisible."†

Another question, probably undecided, is this: What becomes of the Council if the Pope dies while it is sitting? The Council of Trent was not sitting when Paul III. died, nor again at the death of Julius III. During the reign of Marcellus II. it did not sit at all, nor during that of Paul IV. Pius IV. called it together again, and under him it finished the work it had to do.

The fifth Council of the Lateran was sitting when Julius II. died. The fifth session of that Council was held on Wednesday, February 16, 1513, under the presidency of Rafael, Cardinal Bishop of Ostia, supplying the absence of the Pope, who was on his death-bed. On that day the next session was fixed by the Pope for April 2, and in the meanwhile—that is, on the 21st of February—Julius II. was taken out of this world. Now, if the election of the future Pope had not taken place before the day appointed for the sixth session, the Council would have assembled without a Pope, and the question would arise, What power had such a Council? The question, however, did not arise, for Leo X. was elected on the 11th day of March, a month before the adjournment was over, and the

---

* *De Potest. Eccles. Cons.* 12. Oppositorum dogmatizator fuisset de hæretica pravitate vel notatus vel damnatus.

† F. Faber, *Blessed Sacrament*, bk. iv., p. 480.

Council did not reassemble in virtue of its own authority; for the Pope, on Sunday, March 10th, the day before that to which it had been adjourned, issued his Bull, announcing the continuance of the Council. Julius II. had not dissolved it; he had simply prorogued it, four days before his death, to a future day. If Leo X. had not been elected, could the Council have met on the 11th of April, the day appointed by Julius II. for the sixth session?

Many men have written much on the powers of a Council when in opposition to the Pope. Some have held that the Council is supreme in certain cases, and that it can sit in judgment on the Pope. The two cases are, when there is an antipope, and when the Pope is a heretic. These writers have been numerous, but they have not been influential, and their adversaries have always shown them how impossible it is for them to act upon their principles.

In the case of an antipope, it is asked, Who is to convene the Council? Surely not the antipope, for that would be to recognize his claims to be the true Pope. The Pope would not subject his title to discussion, and he would certainly not summon a Council to decide whether he was the Pope or not.

At the election of Alexander III. one of the cardinals became an antipope, and the Emperor called a Council of the German and Italian bishops to decide the dispute between the rebel Cardinal and the Vicar of Christ. The Pope, Alexander III., gave no heed to that Council, neither appeared at it, nor sent anyone to represent him. But the antipope did attend, submitted his claims, and was rewarded for his act by being recognized as Pope by the Emperor. Nevertheless, he was an antipope, and is so regarded to this day.

Again, it has been said, if two persons claim each to be Pope, and if there be no clear evidence as to the title of either, that then a Council is the fitting tribunal for deciding between them. If such a calamity befell the Church, it would be very grave, but as it has not happened in the course of eighteen centuries, we may pray and even hope that God of His infinite mercy may not visit us with so severe a chastisement and so perilous a trial. If it did happen, a Council certainly could give no relief, for there would be no certain Pope to convoke it; and no Council can be convoked by any other person, not even by the Cardinals in their perplexity; and, if at such a time a Council truly summoned were sitting, such a Council could not decide the question, for neither law nor custom has given it a right to elect the Pope or to depose him. The Council, like all the rest of the faithful, is powerless in such a matter, and nothing is left but prayer. There is no power given to any bishop, or any number of bishops, that is not given to all the faithful alike, to decide who is the true Bishop of Rome. The election of the Sovereign Pontiff is, and has ever been, intrusted to the Cardinals, and if they cannot settle all questions concerning that election, there is no human help for it, seeing that nobody has been able to find any law or custom by which any man, not a cardinal, can interfere therein.

It is true that the Cardinals once called a General Council to be held at Pisa, for the purpose of undoing a great evil, which some of them had wantonly caused many months after the election of Urban VI. The Pope not governing the Church according to the opinions of the French Cardinals, was by them renounced, and opposed by the Bishop of Cambrai, whom they set up as antipope to be followed at his death by Pedro de Luna. Under the Pontificate of Gregory XII, deserted by most of his Cardinals, the so-called Council of Pisa assembled, convoked by Cardinals who professed themselves capable of sitting in judgment upon the Pope and the antipope. The result was disastrous in the extreme, for they elected in that assembly another person to be called Pope, and thus there were at least two antipopes in the judgment of all men.*

Gregory XII. in the end resigned, and Martin V. was elected Pope, but after the death of the former. In that election the assembly of Constance interfered,

---

* *Schelstrate, Tract. de Concil. Const.* p. xxviii. Suffecto Alexandro V. schisma non extinctum, sed adauctum fuit, nihilque aliud patres Pisani assecuti sunt, quam ut duobus de Papatu contendentibus tertium adjecerint.

for it appointed certain representatives of the "nations" to enter the conclave with the Cardinals, and with equal powers, but with the special and expressed consent of all the Cardinals. It is certain that the Council of Constance was exceeding its powers, and it is not clear that the Cardinals, by consenting, were not infringing the Papal Constitutions by which their rights were secured. The decree of the Council and the consent of the Cardinals may be regarded as superfluous, which they probably were, for the provisions for a Papal election were ample and express, needing neither correction nor addition, and certainly not to be corrected, nor added to, by an assembly which had not been sanctioned, as it had not been called, by the Sovereign Pontiff. The Cardinals may have submitted to this for the sake of peace; and as the Pope was unanimously chosen by them it mattered little that the intruders agreed with them. The election was legal, because made by the Cardinals who alone have the right to elect, and the suffrages of the intruders, if they were given, were simply superfluous, and could do no harm. Panormitan, however, speaks as if the election had been really the act of the Cardinals only,* and that they made it by their own authority and that of the Council. If they made it by their own authority, that is enough, and the authority of the Council is not necessary, though the Cardinals prudently abstained from saying so, lest more evils still should have fallen on Christendom. In those days some men had persuaded themselves that a General Council had the right to elect the Pope if the Holy See were made vacant, in their sense, by the deposition of the Vicar of Christ. They admitted that only the Cardinals could elect the Pope if the vacancy followed upon death or resignation—for the Popes had provided for those cases. They considered, as the Popes had never made any provision for other vacancies than those caused by death and resignation, that the vacancy

---

* *Cap.* Licet, *de Elect.* Pro evitenda tamen discordia fuit obtentum ut concilium pro illa vice transferret potestatem suam in Collegium Cardinalium, et ita Cardinales elegerunt ex potestate propria et concilii.

caused by deprivation must be at the disposal of a General Council, because there was no law which enabled the cardinals to elect when such a vacancy occurred. Those who held this opinion seem not to have reflected that, if the Popes had provided for two ways only, that there was no third way of making a vacancy in the Holy See, and, therefore, that a General Council has no power or right to depose the Pope.

Even in the evil days of the assemblies of Pisa, Constance, and Basle, it was generally admitted that the Pope was not subject to the censure of a Council except in the case of heresy. That was the only matter which was regarded as a justification for what would otherwise have been a most manifest rebellion. Some of the canonists of those days seem to have been completely under the dominion of that notion whenever they touched upon the relations of the Pope to a Council. They considered that a Pope who fell into heresy became at once subject to a Council, but while they said this, they nowhere said that a Pope might so fall, though the inference from their language is that they probably thought it possible. Those who held this notion admitted that it was not universal, and that a contrary opinion was also held to the effect that the Pope was above all human tribunals. Thus Joannes Andreas,* referring to and reporting the words of Hostiensis,† who held that for the sin of heresy the Pope was subject to an accusation, adds, and in the words of Hostiensis himself, that others held the contrary, maintaining that there was no power vested in any one on earth to try the supreme Pontiff. Hostiensis does not say that the Pope can be tried, but only that he may be accused; that is to say, a process might be instituted in some undefined court, the object of which is to prove heresy against the Pope. He seems to have shrunk back from the full meaning of his words, though that meaning is inevitable,

---

* *Cap.* Proposuit *de Concess. Prœbendœ.* Alii tamen, et si imperator et totus clerus et totus populus conveniant, ipsum non poterunt judicare.

† *Summa Aurea, de Elect. et Elect. Potest. n.* 18. Item de nullo crimine excipi potest contra ipsum, excepta hœresi, de qua accusari potest, etiam consecratus.

for an accusation implies a judge. Guido de Baisio, commonly called the Archdeacon, was less cautious, for he said that the judge of the Pope was a Council. His disciple, Joannes Andreas, did not repeat the daring assertion, for he contented himself with repeating the language of Hostiensis, who had drawn back from it, admitting that the Pope could not be judged by man. His respect for his master, probably, withheld him from expressing his own opinion, if it really differed from that of the archdeacon. For, in another place, he repeats the opinion of his master more fully, but does not say whether he adopts it or not as his own.* Panormitan adopts the opinion of the Archdeacon,† and maintains with him, that a Council can sit in judgment on the Pope accused of heresy. Zabarella, adopting the words of Hostiensis as his own, adds this: That the Pope may be accused of other sins beside heresy, if he continues impenitent,‡ but Zabarella was writing in troublous times, and had himself taken the wrong side.

The only certain attempt to accuse a Pope of heresy was that of Philip le Bel, who laboured hard to compel Clement V. to sit in judgment on his predecessor, Boniface VIII. It is scarcely possible that this memorable fact can have been unknown to the canonists who propounded their theories during the assemblies of Basle, and yet they are not able to find anything in it serviceable for their purpose. Clement V. was sorely pressed, but he never admitted that even a dead Pope could be charged with heresy. He listened to much abuse of Boniface VIII., and made what seemed to be preparations for a legal trial of him, though dead, but he never did anything that

---

* VIto *Cap.* In fidei, *de hæreticis.*

† *Cap.* Proposuit, *de Concess. Præbendæ.* Sed plus placet hæc opinio ut possit ab alio condemnari et deponi in facto fidei, et hanc opinionem expresse tenuit Archidiaconus—et dicit . . . . quod concilium erit judex.

‡ Joan. de Imola, *cap.* Proposuit. Sed doctor Florentinus hic videtur tenere contrarium, nam dicit quod idem dicendum est de quolibet peccato notorio, in quo Papa persisteret, quod dicitur de hæresi. The words of the cardinal are: Sed videtur quod quando persisteret impenitens possit haberi pro male sentiente in fide.

could be interpreted into an admission that the Pope was to be tried for heresy. He left the question undecided; it was all that he could do in the grievous straits to which he had been reduced; but he did that,* and the canonists, who magnified the powers of a Council, were, a hundred years later, left free to argue as they did. Though Clement V. did not decide this question, nor admit, nor deny, the opinion that a Pope might be accused of heresy, yet it is very difficult to maintain that he did not really disown it at the last; for if he did not, it is scarcely credible that he could have borne so patiently and so long the insults of the French lawyers, and the importunities of the King who employed them. He could have released himself in a moment from his difficulties by consenting to the trial. But there is more than this. The *Bull*, announcing the end of the trouble, wherein Clement V. gives the history of the proceedings from the commencement to the close, begins with words which, applied to the facts narrated, seem to imply throughout that it is not lawful to bring accusations against the Sovereign Pontiff, † and Clement V. substantially refused to hear those which the lawyers of Philip le Bel had so maliciously and laboriously forged.

Those canonists who wrote so much in favour of Councils and of their supremacy, wrote probably more under the influence of prejudice, and under the dominion of that necessity which partizanship carries in its train. Panormitan confessed that he had been led astray through his fondness for his nephews, who urged him on, and drove him into schism, and Francis de Zabarellis, when his own theories were presented to him at Constance, embodied in a decree of the assembly there, drew back and refused to read

---

* Non intendentes tamen denuntiatores et objectores prædictos, vel alterum eorundem, aut denuntiationes vel objectiones, vel aliqua proposita per eosdem admittere, nisi si prout et in quantum contra summos Pontifices vivos vel mortuos admittendi forent, et etiam admittendi juxta sanctorum patrum decreta et canonica instituta.—Clement V. Ad Certitudinem.

† Jesus Christus Dominus noster, qui peccatum non fecit, nec vere potest redargui de peccato, disciplinam instituens et humilitatis exemplum, omnibus autem, specialiter pastoribus, Ejus vicariis in Ecclesia Dei futuris, prædicans populo Judæorum dixit, Quis ex vobis me arguet de peccato?

it in the public session. Zabarella saw them in their true colour when he had to act upon them, and Panormitan would not trust himself to die with them.

Chapter XVI.

The Work of Gratian.—The Canons "Anastasius" and "Si Papa."—Worthlessness of the former and non-authority of the latter.—Attempt of the Cardinals to call a Council.—Its failure.—The effect of opposition has been to make the Papal supremacy and infallibility more clear and certain.

Quamvis doctrina Gersonis et Cardinalis de Alliaco caliginem quandam plurimorum Theologorum mentibus in Gallia offuderit: extra Galliam autem jam a longo tempore nullus reperitur Theologus qui infallibilitatem summorum Pontificum eorumque supra concilia auctoritatem non strenue propugnaret.—*Krisper. de Legg. dist.* iv. *q.* 1.

THE chief source of these opinions which prevailed among learned men in the fifteenth century was the compilation of Canons formed by Gratian. That book was found serviceable by the professors of the canon law, and they made it too often a text-book, as if it had really some weight. It is no doubt well arranged, and contains a great mass of matter, but in itself, and as the work of Gratian, it has no authority, and has always been set aside, unless it could be shown that the canons he has quoted are canons which the Pope has sanctioned. The contents of the *Decretum* are not necessarily law because Gratian has brought them together into one book,* but portions of it may be law, because confirmed by the Pope, or because they are decrees issued by him. It is necessary, therefore, to inquire into the authority of each canon in Gratian, before it can be urged ; for it may be an extract from the letter of a bishop, who, of course, had no power to make laws for the Church, or

---

* *Scot.* iv. *dist.* 6, *q.* 8.—Ergo oportet dicere, quod quodcunque capitulum incorporatum in corpore Decretorum a Gratiano confirmatum sit a Papa, vel multa capitula ibi posita non ligant totam ecclesiam. Unde autem possit doceri, quod omnia illa capitula ibi compilata Papa confirmeri, non est manifestum. Nec etiam eo modo quo est manifestum de omnibus capitulis positis in Decretalibus. *Sanchez, de Matrim. lib.* 9. *disp.* 12. *sec.* 5.—Vim canonis minime habent quæ in Decreto continentur, nisi ex Pontificis aut concilii generalis decreto desumpta sint.

it may be a decree of a Provincial Council, never confirmed, or even from the writings of an historian, or from the laws of the Empire, or the opinion of one of the Fathers.

Among the canons brought together by Gratian are two which, accepted without questioning by the canonists, led men into grievous errors touching the authority of the Holy See. They are those cited as *Anastasius* and *Si Papa*. The first teaches that men may withdraw from the communion of the Pope; and the second, that he may be judged of none unless he be found to have swerved from the faith: *à fide devius*. The inferences drawn from these two so-called canons were often most disloyal and irreverent, and those who accepted them came to hold that the Pope might actually teach heresy.

The Canon *Si Papa* has been the most popular, and during the troubles of the fifteenth century, when most of the Bishops, at one time or other, rose up against the Vicar of Christ, it was far better known than the Gospel to a great many eager disputants for the rights of Councils. The gloss upon it went much further, and, if it could be maintained, is an ample justification of the opinion of Zabarella, for it extends the power of the Pope's subjects over him, and enables them to accuse him of other crimes besides heresy. These fictitious canons could do nothing but evil, for men grew accustomed to question the Papal rights, and to take for granted that our Lord would abandon His Vicar and leave him destitute of the special helps which He has promised him.

The gloss when it was pressed as a truth to be acted on, was rejected even by those who were in revolt against the Pope. It was felt to be at least indecent, and then its want of authority was confessed. The Cardinals who came together in Leghorn in 1408, who rejected both the Pope and the antipope, and who were going to take upon themselves the office of the Pope by indicting what they called a General Council, disowned the gloss, and admitted that some rejected it.*

---

* *Martene et Durand. Coll. Ampliss.* vii. 797. Illa glossa, simpliciter posita, non est vera, et reprehenditur a nonnullis.

The influence of the gloss, and of the canon which it professed to explain, was very great among the canonists of the fifteenth century. Perhaps too, a mere legal training which makes men seek speculative solutions of practical doubts, contributed in no small degree to the formation and maintenance of theories which really tended to destroy the constitution of the Church, and to assimilate her to secular communities, corporations, and states, in which the powers of the several members are balanced, as men say, by the presence of a counteracting or rival authority. The assemblies of Pisa, Constance, and Basle, proceeded on theories of ecclesiastical law which were not those of the Church, and which, if admitted, would have changed her constitution and made her a parliamentary monarchy in which the Pope might reign, but in which he could not govern. His decisions would have been questioned in Councils, and probably appeals from him would have become frequent and customary, and the doctrines of the Faith would have become a philosophy.

These theories were built on an unsound foundation, and it may be charitably, if not reasonably, believed that their authors would not have made them known if their minds had been visited by any suspicion that their conclusive canon was no canon at all. *Si Papa* seems to have been taken by Gratian not from the letters of Popes, nor even the decrees of Councils, but from a letter attributed to S. Boniface, Archbishop of Mayence. The Saxon Bishop, a saint and martyr, was not the Pope, and it was not given to him to make laws for the whole Church. That canon is the sole authority for so strange an opinion, and it is not sufficient, however venerable, to impose it on the Church. With that canon falls the building raised upon it, and the elaborate reasoning by which men subjected Popes to Councils at the same time is completely undermined.

The other ground, the so-called canon *Anastasius*, is now known to be worthless; it is an extract from the *Liber Pontificalis*, attributed to the librarian Anastasius, who, being the friend of Photius, accepted from that evil man whatever information he gave him, and handed it down as authentic history, and the facts as stated in the canon *Anastasius*, and as Gratian unhappily repeated them, are known to be no facts,* but either mistakes, or as some think, more likely, deliberate falsehoods, for the purpose of destroying the credit of the Sovereign Pontiffs.†

The Council of Constance attempted to subject the Pope to the authority of the Bishops, and did embarrass the Holy See most seriously, for the troubles occasioned by the Council of Basle were the fruits of its acts, and the Sovereign Pontiff was delivered from his anxieties only after the Council of Florence. The disorder and anarchy which prevailed during the early part of the fifteenth century, when the prelates and the secular princes undertook to govern the Church without the Pope, had their compensation. Great was the scandal, and crying the sin, but out of all the evil there came forth at last the acknowledgment of the Pope's right, and the almost unanimous confession of his supremacy.

One attempt after that of Constance and of Basle was made to throw the Church into confusion. Certain Cardinals, discontented for some reason or other with the Pope, Julius II., and relying on the help of the Emperor and the King of France, which was given them, took upon themselves to call together a general council without the consent, and against the will, of the Pope. They proposed to hold their council at Pisa, and issued their summons; but though the secular powers were favourable, or indifferent, the Bishops throughout the Church were not moved from their duty. Some French Bishops and Abbots came together, but for some time not one from Germany respected the illegal convocation. It was an unlawful

---

* Falsa esse quæ de Anastasio Pontifice Gratianus commemorat.—*Covarruvias, Var. Resol. lib.* iv. c. 13.

† Ut enim erat Photio amicissimus, inito arctissimo fœdere. . . . quemadmodum mutuæ Anastasii et Photii epistolæ testantur, nihil antiquius habuit Anastatius in describendis Romanorum antistitum gestis, quam Græcorum monumentis uti, illis præsertim, quæ a Photio excipere potuisset. At vero quis ignorat Photium codices ecclesiastios depravâsse producendi sui schismatis suæque contentionis gratia, in odium præsertim Pontificum Romanorum, quorum primatum auctoritatemque detestabatur?—*Berardi, Grat. Canones. tom.* 1, p. ii, p. 453.

assembly, unlawfully assembled, and the measure of its folly and its sin was a decree made in its last session at Milan—it had removed from Pisa to that place—by which it professed to suspend the Sovereign Pontiff from his functions. Having done this it migrated to Lyons, and there the Cardinals attempted, but in vain, to continue its sessions.

As soon as men ceased to dispute the supremacy of the Pope, the clouds that hid him from the eyes of men were scattered. They began to see him, not as the judge from whom there is no appeal, though he is that; but as the Father of the faithful and the infallible teacher of the Church. His great office shone out before the eyes of men, and they fell at his feet, and confessed the powers which our Lord had given him. When the lawyers had ceased to discuss his authority, Theologians came forth, as if the noise and tumult of legists had made them hide themselves, and showed people how tender and how true was that authority which the faithful in general always respected, and always maintained to exist. After the troubles of Constance were over, and peace brought back by the Council of Florence, there was no difficulty in determining who were the enemies and who were the children of the Pope. His authority had become so clear, and his dignity so unmistakable, that it was no longer possible, as it had been before, for faithful Christians to dispute his power. The clouds had been scattered, the sun had dispersed the mist, and the confession of the Supremacy led to the confession of the Infallibility. So when the Reformation came, which was nothing else but the fruits of Constance and Basle, the men of simple hearts and humble spirit listened to the storm, but were never troubled; they knew that the Pope was the successor of S. Peter, the Vicar of Christ, the shepherd of all the sheep, and the infallible judge of controversies. God in His anger separated the chaff from the wheat, and by a terrible storm purified the air; but from that day the Papacy has never been misunderstood even by its enemies: they knew it to be the Rock, and, in fighting against the Holy See, they never could find any excuse such as the mediæval lawyers found for themselves. The supremacy of the

Holy See needed really no defence, the conscience of the faithful, released from the trammels within which learned men laboured to confine it, knew the Pope, and though sophistry or want of faith may create difficulties from time to time, the end of each controversy is a clearer view of the power of the Pope, and a more loving submission to his most blessed rule.

APPENDIX.

THE following is the translation and text of the Letter of the Holy Father to the Archbishop of Westminster, in reply to the inquiry of Dr. Cumming, a Scotch Presbyterian Minister, as to whether he could be heard at the Council :—

[TRANSLATION.]
*PIUS PP. IX.

TO OUR VENERABLE BROTHER HENRY EDWARD, ARCHBISHOP OF WESTMINSTER.

Venerable Brother, Health and the Apostolic Blessing.—We have seen from the newspapers that Dr. Cumming, of Scotland, has inquired of you whether leave will be given at the approaching Council to those who dissent from the Catholic Church, to put forward the arguments which they think can be advanced in support of their own opinions; and that, on your replying that this is a matter to be determined by the Holy See, he has written to Us upon the subject.

Now, if the inquirer knows what is the belief of Catholics with respect to the teaching authority which

---

* PIUS PP. IX.
VENERABILI FRATRI, HENRICO EDUARDO, ARCHIEPISCOPO
WESTMONASTERIENSI, WESTMONASTERIUM.

Venerabilis Frater, salutem et Apostolicam Benedictionem.—Per ephemerides accepimus Doctorem Cumming Scotum quæsivisse a te, num in futuro Concilio dissidentibus facienda sit potestas ea proferendi argumenta quæ suæ opinioni suffragari arbitrentur; te autem respondente id a Nobis esse decernendum, ipsum hac de re ad Nos scripsisse. Verum si postulantem non latet Catholicorum fides de

has been given by our Divine Saviour to His Church, and therefore with respect to its infallibility in deciding questions which belong to dogma or to morals, he must know that the Church cannot permit errors which it has carefully considered, judged and condemned, to be again brought under discussion. This, too, is what has already been made known by Our Letters. [Letters Apostolic of Sept. 13, 1868, addressed "to all Protestants and other non-Catholics."] For, when we said, "*it cannot be denied or doubted that Jesus Christ Himself,* in order that He† might apply to all generations of men the fruits o His redemption, *built here on earth upon Peter His only Church,* that is, the one, holy, Catholic and Apostolic Church, *and gave to him all power that was necessary for preserving whole and inviolate the deposit of faith,* and for delivering the same faith to all peoples, and tribes, and nations," We thereby signified that the primacy both of honour and of jurisdiction, which was conferred upon Peter and his successors by the Founder of the Church, is placed *beyond the hazard of disputation.* This, indeed, is the hinge upon which the whole question between Catholics and all who dissent from them turns; and from this dissent, as from a fountain, all the errors of non-Catholics flow, "For, *inasmuch as such bodies of men are destitute of that living and divinely established authority,* which teaches mankind especially the things of faith and the rule of morals, and which also directs and governs them in whatever

---

magisterio a Divino Servatore nostro commisso Ecclesiæ suæ, et de hujus infallibilitate propterea in definiendis quæstionibus de dogmate et moribus, dubitare nequibit quin Ecclesia ipsa, pati non debeat revocari rursum in disceptationem errores quos sedulo expendit, judicavit et damnavit. Nec aliud ei suadere possunt literæ Nostræ. Dum enim diximus "*nemo inficiari ac dubitare potest ipsum Christum Jesum,* ut humanis omnibus generationibus redemptionis suæ fructus applicaret, *suam hic in terris supra Petrum unicam ædificasse Ecclesiam,* id est unam, sanctam, Catholicam, Apostolicam, *eique necessariam omnem contulisse potestatem, ut integrum inviolatumque custodiretur fidei depositum,* ac eadem fides omnibus populis, gentibus, nationibus, traderetur;" hoc ipso diximus *extra disputationis aleam* constitutum esse primatum, non honoris tantum sed et juridictionis Petro ejusque successoribus ab Ecclesiæ institutore collatum. Atqui in. hoc nimirum cardine tota quæstio versatur inter Catholicos et dissentientes quoscumque; et ex hoc dissensu, veluti e fonte omnes acatholicorum errores dimanavit. "*Cum* enim *ejusmodi societates careant viva illa et a Deo constitutâ auctoritate,* quæ homines res fidei morumque disciplinam præsertim docet,

relates to eternal salvation, so *these same bodies of men have ever varied in their teaching,* and their change and instability never cease." If, therefore, your inquirer will consider, either the opinion which is held by the Church as to the infallibility of its judgment in defining whatever belongs to faith or morals, or what We ourselves have written respecting the Primacy and teaching authority of Peter, he will at once perceive that no room can be given at the Council for the defence of errors which have already been condemned; and that we could not have invited non-Catholics to a discussion, but have only urged them "to avail themselves of the opportunity afforded by this Council, in which the Catholic Church, to which their forefathers belonged, gives a new proof of its close unity and invincible vitality, and to satisfy the wants of their souls by withdrawing from a state in which they cannot be sure of their salvation." If, by the inspiration of divine grace, they shall perceive their own danger, and shall seek God with their whole heart, they will easily cast away all preconceived and adverse opinions; and, laying aside all desire of disputation, they will return to the Father from whom they have long unhappily gone astray. We, on our part, will joyfully run to meet them; and embracing them with a father's charity, we shall rejoice, and the Church will rejoice with us, that our children who were dead have come to life again, and that they who were lost have

---

easque dirigit ac moderatur in iis omnibus quæ ad æternam salutem pertinent, tum *societates ipsæ in suis doctrinis continenter variarunt,* et hæc mobilitas atque instabilitas apud easdem societates nunquam cessat." Sive ergo qui te interrogavit sententiam consideret quam de infallibilitate judicii sui in definitione rerum spectantium fidem et mores tenet Ecclesia, sive quæ Nos de non revocando in dubium Petri primatu et magisterio scripsimus, intelliget illico nulli damnatorum errorum patrocinio locum esse posse in Concilii; nec Nos acatholicos invitare potuisse ad disceptandum, sed dumtaxat ut "occasionem amplectantur hujus Concilii quo Ecclesia Catholica, cui eorum majores adscripti erant, novum intimæ unitatis et inexpugnabilis vitalis sui roboris exhibit argumentum; ac indigentiis eorum cordis respondentes, ab eo statu se eripere studeant in quo de suâ propria salute securi esse non possunt." Si ipsi, divina gratia afflante, proprium discrimen percipiant, si toto corde Deum quærant, facile abjicient præconceptam quamvis adversam opinionem; et omni statim disceptandi cupidine deposita, redibunt ad Patrem a quo jamdiu infeliciter discesserunt. Nos autem læti occurremus ipsis eosque paternâ caritate complexi gaudebimus, Ecclesiam universam gratulari Nobis, quod filii nostri qui mortui erant revixerint, et

been found. This indeed we earnestly ask of God; and do you, Venerable Brother, join your prayers to ours. In the meanwhile, as a token of the Divine favour, and of Our own special benevolence, We most lovingly give to you and to your diocese our Apostolic blessing. Given at St. Peter's, in Rome, this 4th day of September, 1869, in the 24th year of our Pontificate.

PIUS PP. IX.

LETTER FROM THE HOLY FATHER TO THE ARCHBISHOP OF WESTMINSTER
CONCERNING THOSE WHO ARE
WITHOUT THE CATHOLIC CHURCH.

PIUS PP. IX.

TO OUR VENERABLE BROTHER, HENRY EDWARD, ARCHBISHOP OF WESTMINSTER.

Venerable Brother, Health and the Apostolic Blessing.—Having said in the letter which We addressed to you, Venerable Brother, on the fourth day of September last, that subjects which had already been carefully examined and decided by an Œcumenical Council could not again be called in question, that therefore no place could be given in the approaching Council for any defence of errors which had been condemned, and that for this reason we could not

---

qui perierant sint inventi. Id certe a Deo poscimus enixe; et tu, Venerabilis Frater, preces tuas junge nostris. Interim vero, Divini favoris auspicem et præcipuæ nostræ benevolentiæ pignus, Apostolicam Benedictionem tibi totique Diœcesi tuæ permanter impertimus. Datum Romæ apud S. Petrum, die 4 septembris, 1869. Pontificatus Nostri Anno XXIV. PIUS PP. IX.

PIUS PP. IX.
VENERABILI FRATRI, HENRICO EDUARDO, ARCHIEPISCOPO WESTMONASTERIENSI.

Venerabilis Frater, salutem et Apostolicam Benedictionem.—Cum in litteris ad te, Venerabilis Frater, datis die 4 præteriti Septembris dixerimus, revocanda non esse in dubium quæ ab Œcumenico Concilio jam expensa fuerunt et judicata, nullique propterea damnatorum errorum patrocinio locum esse posse in novo Concilio, Nosque idcirco nequivisse

have invited non-Catholics to a discussion, we now learn that some of those who dissent from our faith have so understood those words as to believe that no way is left open to them of making known the difficulties which keep them separated from the Catholic Church, and that almost all approach to us is cut off. But so far are We, the Vicar upon earth, although unworthily, of Him who came to save that which was lost, from repelling them in any way whatever, that We even go forth to meet them, and nothing do We seek for with a more ardent wish than to be able to stretch out Our arms with a father's love to any one who shall return to Us. And never, certainly, have We wished to impose silence upon those who, misled by their education, and believing their opinions to be right, think that their dissent from Us rests upon strong arguments which they would wish to be examined by wise and prudent men. For although this cannot be done in the Council, there will not be wanting learned divines, appointed by ourselves, to whom they may open their minds, and may with confidence make known the reasons of their own belief; so that even out of the contest of a discussion, undertaken solely with a desire of finding out the truth, they may receive a more abundant light to guide them to it. And may very many propose this to themselves, and carry it out in good faith! For it could not be done without great profit to themselves and to others; to

---

acatholicos invitare ad disceptandum, discimus aliquot e dissentientibus sic ea verba intellexisse ut omnem sibi præclusam existimarent viam ad exponendas difficultates quibus detinentur ne ad catholicas partes accedant, interceptumque sibi ferme conserent ad Nos aditum. Adeo vero Nos, qui, licet immerentes, Illius vices gerimus in terris qui venit salvum facere quod perierat, absumus ab iis quoquo modo repellendis, ut imo occurramus ipsis, nihilque votis incensioribus expetamus quam ut reverteneti cuilibet paterno affectu brachia protendere possimus. Nec unquam certe silentium illis indicere voluimus qui, prava institutione decepti, putantesque se recte sentire, dissensum suum a Nobis validis initi argumentis arbitrentur, quæ propterea a sapientibus prudentibusque serio expendi desiderent. Licet enim id fieri nequeat in Concilio, viri tamen divinarum rerum periti a Nobis designandi ipsis non deerunt, quibus mentem suam aperire possint omniaque rationum momenta sententiæ suæ fidenter exponere, ut, ex ipso disceptationis, solo veritatis assequendæ studio institutæ, conflictu, uberiori luce perfundi valeant qua ad illam perducantur. Utinam id plurimi sibi proponant bonaque fide exequantur: cum id contingere nequeat sine magno

themselves, indeed, because God will show His face to those that seek Him with their whole heart, and will give them what they long for: to others, because not only the example of eminent men cannot fail of its efficacy, but also the more diligently they shall have laboured to obtain the benefit of truth the more earnestly will they strive to impart the same benefit to the rest. Earnestly praying the God of Mercy for this most happy issue, we desire you to receive, Venerable Brother, the Apostolic Blessing which, as a token of the Divine favour and of our own especial goodwill, We most lovingly grant to you and to your whole diocese. Given at St. Peter's, in Rome, on the 30th day of October, 1869, in the 24th year of Our Pontificate. PIUS PP. IX.

---

ipsorum ceterorumque proventu. Ipsorum quidem, quia Deus requirentibus se toto corde faciem suam ostendet, iisdemque præstabit quod cupiunt. Aliorum vero, tum quia præstantium virorum exemplum efficacia sua carere non poterit, tum etiam quia isti quo majore diligentia et labore veritatis beneficium sibi compararunt eo impensiore studio, beneficium idem ad ceteros porrigere nitentur. Dum autem faustissimum hunc successum a divina clementia poscimus enixe, excipe, Venerabilis Frater, Apostolicam Benedictionem, quam superni favoris auspicem et præcipuæ Nostræ benevolentiæ pignus tibi totique diœcesi tuæ peramanter impertimus. Datum Romæ, apud S. Petrum, die 30 Octobris, 1869, Pontificatus Nostri anno XXIV.

PIUS PP. IX.

THE END.

www.ingramcontent.com/pod-product-compliance
Lightning Source LLC
Chambersburg PA
CBHW020242170426
43202CB00008B/195